POMS AND COBBERS

POMS AND COBBERS

The Ashes 1997 – An Inside View

Rob Steen
with Robert Croft and Matthew Elliott

ANDRE DEUTSCH

To Laura and Josef
See you in the Gatting Stand in 2007

First published in 1997 by
André Deutsch
106 Great Russell Street
London WC1B 3LJ

www.vci.co.uk

André Deutsch Ltd is a subsidiary of VCI plc

Typeset by Derek Doyle & Associates
Mold, Flintshire.
Printed and bound by MPG Books,
Bodmin, Cornwall

A catalogue record for this book is available from the British Library

ISBN 0 233 99210 3

Acknowledgements

To anyone and everyone who availed me of their help, wittingly or otherwise: Stan and Hilda Accrington, Qamar Ahmed, Rob Aivatoglou, Mr and Mrs Apple Macintosh, Andrew Archer, Carrie Barlow, Greg Baum, Sir Alec Bedser, Eddie Bevan, Sir Geoffrey of Boycottshire, Shaun Bradley and family, Mike Brearley, Tom Brooks, Bill Brown, Mark Butcher, Michael (No Relation) Caine, Chris Campling, Ron Carter, Nim Caswell, Ian Chadband, Ian Chappell, Derek Clements, Malcolm Conn, Cornhill Insurance, Marie Croft, Alan Crompton, Tim De Lisle, Mike Denness, Barry Dudleston, Shirley and Ralph Dymond, Eglinton CC, Megan Elliott, Matthew Engel, Colin Evans, Clare Fathers, Paul Filer, Fiona Foster, Charles Frewin and all at Inside Edge, Noam Friedlander, David Frith (bitterness doesn't suit you), Kevin Garside, Graham Goldwater (see you at Cripple Creek), Tony Greig, Bobby and Carina Grossmark (may your loins be fruitful), John Hampshire, Ian Hawkey, Michael Henderson, Andrew Hignell, John Holder, Richard Huntley, Roz Isaacs, Ian Jessup, Chris Kaklamanis, Alison Kirkham, Peter Johnson, Tim Lamb, Dorothy Lamour, Christopher Lane, Geoff Lawson, David Lemmon, Howard and Alex Levi, Richard Little, Mike Marqusee, Keith Miller, Jim Munro, Brian Murgatroyd, the New York Mets, Paul Newman, Jeremy Novick (meet the new boss . . .), Laura Nyro (RIP), Gary Oliver, Jill Otway, Michael Parkinson, Nick Pitt, Rachel, Glen and Billy in E2 Stand at Old Trafford, Anne-Marie Ransom, Paul Rayer, Simon Redfearn, Huw

Richards, Keith Roberts, Dave Rose, Graham Rose, Alasdair Ross, Todd Rundgren, Larry Sanders, Martin Searby, Jerry Seinfeld, Don Shepherd, Sky Sports, Tony Smith, the South African bartender in the Middlesex Room who wanted to remain anonymous, Barney Spender, John Steen (how's the Prozac?), Bob Taylor, Colin and Carol Taylor, Jill and Peter Taylor, Ivo Tennant, Jim Tucker, Pete Watts, Paul Weaver, Pete Wilson, Wendy Wimbush, Andy Woodend (happy 40th).

To Graham and Diana Morris, a team for all seasons.

To Tim Forrester and all at André Deutsch, for your patience and indulgence.

To my agent John Pawsey, a pillar among pillars.

To Matthew and Croftie (and your fellow flannelled fools) – may your jockstraps always be full.

To Mark Ray, Ulysses of the lens and the big brother I never had (there's this great Blodwyn Pig album you simply have to hear . . .).

To Anne, my rock and my redeemer.

Contents

The Cast and Players

Croftie	Robert Croft
Matthew	Matthew Elliott
Stinger	Mark Ray
Tubs	Mark Taylor
Bev	Michael Bevan
Pigeon	Glenn McGrath
Punter	Ricky Ponting
Pistol	Paul Reiffel
Slats	Michael Slater
Warney	Shane Warne
Kasper	Michael Kasprowicz
Junior	Mark Waugh
Tugga	Steve Waugh
Heals	Ian Healy
Dizzy	Jason Gillespie
Gilly	Adam Gilchrist
Bick	Andy Bichel
BJ	Brendon Julien
Alfie	Justin Langer
Blewie	Greg Blewett
Chuck	Darren Berry
Crommo	Alan Crompton
Hooter	Errol Alcott
Swampy	Geoff Marsh
Lord Tesco	Lord MacLaurin (chairman, England and Wales Cricket Board)
The Right-On Tim	Tim Lamb (chief executive, England and Wales Cricket Board)
Richie	Richie Benaud (former Australian captain)
Chappelli	Ian Chappell (former Australian captain)

1

ROBERT DAMIAN BALE CROFT

b Swansea, 25/5/70. RHB, OB. Tests: 5. HS: 143 (for Glamorgan); BB: 8–66 (for Glamorgan). Favourite colour: blue. Favourite hobby: fishing. Favourite cricketer: Ian Botham.

'As a rule, talent tends to sneak up from behind, nudging and prodding over a prolonged period until an unanswerable case has been presented. Robert Croft has already demonstrated that he is not one for the soft sell.' I wrote those words for the *Independent* in March 1992, midway through England A's less than jolly jaunt round the Caribbean. The subject was 21; his maiden representative mission was going swimmingly. 'Croftie knows himself,' vouchsafed Hugh Morris, his tour captain and Glamorgan colleague, 'knows where he's going.' Six Aprils later, he has finally arrived. Among contemporary Welsh sporting icons, only Ieuan Evans and Ryan Giggs occupy a loftier pedestal. It would be convenient to claim that my faith never wavered, but wholly dishonest.

Raised in the South Wales village of Hendy, where his grandparents ran the Bird in Hand pub, Croftie acquired half a dozen O levels at St John Lloyd Catholic School, a rugby-playing comprehensive. 'Where I grew up,' he recalls, 'you had a rugby ball in one hand and a cricket ball in the other.' Gaining a name for himself as a lively and forceful scrum-half, this waspish welterweight represented Llanelli Schools, partnering Colin Stephens, a future Wales fly-half. Then he jettisoned seam-up for off-spin and eyebrows were quick to take off in another arena. While doing a stint as PE teacher at St John Lloyd, Phil May, the former Wales and Llanelli lock, whisked him off to the local trials, from where he progressed into the Welsh Schools XI, coming up against the likes of Graham Thorpe, Nick Knight and Mark Ilott. 'The crunch came when I was picked for the Glamorgan 2nd

2

XI at 16. The injury risk was too great. I'd always wanted to run out at Cardiff Arms Park but I also wanted to play cricket for England, so I ended up making sacrifices.'

The benefits were not slow to materialize. In 1989 he was named Player of the Tournament after leading England South to victory in an international youth event, and also made his first-class debut. At Swansea the following summer he dismissed India's latest prodigy, Sachin Tendulkar, then stirred the tail with an unconquered fifty; at St Helen's a year later he had Richie Richardson stumped. 'I was out of my depth,' he now says of that first A tour, but most of the boxes appeared to have been ticked. An impish chatterbox, exuding vim and vigour, self-belief and commitment oozed from every pore. Already hailed by judges as esteemed as Lance Gibbs and Bishen Bedi to be the best of his breed in the shires, those unquenchably optimistic offbreaks were full of loop and flight and fizz. The batting was purposeful and plucky, uncowed by the forbidding likes of Courtney Walsh and Kenny Benjamin. What were a few bouncers compared to taking on all those mountainous props and locks?

But it was the spirit that impressed most. With the hosts requiring just 48 to win the second international in St Vincent, it would have been forgivable had motions been gone through. Not our Croftie. After every delivery he would bounce down the pitch, itching to reclaim the ball, eager for another bash. The wicket of Clayton Lambert, his fifth of the match, was due reward, but this was no average-glossing exercise. When Robert Samuels stroked Tim Munton towards the long-on boundary, Croftie hared off in pursuit, bounding sixty yards to save one measly, meaningless run. Everything he did, on the field and off, carried an air of boundless, almost innocent zeal. Armed with an HND in business studies and a diploma in press seduction, chirpier than a chaffinch in season, here, it indeed appeared, was a young man absolutely certain of his destiny.

Then he vanished. Or so it seemed. There was one blindingly obvious factor, claimed my good friend Huw Richards, voicing the convictions of every man, woman and child who has ever rooted for the squires of Sophia Gardens. Tradition has it that playing for Glamorgan offers about as viable a route to wider recognition as a penchant for cross-dressing; even though Matthew Maynard, Steve Watkin and Morris himself had all won caps, there was no dissuading their compatriots from the view that they would have won dozens more had they been plying their trade on the other side of the Severn. It can scarcely have alleviated Croftie's fears of prejudice to know that his bowling mentor, Don Shepherd, went capless despite tallying 2,218 victims, the most in first-class history to go so manifestly unrewarded.

Over the next few seasons, whenever I saw him, Croftie looked to be suffering from two-stoolitis, the ailment that has plagued county bowlers of every hue since the advent of the Sunday League. He appeared to be putting thrift before penetration, runs against ahead of wickets for. The wickets certainly flowed in 1992, 68 in the first-class fray, including 8 for 66 against Warwickshire, but the arc was flatter, the fizz less pronounced. Viv Richards graced the Glamorgan ranks the following summer, infecting all with his swagger and fire as the county took the Sunday League, their first trophy for twenty-four seasons, and Croftie duly earned another A tour, this time to South Africa, where 14 first-class wickets at 28.35 saw him eclipse the party's other off-spinner, Peter Such. Come the first Test against New Zealand, though, Such got the nod and anticlimax bit deep. In July Glamorgan dropped him: 'It was the biggest shock of my career. And the biggest lesson. Perhaps I needed it. Perhaps I thought I was fireproof. It certainly taught me never to take anything for granted. I returned from South Africa only to be leapfrogged. I found that hard to take. I began to believe I was treading water, that it was never going to happen for me.'

That next season was little better, but 1996 brought renewal. Summoned for the final Test against Pakistan at The Oval, here, they said, was a craftier Croftie. Though still frisky and jaunty of run and skip, the angle of approach had straightened. The grip, moreover, had loosened, enabling him to impart more turn. On the day before the game, however, he had resigned himself. Only one twirler would make the final XI, and that man would be the leg-spinner, Ian Salisbury. 'I'd packed my bags, checked out of the hotel. I was ready to go back to Cardiff to play against Kent. Then, on the morning of the game I went to have a look at the wicket and thought, "Hello, that looks a bit browner." Might play us both now. But even when Athers came over to me I was expecting disappointment. I didn't want to hear it but I couldn't avoid him. I'd been trying the Phil Bennett sidestep but I couldn't keep it up for ever. But he just put his hand out. 'Good luck, pal, you're playing, make sure you enjoy it.' Dream come true.'

In the event, Mushtaq Ahmed was the twirler who decided the outcome and Croftie finished with 2 for plenty, yet the newcomer tickled the fancy of commentators and public alike. Dash it all, the lad actually seemed to be enjoying himself. And on it went. The ensuing one-dayers brought 5 prime scalps at 22 apiece and a concession rate of fewer than 4 runs an over, emphasizing the adaptability, expanding the fan base. Finishing the season with 76 first-class wickets from 955.4 overs (Phil Tufnell was the circuit's next hardest-worked bowler with 839.1), he gained a berth on the senior tour to Zimbabwe and New Zealand, taking 18 wickets at under 19 apiece in four Tests while striking up an empathetic alliance with Tufnell. The variety was there, ditto intelligence and maturity. Overlooked for the first Test in Auckland, an error the selectors openly regretted, he amplified the oversight at Wellington with a spell of 3 wickets in 14 balls, persuading him that he might well have a future 'at this international lark'. In Christchurch he smoothed the path to another win with 5 for 95 in the Kiwis' first dig, thus ending a protracted famine; four years and forty-three Tests had passed since an England slow bowler last contrived a 'five-fer'.

Virtually every breath he took was monitored by a film crew working on a three-part documentary for BBC Wales on his rise to celebrityhood. Reunited with Gough, a former A-tour confrère and a bird of an extremely similar feather, their fast friendship and boisterous demeanour prompted the coach, David Lloyd, to dub them 'the children', with affection rather than impatience. He also struck up a rapport with the spectators, who responded to his energy and theatrics. Although limited of footwork and indecisive on occasion – an admirable show of restraint in Christchurch ended when he spooned a high full-toss to mid-on, caught between nature and duty – there was sufficient promise in his batting to suggest a Test number seven in the making. By the end of the trip, better still, he had superseded Tufnell as the premier spinner, a whirligig of a career back on the rails and steaming along. He still can't quite credit it. 'When we were in New Zealand, Ian Botham came up to me in the dressing room and said, "Hi Croftie." Then Richard Hadlee did the same. I couldn't get over that. Legends like that, talking to me as an equal.'

Asked to select a ditty to accompany him to the crease during the one-day rock 'n' roll carnival in New Zealand, he eschewed the modern and the hip, opting for 'Delilah', made famous before his birth by the Elvis of the Valleys, Tom Jones. A Welsh speaker since childhood, the pride in the land of his fathers is fierce and undying. Indeed, should Wales decide to enter a team for 1998's inaugural Commonwealth Games cricket tourney in Kuala Lumpur, he may well be confronted by a tricky test of allegiance. 'I don't want to come out and suggest we should play Test matches as Britain. There's probably too much water under the bridge. The way I see it, playing for Glamorgan is like playing for Wales and playing for England is like playing for the British Lions. And when I'm representing England, I'm also representing the whole of Wales.'

With no expense whatsoever having been spared to bring Waqar Younis and his blistering yorkers to the Principality, this could well be a summer to cherish for the Taffs. Croftie, who is slated to bat at six and open in the biff-bangers, is hardly speaking out of turn when he talks up Glamorgan's prospects of wresting their third county pennant in seventy-six summers. Nor is he chary of pointing out that he could ultimately carve his own niche in Welsh folklore: 'I've won five caps, ten short of the Glamorgan record shared by Alan Watkins and Jeff Jones. Mind you, even if I finish up with ten, that would still be more than most.' While some might regard this as a modest ambition, the command of perspective is unmistakable.

For all his devotion to Liverpool FC and Llanelli RFC (he and wife Marie live three miles from Stradey Park), fishing is his abiding passion, has been since he was a bairn, his heftiest catch a ten-and-a-half-pound rainbow trout. 'I've always found it valuable training for bowling spin. It's taught me patience. There are days when you don't catch anything, days when you don't get a wicket, but you keep trying, keep believing you'll succeed in the end.' His entry in the 'Opinions' column of the *Cricketers' Who's Who*, unchanged from spring to spring, is entirely in character: 'Enjoyment is of the utmost importance.' Coming from a man who derives such palpable pleasure from every aspect of his calling, who doesn't have the remotest idea how to give less than everything, only the churlish could doubt the sincerity. Zimbabwe and New Zealand, however, are one thing. That creed is poised for its most searching test.

MATTHEW THOMAS GRAY 'MATTY' ELLIOTT
b Kyabram, Victoria, 28/9/71. LHB, SLA. Tests: 5. HS: 203 (for Victoria); BB: 1–27 (for Victoria). Favourite colour: navy blue. Favourite hobby: fishing. Favourite cricketer: Dean Jones.

Sometimes, just sometimes, all it takes is a single shot. With David Gower, of course, it was that velvety pull off Liaquat Ali at Edgbaston; in Matthew's case it was a thunderclap of a hook in Johannesburg, off a dumbstruck Allan Donald, the most feared fast bowler in Christendom. Off the *front* foot.

Close your eyes. Now imagine, if you can, a left-hander blessed with Gower's fluency, John Edrich's cussedness and the physical characteristics of Bill Lawry, notably his nose. Meet the young man widely acclaimed as the best opener in Australia since, well, Mark Taylor. That this gaunt 25-year-old with the proud chin is the likeliest to profit from his captain's run famine adds spice to a well-seasoned debate. He is expected to go in first drop for the Ashes tour: back home, this is the source of much ire. 'What's our best opener doing at number three?' wondered Ian Chappell, getting to the crux with customary precision. Others went further. Lawry's erstwhile opening partner for state and country, Keith Stackpole, the fellow Victorian whom Elliott cites as one of his foremost influences, declares him to be 'probably the best batsman in Australia'.

That rousing blow at the Wanderers in March was enough to convert the sceptical. Taylor himself had gone for 16. It was the first Test of the series, a rubber billed as a showdown for the unofficial world crown, and it was Matthew's audacious gesture that grabbed the initiative, giving the Cobbers an edge they would not relinquish until the series had been won.

Matthew may be on the verge of his maiden Ashes tour, but like so many of his colleagues he has extensive knowledge of the terrain, particularly Bedfordshire and North London. After winning a scholarship in his teens, he found himself seconded first to Leighton Buzzard CC then Eastcote CC. He also came over as a member of the Australian Under-19 and A sides. County cricket holds a strong allure, although he would ideally like to see the rules changed first. 'Two imports per county would make much more sense. That way we could give our utmost for a couple of months without getting exhausted.'

A keen golfer and fisherman, Matthew also has a flair for arithmetic, hence his uncanny knack of remembering his own scores, boastworthy or otherwise. His formative cricketing experiences in the Victorian backwoods had a considerable bearing on that thirst to open. He grew up in Kyabram, a fruit-growing area in the heart of the aptly named Golden Valley, half an hour from the Murray River on the border with New South Wales. His first taste of the game came on the family hobby farm at Lancaster, where he and his two younger brothers would while away the summer days on a half-length concrete pitch laid by their father, John, a secondary schoolteacher and qualified coach whose services in the latter capacity prompted him to apply for the post at Warwickshire left vacant by Bob Woolmer (in the event, shamefully, he was denied even the courtesy of a reply). Matthew's spindly arms, impairing as they did the cross-batted swipes regarded with such fondness by boys the world over, ensured he played straight from the outset. When John batted for the local team in the intimate confines of the Wyuna-Lancaster Oval, the boys would all be in attendance, honing their fledgling skills on the boundary edge. 'We'd bat in order of age, youngest first,' Matthew recalls. 'They'd usually run off when it was my turn, so I'd end up chasing after them.' How could he not want to open, to get in first?

John Elliott may have been less than impressed when his eldest son ditched his physiotherapy studies in order to spend a second summer in England, but the choice proved fruitful ... eventually. In 1990 Matthew was selected to enlist at the Australian Cricket Academy, along with Shane Warne and Greg Blewett, only to be persuaded that his cause would be better served by a season in England. The following winter his form slumped horribly, attributed by the *Sunday Age* to an 'overdose of mediocre club cricket in England', leaving him 'flat and bloated'. The *deus ex machina* turned up one Thursday evening, two days before Collingwood's game at North Melbourne. Before training, Neil Buszard, the coach, had told him he had been dropped. Fortunately, his replacement proved as reluctant and unreliable a trainer as feared and failed to show up. Matthew played at North Melbourne after all, 'made twenty-five of the worst runs ever, all edges', and was retained for the one-day tilt with Waverley-Dandenong. Pushed down the order by Buszard, who wanted to encourage him to play his strokes, he made a half-century. The slump was over.

There have been times, understandably, when he has regretted not enrolling at the Academy. 'Not going there did act as a motivation. If you graduate from the Academy you do get preferential treatment when it comes to national selection. If you don't, you have to play better for longer to prove yourself. Now, if I go there for the spinners' week to learn about playing slow bowling, I see all the photos of the graduates in the breakfast hall and it all comes home. But in some ways I wouldn't change it. The Academy may make you a better player quicker but the best come through anyway. There's a lot you have to learn yourself, and going there means you miss out on district cricket, which is very tough, a terrific education. You see the pitfalls yourself and learn more.'

The evidence was plain to see on his first-class bow against South Australia at the fag-end of the 1992–93 campaign, when he thrashed 66 to set up a declaration, displaying a levity Lawry would never have countenanced. Thereafter, hunger subsumed extravagance. Long and lean, correct rather than pretty, equally at home on front foot and back, Matthew soon acquired a reputation as a constructor of innings, digging deep roots and flowering at length: his maiden first-class hundred was an unbeaten 175. Progress, though, was hindered in 1993–94 by a prolapsed disc in his lower back, which kept him out for eight weeks, depriving him of a place in the Prime Minister's XI against the touring South Africans. The injury stemmed from 'mucking around while bowling in the nets'. It would not be his first avoidable lay-off.

The following season he atoned with a will, notably a sturdy 73 against the Poms at Bendigo during the course of which he took an especial fancy to Devon Malcolm, hooking him to distraction. That winter brought 1,029 runs at a shade

10

under 50 and a berth on the A tour to Blighty, where he impressed rather than dazzled. Despite playing for the Shield's arch-duffers, he overcame a knee complaint to head the 1995–96 national averages with 1,233 runs at 68.50, including two double-hundreds and a century in each innings – carrying his bat in the first – to deny Western Australia, the eventual champions. The Player of the Year garlands were his, from both players and umpires. South Australia made 'a fairly good offer' for his services but Warne advised him that the flat tracks of Adelaide would do little for his development or profile. Opening the next Shield campaign with 187 against New South Wales, he was chosen for an Australian XI against the touring West Indians. Ramming home that talent for substance, he batted throughout the opening day in a stand of 323 with Matthew Hayden, his rival suitor for Taylor's hand at the top of the Test order. Hayden did the bulk of the scoring, 224 to 158, but come the first Test in Brisbane it was Matthew, in deference to class, who got the nod.

A grand entrance it was not. 'Given out for a duck, caught behind off Ambrose,' he relates, tact beating dissent by a nose. 'I thought I missed it, but the umpire didn't.' Second time round, with quick runs the priority, he contributed a perky 21, then swept to 78 in the second innings at Sydney whereupon confusion over a single saw him collide with Mark Waugh, damage his right knee and retire hurt. 'Retired embarrassed' would have been more apt. Not that this was the first time this had happened. 'In the first innings against New South Wales I'd been run out after colliding with Warren Ayres. None of the NSW players could believe it could happen again. Junior and I were both watching the ball. We got a hundred million things wrong. It was a total cock-up. What I really couldn't believe was that the Windies had time to run us both out but somehow didn't get either.' Wracked with pain as he was, Matthew dived home, beating the throw, but trudged back anyway.

He flew back to Melbourne the next day for an operation

and missed the rest of the series. 'It was a bit of a concern. I was out for eight weeks, though it could have been less. The surgeon performed a procedure which should prevent a recurrence but that meant missing a few Tests. In the long term, hopefully, it was worth it.' His lecturer wife Megan, who is expecting their first child in December, saw a side to him she had never hitherto glimpsed. 'He just became very depressed. He couldn't do anything. I had to take a week off work to help him, feed him. There was a lot of press criticism, too, and that wasn't helping. He's always been terribly easy-going, very laid-back, a real country boy, so it was really hard at first. I rang his dad a few times, saying 'please come down, I need some help'. Then I rang Warne, and asked him to ring Matthew, to come and see him. But he was OK in the end. It was a good experience to come through such a testing time.'

By the time Matthew returned for the South Africa trek, Hayden had cashed in, making his maiden Test hundred. Fortunately, a void gaped at number three. In ten innings against Ambrose and Co., Ponting, Langer and Blewett had aggregated 158 runs: filling David Boon's seven-league boots was proving every bit as tall an order as envisaged. Johannesburg, where Matthew made 85 off 113 balls all told, provided the first indication that somebody might be up to it. Reflections, nevertheless, are sheepish. 'I was going a million miles an hour. It was out of character. It was my first game back, so I suppose I wanted to prove a point, but you won't see me bat like that too often.' Pity. Measured or otherwise, the Poms may still be in for a pummelling.

MARK 'STINGER' RAY

b Surrey Hills, Sydney, 2/10/52. LHB, SLA. Tests: 0. HS: 94 (for Tasmania); BB: 5–79 (for Tasmania). Favourite colour: black and white. Favourite hobby: re-reading James Joyce. Favourite cricketer: Victor Trumper. Beard: shaggy.

Described in the *Oxford Companion to Australian Cricket* as 'a dour, self-taught batsman with limited strokes . . . an accu-

12

rate, economic bowler who relied on flight rather than spin', Stinger gained a degree in English from the University of New South Wales and won a place in the state XI in 1981–82. Lack of opportunity prompted a move to Tasmania, where he spent four seasons, rising to opener and captain, compiling career returns of 1,948 runs at 27.05 and 41 wickets at 49.91 before joining the *Launceston Examiner* as a reporter and photographer. Graduating to cricket correspondent at the Melbourne *Herald,* he assumed the same post at the Melbourne *Sunday Age* in 1989 and has covered every home Test since. Widely respected by colleagues and players alike as an astute, unfailingly fair observer, he has written a number of books on the game, including *Border and Beyond,* a perceptive and revealing account of Australian cricket from 1984–94. His favoured mode of expression, though, is photography. A collection of his work, *Cricket: The Game behind the Game,* published in 1994, testifies to a keen eye and a rare talent.

ROBERT MORRISON 'STEENIE' STEEN
b London, 23/11/57. RHB, OB. Tests: 0. HS: 49 not out (for John Lyon School); BB: 8–30 (for *Marketing Week*). Favourite colour: Royal blue. Favourite hobby: Guilt. Favourite cricketer: David Gower (then), Phil Tufnell (now). Beard: bushy.

Played colts cricket against Mike Gatting and came within a couple of withdrawals of a Middlesex Under-13 trial. Motto: You can take the man out of the boy, but you can never take the boy out of the man.

PROLOGUE

Sir Roger Carrick was hurtling past indignation and heading straight for apoplexy. 'They're introducing things into the UK called Bar Oz and taking out old English pubs. And they're ripping them out and hanging surf boats from the ceiling so you can eat peanuts. And they're putting up notices saying Earls Court and all these ghastly out-of-date images the Poms have of Aussies.' How perverse, noted Luke Slattery in *The Australian* newspaper, that such effrontery should have sprung from the quivering lips of the British High Commissioner.

For all the contrasting influence and impact of Rupert Murdoch, Germaine Greer, Clive James and Alan 'Fluff' Freeman, for all that Bryan Brown's icy charm is employed to sell us cars, and millions tune in to watch Rolf Harris tending sick animals, the average Pom pigeonholes the average Cobber as conforming to a number of aspic-set caricatures: Crocodile Dundee's no-worries bushman; *nouveau riche* Noelene, the coarse matriarch from *Sylvania Waters*; Shane Warne the bleach-blond beach bum; Sir Les Patterson's drunken, dribbling vulgarian. ('The image of the vulgar Australian,' contended Slattery with no little justification, 'is really the Mr Hyde that is there, all the while, in the Dr Jekyll of the British personality.') Stereotypical images, needless to add, also hold sway Down Under: Trevor Howard's starched upper lip in *Brief Encounter*; Stan Ogden's indolent slobbery in *Coronation Street*; Jeeves and Wooster. Phillip Knightley, the eminent Australian journalist who used the proceeds of a lottery win to pay for his passage to London and has remained ever since, summed it

14

up with customary deftness: 'The two countries are so far apart that the clichés are all that's left to bind us.'

Happily, there is evidence of a desire to move beyond these clichés. NewIMAGES, a programme encompassing the best part of 200 projects bringing together scientists, students and artists from both nations, may well help drag the special relationship into the twenty-first century. Of late, nonetheless, the umbilical cord has been stretched to breaking point. Granted, Canberra recently supported Whitehall at the Association of South-East Asian Nations regional forum, and continues to regard Gerry Adams as *persona* extremely *non grata*. Paul Keating's term as prime minister, however, left scars that may take an inordinate time to heal. For having the brazen audacity to drape an arm around the Queen, this working-class Catholic found himself dubbed the Lizard of Oz. Advancing the cause of republicanism also did him few favours; nor did his refusal to play ball over Singapore. These are testing days indeed. As China prepares to take over Hong Kong, ringing down the curtain on the British empire, the Labour government here is hell-bent on devolution for Scotland and Wales and cosier links with Europe; as its counterparts Down Under twist and turn over the attractions of the Commonwealth, the shadow of Asia lurks and looms. Pom and Cobber, it would appear, are now united more by a crisis of identity than mutual affection.

Which is why, as ever, we look to cricket to bind us. Now let's not get too carried away. Steve Waugh would probably be quite content to spend the rest of his life pounding Poms into a squishy pulp (he once averred that he would rather spend Ashes tours in Ireland, venturing east only for the Tests). Victory over the Poms' bravest and bestest will probably always mean more to a Cobber. Defeat is a reminder of the past, of convict ships, of anonymity, of subservience; success an affirmation of nationhood, of adulthood. Yet the ties have never been severed. Frayed at times, yes, but never broken. Rivalries have been buried and friendships forged. Two lands divided by a common obsession? Peel away those divisions and the obsession remains.

Look at all those kindred spirits. Until the latter's death a couple of weeks ago, Keith Miller and Denis Compton were forever drinking each other under the table. Sir Alec Bedser and Sir Donald Bradman still phone each other every month. And then there was Harold Larwood. In March 1953, shortly before Lindsay Hassett and his fellow Cobbers set sail from Sydney to Southampton, who should join them for a farewell ale but the principal agent of Bodyline. For Douglas Jardine's puppet it was the end of a new beginning, the ultimate proof of forgiveness. Five years earlier, in Blackpool, Larwood had been reunited with Jack Fingleton, once the object of his fiendishly guided missiles but now a renowned commentator on all things flannelled and foolish. The pair had been corresponding for years. 'Larwood was living in almost complete obscurity,' noted Fingleton in his diary. 'Disillusioned, felt unwanted . . . could not be induced to talk of cricket.' Two years later Fingleton received a cable that 'clean-bowled me':

Leaving London Tomorrow Stop Can You Arrange Accommodation For Self Wife Five Daughters Eldest Daughter's Fiancee Stop Also Jobs Larwood

Not long afterwards, as luck would have it, Fingleton bumped into J B Chiffley, the erstwhile Australian prime minister, and mentioned Larwood's request. Chiffley duly contacted a few of his influential pals and all was arranged. Larwood spent the rest of his days Down Under, an enduring symbol of the healing powers of a common affliction.

Ah, you say, but that was then. Yet even in these ultra-professional, hyper-competitive, no-holds-barred times, there was Warne, sending a telegram to Darren Gough, urging him 'to be yourself'. The two will cross swords again this summer, the Ashes at stake, an omnipresent reminder of a shared heritage. And a heritage shared, of course, is a heritage squared.

Rob Steen
May 1997

ACT 1

Lord Tesco
Chairman
England and Wales Cricket Board
Lord's
1 April 1997

Dear Lord Tesco,

People tell me you're a tough cookie with a Thatcherite streak. Granted, there is more chance of Ian Paisley setting up a Gerry Adams fan club than of my forgiving dearest Margaret, but I welcome that. Loath as I am to admit it, cricket on these islands cannot survive without an element of ruthlessness. But beware. Persuading Sir Jack Cohen to renounce Green Shield stamps was a doddle next to convincing the first-class counties to look beyond the end of their noses.

Hence this heartfelt missive. It is now three months since the advent of the ECB (why not ECWB, pray?). Over the next three months, as you prepare your blueprint for the future, you will hear all manner of guff and nonsense about how and why revolution is unnecessary. Listen and ignore. Well-meaning people with amply stocked wine cellars will tell you that all that is required is a spot of nipping and tucking, or some fine-tuning. Listen and ignore. Some will castigate, others will mock. 'Look at Lord Tesco,' they'll say. 'Thinks he can turn cricket into a product to stack on his bloody supermarket shelves.' Forget 'em. Others will assure you that Test matches are occasions, institutions, impervious to the cyclical nature of success and failure. Balderdash and

17

poppycock. Carry on regardless.

That said, there are ground rules that need following if you are to fulfil your wishes: resist the urge to laugh, mind your p's and q's, and don't, whatever you do, issue any more threats. So you'll flounce off into the sunset if your proposals aren't accepted, will you? The merest hint of bullying will simply harden their resolve. Last summer I asked your chief executive, the Right-On Tim, whether any legal machinations could be brought to bear in order to deprive the counties of their veto over structural alterations. He shook his head, more in sadness than anger. Nothing, nowt, niet, nada. Short of a breakaway by the Test grounds, the revolution will only be possible if you play your cards precisely right.

Before I reveal the steps that must be taken, and how you may best achieve them, it seems only right and proper for me to tell you something about myself. I am fast approaching 40, going on 14. I have a wonderful wife, a gorgeous 4-year-old daughter, an irresistible 15-month-old son, an impossibly cute cocker spaniel and a breathtakingly loose tongue. For the past dozen years, I have been privileged to earn a crust as a sportswriter, arguably the best job in the world for anyone seeking to keep adulthood at bay. There is a scene in Woody Allen's *The Purple Rose of Cairo* wherein moviegoers line up at the box office during the Depression, request two tickets, then go in alone. My attitude to cricket is much the same. Outside the press box, very few people I know share my fascination. It has always felt such a lonely obsession. All you really need to know, however, is that I want the Cobbers to retain the Ashes. Should they fail, either through fatigue or *force majeure*, the chances of the counties consenting to anything more than a nose job will be less than zero.

The form book, happily, should allay such concerns. Whereas we wound up the winter by beating the Kiwis in successive Tests (having failed to lower Zimbabwe's colours in five attempts), the Cobbers made short work of both the West Indies and South Africa. Now don't get me wrong. Of course it galls me that the baggy green cappers are within reach of a fifth consecutive victorious series against our bonny boys. This would, after all, be a measure of superiority neither side has accomplished this century. It would confirm that the gap in standards has reached unprecedented levels; that what was once a sliver has now become a canyon, and not a particularly grand one at that. Why should this be? Because our nation is stifled by the past while theirs is liberated by the present and empowered by the future? Because playing a game exclusively with members of the Commonwealth will always give the opposition the edge in motivation? It surely cannot be a coincidence that our Test fortunes have declined ever since Kerry Packer levelled the playing field.

Aesthetic considerations aside, one of the main reasons I care about our national team with a passion I cannot muster for their counterparts in other sporting spheres is that the game's future depends on them. Another is the fact that they are on parade so frequently; what with a dozen Tests, as many one-dayers and sundry other overseas assignments, they represent us for the thick end of 500 hours a year, rendering their burden immeasurably heavier than that of the Shearers and Guscotts. Another factor is my empathy for the players. During the course of eleven years on the circuit and three A tours, I have developed a respect for them, in many cases downright affection. I have known Graham Thorpe and Nasser Hussain since they were teenagers. Having witnessed their struggles – with themselves, with opponents, with a system that conspires against them – the sight of them prospering is intensely gratifying as well as exceedingly pleasurable. Wishing them ill is not something I do lightly. Which is why I have a compromise plan: victory at Edgbaston while the Cobbers are still knackered after their winter's labours, some patriotic downpours at Lord's and Old Trafford then a good scrap over the last three Tests. Given your connections, I'm sure you can arrange it.

The point is that I am petrified. Ten years have passed

since our boys last won a five-Test rubber. Their only series victories of any persuasion in that time have come against India and New Zealand, lands where one-dayers outnumber the full Monty by three to one. Unless those results improve drastically, and sharpish, an entire generation will grow up believing that the phrases 'English cricket' and 'national joke' are synonymous. A generation that will lack the vaguest desire to attend the five-day play. How will I persuade my children that this is one of the most enriching of all experiences if it doesn't exist?

If Laura and Josef asked me to furnish them with a list of all the things that make life worth living I would be obliged to rape a rainforest. I would kick off with the obvious – love, sex, honesty, fairness, compassion, Peking duck, lockshen pudding, good pot – then regale them with all the cultural musts: ee cummings and Gerard Manley Hopkins; *The Great Gatsby* and *The Catcher in the Rye*; Elliott Gould in *The Long Goodbye*; Walter Matthau, James Bolam and Robbie Coltrane in anything; anything by Mamet, Manet or Monet, Ali or Dali; almost anything by Morrison (Jim) or Morrison (Van); *Frasier*, *Seinfeld* and *Homicide*; Todd Rundgren's vision, Laura Nyro's voice, Sid James's laugh, Rene Russo's eyes, Keith Jarrett's fingers, Charlie Parker's breath, Pelé's instep, John McEnroe's backhand, Charlie Hough's knuckleball. And then I'd rape another rainforest to avail them of the wonders of Test cricket. The timeless timbres and supple rhythms; the exquisite simplicity and compelling nuances; the sense of space and refuge, of past and present in harmony; the sudden twists and turns; the infinite possibilities; the mind games and physical trials; the stoicism and the self-expression; and, above all, the sheer unadulterated beauty. A cover drive from Gower or an on-drive from Chappell G; a googly from Warne or an arm ball from Bedi; the stillness and calm; the decorum and decency. 'If everything else in this nation of ours were lost but cricket,' asserted Cardus, 'it would still be possible to reconstruct from the theory and practice of cricket all the eternal

20

Englishness which has gone to the establishment of [the] Constitution and the laws.' Maybe that's the trouble. As the Venetian ambassador reported 500 years ago: 'The English are great lovers of themselves and of everything belonging to them. They think there are no other men like themselves and no other world but England.'

Mark Butcher, one of the stars of the recent England A tour Down Under, made some frank observations to me the other day. 'Whenever I go away anywhere, all people do, to a man, is say English cricket is no good, county cricket is no good. It hurts. You try to defend it but there isn't a great deal to defend. I can understand exactly what they mean, which is why I don't bother defending it any more. I wouldn't say that the Aussies compete harder than us. What makes it appear that way is that the level of competition there is much higher; individuals are more focused. Because there are only six state sides, if you want to survive you have to be competitive. You have to produce results or you don't play. The system *makes* them want to win more. What's required is something absolutely drastic. Someone's going to have to say, "right, stop". It's going to hurt some people but if we want a successful England team, sacrifices must be made. The only thing I can envisage making any significant difference is to lose ten counties and pool the players among the other eight. But it'll never happen.'

He's right, of course. Besides, why dispense with tradition unless all other options have been examined? The fact that we continue to support eighteen professional clubs is one of the miracles of the age, a rare example of bona fide British socialism. Which brings me to my proposals. The priority is self-evident: improve our Test performances by hook or crook. To achieve this, you must start at the top, which means following the Australian and South African example and contracting the leading players to the ECB, putting an end to split loyalties (that wheeze of offering the counties £2,500 for every championship match Atherton misses because he has been told to rest goes only part of the way,

I'm afraid). It also means raising standards in the shires, which in turn means: (a) increasing the demands on the brain, and (b) reducing those on the body. A two-divisional county championship, complete with playoffs for promotion and relegation (four up, four down), is far and away the best bet. Since this need not involve more than a dozen matches per county, both aims would be met. The protracted dramatics would also make the 'product' more enticing to television and punters alike.

Unfortunately, as you well know, the notion of being mired in the second division will generate no end of panic among the lesser-heeled. Their fears must be assuaged. Carrots must be proffered. You could recommend two parallel divisions, divided regionally and retaining the playoff concept, but better, surely, to examine ways of generating extra revenue and, more importantly, of promoting self-sufficiency. Staging more one-day internationals (this summer's ration of three is pitiful) and doubling capacities at the Test venues (or developing purpose-built sites like the one currently being mooted at Wakefield) would help no end. Installing floodlights at every county HQ (if local council palms need greasing, so be it) would be even more astute. Peter Hennessy, Professor of Contemporary History at London's Queen Mary and Westfield College, made a salient point: 'So powerful have been the drumbeats of [the] past that it can be no surprise that we find it so hard to make the leap to modernity. But perhaps it's because we don't really want to try; that muddling through is our preferred way.' Roger Waters was more succinct: 'Hanging on in quiet desperation is the English way'. Muddling through and hanging on? No more, señor.

The other day I reproached my mother for aiding and abetting her local Conservative Party in the run-up to the election. 'Well, darling,' she retorted, 'what about you, with your left-wing views, obsessing over a conservative game like cricket?' I didn't have an answer. I would be forever in your debt if you could prove her wrong.

I'll leave you with the wise words of Paddy McAloon:

> *This ghost is here to stay*
> *I survived the blast*
> *Get ready, get ready to pay*
> *I'm taking you at last*
> *A prisoner of the past*

You have the key. Help us unlock the door. Please.

Yours expectantly

A Well-Wisher

15 April 'The stars really are younger than the universe'
(Guardian)

EEC Council Directive (89/633/ECB): reading the following may cause heart failure, particularly to those labouring under the illusion that historians can be trusted.

Ken Dodd summed it up best. Tattyfilarious. The rough translation for which, according to my official 'How To Be A Diddyman' guidebook, is tickled pink. Which is essentially how I feel about cricket in the twilight of the twentieth century.

Stuff all that nonsense about pyjama parties eroding techniques. Forget all that guff your Great Uncle Bertie spouts about the glories of uncovered pitches and timeless Tests. The here and now easily outstrips the there and then. Consider the uncommon deeds and unlikely doers of the never-ending 1996–97 campaign. Everywhere you look, someone, somewhere, has been straining credulity. In Zimbabwe, for the first time in almost 1,300 Tests, a game was drawn with the scores level. In New Zealand, Danny Morrison, the rabbit's rabbit, staved off defeat against the Poms by stapling himself to the crease for two and three-quarter hours. In Pakistan, in one and the same Test, Paul Strang, a leg-spinner, picked up a five-fer and a century while Wasim Akram, the world's niftiest left-arm quick, walloped 257 not out, the highest by a number eight in five-day annals. These are merely manifestations of a vibrant whole. Scoring rates, slumbering at 40 runs per 100 balls and below for so long, now regularly exceed 50 per 100. Gathering, throwing and catching have attained unparalleled heights of gymnastic precision. Draws are going out of fashion (down from 45 per cent of Tests in the sixties to 39 per cent in the nineties, no mean feat given the sluggish over rates and covered tracks). Best of all, five of the six leading national XIs field wrist-spinners, not as a concession to nostalgia, nor even as an apology for all those years of rib-bending macho men, but as a focal point, a policy statement. Deception is now as potent as intimidation.

The reasons are not immediately apparent. Unlike athletics, cricket is an activity in which mind matters more than body, so there is no reason why its records should have a limited shelf life. Even when it comes to naked velocity, a category in which one might reasonably assume the anatomical development of the species to have ensured a sizeable advance, the fastest recorded delivery remains the 93 m.p.h. Jeff Thomson clocked more than two decades ago. Yet fresh peaks, all the same, are being scaled. Three years ago, the highest individual scores, Test and first-class, having endured for almost four decades, were erased by the same genius in the space of six weeks. Of those batsmen winning 10 or more caps, 22 have averaged 50 over a Test career; 5 men ended last summer doing likewise. The balance between bat and ball, nevertheless, has seldom been keener. Thirty-one men in the history of the game have finished their careers with 100 Test wickets at less than 25 runs apiece; 9 current players have taken 50 or more at under 25. No bowler this century can approach Waqar Younis's exchange rate of 39 balls per scalp. Technical innovation, admittedly, has aided batsmen and keepers: all that improved armour has certainly emboldened the former; and at least some of the wonders wrought by the latter can be attributed to lighter and comfier equipment. The most significant factors, though, are the ones nobody likes to admit to.

First, there's the money. Goals are greater, competition fiercer. The playing field, as a result, is more level than ever. New Zealand took twenty-six years to record their first Test win; Sri Lanka expended four; Zimbabwe two. Sri Lanka, moreover, are currently the game's closest approximation to a world champion. Religiously derided for celebrating athletics at the expense of aesthetics, the one-day japes also have a lot to answer for. Far from presaging the extinction of the five-day play, the box-office success of the biff-bang game has sustained growth: from 1896 to 1912, the so-called Golden Age, 51 Tests were played in 3 lands; from June 1930 to the outbreak of the Second World War there were 85 in 6; the nineties are likely to stage close to 300 – in 9 countries. The accent on urgency and invention in the abbreviated game has also had a ripple effect. Similarly, the emphasis on fitness and accuracy teaches fielders to be proactive as well as reactive, to be less submissive. Heightened awareness of an audience's demands, of the pleasures of shaking one's booty in front of the cameras, has accelerated the process.

After all, thanks to BSkyB, Star TV *et al.*, it is now possible to watch Ambrose and Tendulkar lock antlers from an armchair in Bombay or Torbay. No more relying on the judgment of jaundiced journos to decide whether Whoever really is the best thing since Whatsisface. No more blind acceptance of scorecards and averages. Welcome to the good old days. All we need now is for the original masters to get their act together.

16 April 'Cricket back with sunshine, plenty of runs . . . and four short legs'

(Daily Telegraph)

The back page of this morning's *Telegraph* features two deckchaired chappies on the boundary at The Parks, accompanied by what looks like a miniature Cairn terrier fresh from a close encounter with a washer-dryer. The *Guardian* opts for something not terribly different, shorn only of the dog, below it some characteristically pastoral paragraphs from David Foot, that unfailingly generous and modest West Country wordsmith, not only a peerless chronicler of the game's artistry and character but an acute, sympathetic observer of its shadowy undertow. The Parks is as splendid a venue for nineteenth-century cricket as could possibly be imagined. Entrance is still free – given the standard of the average county XIs that turn up there, this seems only fair – although keen-looking bods in macs are always lurking around the pavilion steps, jangling wooden collection boxes, furtively soliciting donations to the Oxford University Cricket Club. 'Lack of runs did you say,' Adela Main, 82, gently chided Foot as she occupied her customary perch for the fifty-first spring in a row, drinking in the history and tranquillity. 'It's a winner,' she exclaimed, 'just to be here in this atmosphere.' All that said, if you were seeking one symbol of English cricket's inability to unglue itself from the past, the continuing first-class status of the Varsities would do nicely.

Play has resumed. Not that it ever went away. It may have been 206 days since my last first-hand encounter with beflannelled tomfoolery, yet by kind courtesy of my principal mortgage-financer, Rupert Murdoch, not to mention John Logie Baird, I have spent a good many of them watching googlies glance off glinting bats. From Asia and Africa. From the Caribbean to the Cape. From Wellington to Hong Kong. In fact, not until 24 June, when Sri Lanka and the West Indies finally down tools in Sabina Park, will the curtain descend on the winter campaign. By then, uniquely, the *second* Test of an English summer will be over. It's official: the seasons have formally merged into one endless cycle, an ever-present global advertisement for the best game you can play with a ball without actually stroking it.

The focal point of the game, moreover, has switched,

irreversibly. On 14 March, three Tests began simultaneously in the Southern Hemisphere, not one involving a Pom. And nothing reflects that change more surreptitiously than *Wisden*, the Bible, Talmud and Koran of cricket. The '38, the ripest on my shelf, granted 77-and-a-bit of its 990 pages to 'Cricket In The Empire'; 87 were reserved for the public schools. Of this year's whopping 1,440 pages, the 'Overseas' section accounts for 293 (plus a further 8 in the form of a stop-press containing as many Tests played during the winter as was humanly possible to include without putting that nice distribution deal with Penguin at risk). Better still, the 'Public Schools' are now simply 'The Schools' – with Roedean flying a lone flag for the fillies – their alotment spans just twenty reams. As strides go, we're talking eight-league boots. At a time when an Indian businessman, Jagmohan Dalmiya, is about to become the ICC's first elected chairman, when Calcutta is challenging Lord's as the game's Mecca, it seems only right and proper.

Matthew Engel, the editor of the almanack, is a man of mostly unwavering views. His humour may verge on the sulphuric but the humanity shines through. So when he suggests his readers 'give thanks for a wonderful game', one that 'needs to change' but which must do so 'with care and love', it seems fair to assume that he has the welfare of that game in mind. Then to state, as he proceeds to do in his latest Notes, that that selfsame game is 'widely perceived as elitist, exclusionist and dull' is surely a *cri de coeur*. Judging by the way it was greeted in the crustier crannies of the popular prints, he might just as well have bombed Balmoral.

But let's get back to basics. Spring has officially sprung. The grass is officially riz. It is good to be aware of such land-marks as they happen. In *The Great Gatsby*, Daisy Buchanan complains that she always looks forward to the longest day and then misses it. Same goes for me with cricket seasons. The nearest I came to The Parks or Fenner's yesterday was a three-minute drive west from the bowels of Alexandra Palace to Marks & Spencer on Muswell Hill Broadway. Even though I can summon the Press Association wires on my spanking new Apple Mac with the merest flick of my trusty mouse, the first time the momentousness of the day truly registered was when Martin Searby, a *Sunday Times* colleague, availed me of the news that Jon Lewis had made 210 not out on his debut for Durham, breaking the county record in the process. Five days in the country and already David Boon is refreshing parts many thought beyond salvation. Trouble is, slapping students around is about as accurate a barometer of the right stuff as a degree in woodwork. Whichever marketing mastermind recommended that our national summer game should reopen for business with a couple of matches offering nothing in the way of significance, or even charity, must surely have known something we didn't.

For the first time since 1981, the Cobbers are venturing here without the Tasmanian Walrus. Of course Boon wished he could still be in the thick of it, but here was a fresh peak to conquer, if anything a more demanding one. He reckoned it would be 'a bit like my first six or seven seasons with Tassy': patience was paramount. Our telephone conversation revealed him to be as sanguine as I'd imagined, the sentences every bit as deliberate and dogged. Those beefy clumps through the V had been a masterclass in technical excellence yet, as with Allan Border, it was the cussedness that lingered. That this pair also happen to be holding down the number one and two spots in the all-time Australian run charts seems entirely uncoincidental.

The spur was plain enough, most obviously on these shores. Having sampled endless duffings at the hands of the Pom, neither had the vaguest intention of doing so again when they touched down at Heathrow in the spring of 1989. Border had lost four of his first five Ashes series; in his first five Ashes innings, Boon had mustered 56 runs; in both his previous rubbers against the oldest foe, his side had finished second by a lap. Which may or may not have had something to do with his record-breaking consumption of lager en

28

route to Terminal 3. Whereupon the world's longest-running sporting soap opera entered an era unmatched for onesidedness: by the time Boon signed off in 1994–95, surviving his erstwhile captain by a winter, the Cobbers had taken their fourth series off the reel, equalling the twentieth-century record set by Joe Darling's 1902 indomitables. Of the last 23 Ashes encounters, the Cobbers have won 14 to the Poms' 2. Before long, they'll be telling us to draft in some Danes and Dutchmen.

The statistics, for once, lack nothing in veracity. We're hardly talking close-run things here. Three of those victories have been by an innings, 1 by 10 wickets, 2 by 9, 2 by 8, 1 by 6, and the remaining 5 by 100 runs or more. The Cobbers have also totted up 27 centuries in 356 innings (1 in 13) to the Poms' 14 in 448 (1 in 32). Eight of their batsmen have averaged 50 or more; the Poms' best is Graham Thorpe's 48.14. Four Cobbers have claimed 50 wickets or more (Merv Hughes, with 65, heads the list, though Warney, with a breathless 61 in just 11 appearances, is closing fast); the most proficient Pom is Angus Fraser, with 42. Only once has a Pom – Darren Gough with 20 in 1994–95 – claimed a score of victims in a rubber; the Cobbers have managed it 8 times. While the Cobbers have employed 27 players – Boon, Tubs and Heals are all ever-presents – 48 Poms have been deployed, of whom 7 have been granted 1 chance, 18 more 3 or fewer.

All of which may well explain why the task now facing Boon appears not to faze him in the slightest. Yet doubts persist. Granted, anyone who has spent a decent proportion of his life fending off Marshall, Ambrose and Walsh has no earthly right to be deterred by a job that revolves around motivation. Instilling instinct, though, is the devil's own job. Gower couldn't manage it. Nor Botham. Nor Sobers. Which is why Lara has his hands full, Tendulkar too. When self-starters are in short supply, as Atherton would surely testify, the odds grow that much longer.

Atherton has been retained as captain of the Poms for the entire summer. After such an uplifting end to the winter, this will seem wise to most. He has certainly overseen a marked rise in resilience (5 defeats in the last 22 Tests compared with 8 in the 9 immediately prior to him succeeding Graham Gooch two-thirds of the way through the Cobbers' last visit). Those who have played under him, moreover, are unstinting in their respect. Personally, I think he should have returned to the ranks a year ago, after the Mushtaq Ahmed–Wasim Akram demolition derby at The Oval. As distinct from enablers such as Brearley and Worrell, he is an exemplar, the one obvious shortcoming an inability to rouse, to lift bowed heads. Too much can be made of body language, yet surely a captain of a struggling side cannot afford to appear passive. In 40 Tests, one shy of Peter May's national record, for all that holes have been plugged, he has commanded just 5 victories. A captain can only make so much difference, but does he truly possess the enterprise and drive to take his team to the next level? I doubt it. Which is why a trip to Test cricket's most impoverished realms would surely have been the ideal way to knock in a successor (Hussain) or even an interim one (Stewart). Given the nature of the upcoming itinerary – Cobbers (home), West Indies (away), South Africa (home) and Cobbers (away) – what riper moment could there possibly have been?

Yet even now an opportunity has been spurned. Adam Hollioake, who led England A with such distinction on their productive winter trek Down Under, ought to have had his mettle tested in the forthcoming one-dayers. Atherton, after all, has never made any secret of his preference for the elongated game. His leadership in the last World Cup, albeit hampered by fatigue after an arduous tour of South Africa, was wholly uninspiring. Besides, a break might have done the juices no end of good. That said, it is not hard to imagine him bridling at such a division of duties, and this may have forced the selectors' hand. The fact remains that his winter form was mediocre, against attacks he would normally expect to have mastered with one hand trussed behind his back. Those perennial back problems may have been a factor, but it was hard to avoid the suspicion that the burden of responsibility may have become more of a distraction than hitherto. If he is to reclaim his standing as the rock of the batting order, that load must be lightened.

17 April 'Trust me, Honest John tells the voters'
(Daily Telegraph)

Frederick Gale had several pertinent points to make about this blessed game of ours. In his 1887 treatise, *The Game of Cricket*, his Twenty Golden Rules for Young Cricketers contain pearls such as: 'After drawing your partner past recall you are bound to go and run yourself out if necessary – be you who you may.' (Are you listening, Mr Boycott?) Then there's No. 19: 'Remember cricket is an amusement and manly sport intended for good fellowship and not at all a vehicle for envy, hatred, malice or uncharitableness. If you have any complaint against your captain tell him to his face quietly what you think but do not form conspiracies behind his back. The grumblers and mischief makers are always the greatest muffs and worst enemies of cricket.' Tubs may well find that rule being broken rather frequently this summer.

In Jo'burg a month ago, Blewie and Tugga, the handsome and the rugged, became the thirteenth pair to bat through an entire day of a Test, paving the way for Tubs and his coolly efficient assassins to go dormie two in the rubber against South Africa. Since then, however, the mutterings have become darker, the cracks in that seemingly flawless edifice wider. Defying tradition's diktat, the Cobbers have retained Tubs as captain, opener and peerless first slip, even though he has failed to reach 50 in his last 20 occupations of a Test crease and, for the moment, is palpably not one of the leading 17 players in the land, let alone the best 11. Dennis Lillee was but one noteworthy who urged the selectors to bid him a heartfelt thank-you and a firm goodnight. A fair few of Tubs's colleagues, it is said, are of much the same mind. Did the imploring of the

Prime Minister, John Howard, really sway the day?

If it did, all power to those concerned. If there is a more astute, personable or enterprising captain on the high seas of international cricket right now, he is certainly doing his damnedest to disguise his presence. Tubs has lost but one series since succeeding Border in August 1994, and that under exceedingly controversial circumstances in Pakistan, on his maiden mission. Under his stewardship, the Cobbers have become the game's pre-eminent force. How many other leaders would have had the enterprise to give Punter, a part-time bowler new on the scene, an over against the West Indies? His reward was a wicket. How many would have had the ingenuity, still less the faith, to give Bev's chinamen an airing? The fruits, 21 wickets at 22 apiece, including one series-deciding spell against the West Indies in Adelaide and another matchwinning turn in South Africa, spoke volumes, for producer no less than star. Subtract those relatively trifling dead-rubber games and the Cobbers have won 13 and lost 2 of their last 18 meaningful Tests. The last 17, astonishingly, have been entirely bereft of draws. Which is the sort of state in which one might well expect to find Brian Rix on a visit to the Whitehall Theatre. It certainly isn't cricket. Or, at least, not as we knew it. Does selectorial faith denote a lack of conviction about the alternatives and their more overtly passionate ways? Or is it evidence of a belief that only such an accomplished leader can wring the best from his weary charges?

The announcement of the touring party has finally put the counties out of their misery. Slats and BJ are in, which will peeve Yorkshire and Surrey no end; Matthew Hayden and Stuart Law, who would probably walk into the host XI, are not, which will delight Hampshire and Essex; Middlesex were already resigned to losing Blewie after Jo'burg. Not that there will be any shortage of Anglo–Antipodean fusion. Shaun Young, a useful all-rounder by all accounts, is due at Bristol, three counties are being led by Cobbers (Boon at Durham, Dean Jones at Derby, Tom Moody at Worcester) and three coached by them (Les Stillman at Derby, Dave Gilbert at Surrey and Dav Whatmore at Lancashire). Cross-fertilization between the kinsmen has never been keener.

A ratepayer in cloud-cuckoo land would digest the seventeen-strong squad and declare him or herself rather chuffed. Gilly, the reserve stumper, a dab hand with the bat and a decent bet to lead the side one day, may be the only uncapped member, yet eight of his colleagues have won fewer than ten caps. Hence the widespread criticism of the omission, purportedly on grounds of fitness, of Pistol, whose eight scalps at Leeds and 6 for 71 at Edgbaston in 1993 affirmed his affinity for the greener grass of the old country. Nor is his batting negligible. Should Pigeon break down, BJ, with 15 wickets in 7 Tests spanning 4 years, will be the most experienced manipulator of the seam, not to mention the only one to have figured in five-day play on English soil. Between them, Kasper and Bick boast one victim in four Tests.

Some of the batsmen, furthermore, appear to be in a bit of a pickle. Tubs is apparently in no shape to recapture the acquisitive assurance of 1993 (a century in each of the first two, victorious Tests), let alone his maiden voyage four years earlier (839 runs in total, the third most bountiful in any series anywhere). Slats' *joie de vivre* has faded. Despite a Test average of 47, an indiscreet shot in Madras cost him his opening berth for the rest of the winter, though there have been murmurs about off-field naughtiness. Judging by the almost feverish manner in which the middle-order has been chopped and changed of late, the selectors have thus far been unconvinced by either Punter or Alfie, while Bev would almost certainly have returned to Yorkshire but for his newly discovered extra string. All told, nine batsmen have been named. They *must* be worried, mustn't they?

The straw-clutching stops there. Since having Atherton caught behind in both innings at Perth during the final episode of the last Ashes series, Pigeon, the lean, mean New South Walian farm boy and bird-fancier with the deceptively serene eyes, has scaled Kilimanjaros. 'The team has found the clown it needs,' rejoiced Rupert McCall in his poem 'The Last Bus Out of Lahore's Almost Gone (The Spirit of the Southern Cross)', 'the kid's fair dinkum loony.' Loony enough, certainly, to strike up some chin music for the Caribbean flamethrowers in 1995, knowing full well that the favour would be returned with interest, an act of considerable derring-do given that his own batting is more suitable to warren than crease. He was blowing a raspberry. Make that an entire punnet. The West Indies' thirteen-year unbeaten series record, as inspiring to some as it was galling to others, was probably doomed from then on.

When Ambrose and his compadres ventured Down Under this winter the impact was no less decisive. Quite simply, Pigeon handcuffed Lara and threw away the key, dismissing him five times in his first six innings of the series, for 26, 2, 1, 2 and 2. On each occasion he persistently cramped him with accuracy, then delivered the sucker punch with something tempting and wide that invariably drew a frazzled and fatal response. First impressions are deceptive. He rumbles to the stumps stiffly, as if his boots were one size too small. Straight-backed and economic of action, he deploys the full extent of his six-and-a-half-foot at the point of delivery yet there is no obvious menace, no hint of devilry. The end product, all the same, is proving increasingly irresistible, as evinced by his acquisition of his hundredth scalp in his twenty-third Test, a rate of proficiency on a par with Warney. Seldom shy with bouncers or badinage, his stock-in-trade is the outswinger, yet he also moves the ball through the air, all at a more hasty lick than the body language portends. Ignorance of the terrain may put him at a disadvantage at first, but six Tests should give him ample time to find his feet.

His latest new-ball partner is Dizzy, a sharp, slow-talking Daddy Longlegs with an earring per lobe who measures out his run with a tape measure. 'With his new short hairstyle, wispy goatee, dark eyes and long face,' observed Stinger in

Wisden Cricket Monthly, 'he bears a striking resemblance to Fred "The Demon" Spofforth.' (Who, incidentally, once lived at 111 Broadhurst Gardens, West Hampstead, the self-same premises where Anne gave birth to Laura the best part of a century later.) Warney described his opening assault at Port Elizabeth – 5 for 32 in 14 overs – as 'one of the fastest by an Australian for a long time . . . the best thing is the passion in his eyes . . . he's emotional about playing for his country'. Off the field, another story. Twenty-two the day after tomorrow, Dizzy is as laid-back as they come, a cricketer for the New Age. His daughters' names are Star and Sapphire. In his early outings for South Australia, he sported a ponytail. 'He still misses it,' noted Stinger. Time to conform.

So tireless and potent were the new-ball duo on the Veldt, the lack of a third seamer went virtually unnoticed, allowing Bev's 70 m.p.h. allsorts to pick up from where they'd left off against the Windies. Still, for all that he polished off Hansie Cronje's men in Jo'burg, it is hard to picture this intense, tense, introverted phenomenon proving as effective on the more sedate surfaces prevalent over here. In truth, watching on TV, one never quite believed Bev knew what he was doing. Or, at least, how he was doing it. On occasion, even as fearless a foil as Heals was chary of going up to the stumps to face those fizzing unpredictables, and occasionally rammed on a helmet. All the same, one suspects this stony-faced son of Canberra's turbulent mix of burning pride and fragile confidence will be the deciding factor. The gifts and dedication have never been in dispute; the one constant source of criticism has been his habit, as one writer put it, of 'catastrophizing' every failure. For all his struggles at Test level – Gough, a Yorkshire colleague for the past two summers, believes he is ripe for the plucking against the short stuff – the world's most consistent one-day thrasher still regards himself as a batter first, second and last. What was that he said recently, 'I don't give a rat's arse about my bowling'? Why not accept you have a rare gift and concentrate on that for a while?

What, then, of the main men? In Warney, Heals and the Waughs, after all, the Cobbers have at their centre the finest core since Granny Smith went into the apple business. Not since Ringo replaced Pete Best can one quartet of talent have meant so much to one nation. Warney, of course, is Lennon personified. Innovative, apt to get up noses, bent on changing the world and having a ball while he's about it. Imagining him as a father-in-waiting is tricky (his wife Simone is due to give birth in late June), though not half as bothersome as that arsenal of revolving grenades. True, it has been quite some time since he last took five wickets in a Test innings – against Pakistan in Brisbane, November 1995 – yet how many batsmen have lapsed against others in their relief to get away from him? All the same, he is no longer the force he was before his ring finger buckled under the strain and compelled an extended layoff during the autumn. Indeed, so jam-packed is the calendar, and so immense the burden of expectation, he has hinted that he may not be around for much longer, for all that, at 27, he remains a veritable whippersnapper (at that age, Clarrie Grimmett was six years from his maiden Test scalp). The flipper, constrained by shoulder trouble, is rarely sighted. All the same, he can still baffle and bemuse, and enchant the partisan as well as the neutral. Ian Dury had it about right: 'There ain't 'arf been some clever bastards.'

Naturally, there are more than a few blinkered, envious types who see a cocksure beach bum instead of a master craftsman, and stoutly resist any appreciation of the most significant cricketer of the late twentieth century. Maybe he did overdo the sniggering after dismissing Paul Adams in Jo'burg, but then if you were the most respected bowler in the universe and you'd just had some uppity young pup dare to attempt to reverse sweep you, wouldn't you have a titter? There are those who contend that Atherton and the chaps mastered him as the last two Ashes series wore on, yet in each case he had already decided the outcome. In the first two Tests of each rubber, he claimed 35 victims at under 14

36

apiece. The memory of that dominance should keep that swagger oiled for a good while yet. God knows we need him.

The Waughs, of course, are twins in name alone. Tugga takes after their mother, Junior after her ex-husband. To me, for all that the gait is purest Chaplin, Tugga will always be Buster Keaton, Ol' Stoneface. Wally Grout said famously of Ken Barrington that he marched to the crease with a Union Jack trailing from his back pocket; the man who reminded Bill O'Reilly of Stan McCabe waddles in with a dingo in his jockstrap. The slits beneath those gently flowing eyebrows are lakes of single-minded intent; the hair cropped and religiously kempt. In Stinger's telling photo, a fly grazes on his right cheek, insignificant and ignored.

After withstanding three successive bouncers from him at Melbourne in 1988, Viv Richards dubbed Tugga 'Mr Cricket'. All you need to know about the man is that whenever he bumps into Tony Crafter, he reminds the former Test umpire of the leg-before he denied him against the Antiguan Attila during that same long-gone winter. To watch him is to admire, to respect, never delight. The technique is airtight, the concentration limitless, the joy negligible. Here is batsmanship in monochrome, stark and spare, dutiful and undemonstrative. Those sumptuous cover drives of 1989 have long been subsumed by the drive to eliminate risk, as if he sensed the size of the void Border would eventually leave for him to fill. It's an unglamorous job, but somebody has to do it. Here, more instructively, is the fiercely patriotic history student who proposed that the baggy green cap be *de rigueur* during the first fielding session of every Test. Not until his twenty-seventh Test, lest it be forgotten, did he acquire his maiden century, yet his five-day average since being dropped in 1991 exceeds 80. To ask for charm and elegance would be greedy. As the new second-in-command, moreover, he is bound to monitor Tubs's progress more keenly than most. He undoubtedly has the edge in experience. No other member of the party has tasted second-best in an Ashes series.

How intriguing to look back at those early notices: 'The

new Dougie Walters', indeed. In terms of approach, the two New South Walians are sugar and pepper. Walters exists for fags, poker and risk; Tugga is a clean-living pragmatist whose only vice is a lust for cricketana and whose greatest ambition was achieved when he shook hands with Mother Teresa. Ella May, his paternal grandmother, was doubtless another source of inspiration. She contracted polio at 18 and was told she would never talk again, never mind bear children. The turning point of his career, arguably, came in Pakistan in the autumn of 1988. Convinced everyone was against them, the Cobbers came perilously close to aborting the expedition. Its timing, it must be said, had been less than impeccable. The president of Pakistan, General Zia, had just died in a plane crash; an election was looming; Karachi and Hyderabad had been plunged into ethnic violence, hence the cancellation of two one-day internationals; fears of civil war were mounting. 'There was no way we were going to win, no matter what we did,' Tugga assured me on a sunpecked morning at Northampton ten months later, shortly after he had acquired his maiden Test hundred at Headingley and followed it with another unbeaten ton at Lord's. 'I wouldn't say they were cheating, but . . .' The voice trailed off discreetly. 'I got depressed, I let myself down in every way. I like to think it wouldn't happen again.'

Nor has it. Unless, of course, one counts that fleeting spell when he made way for his twin after forty-two successive Tests (and, arguably, when he claimed that highly dubious catch off Lara in Bridgetown two springs ago). It could be said, conversely, that Junior, the younger by four minutes, has let himself down rather too often. He is, after all, Mohammad Azharuddin's only serious rival for the crown of World's Most Sublime Batsman, and its most prehensile slip to boot. To see him flit in and out of the bookies' tent at Ilford during his sojourn at Essex was to witness a man born to play for a living. He bets like a billionaire, and flourishes willow in much the same vein. He has drawn more from his

38

extroverted father, an accomplished, stylish prowler on a tennis court. Reposeful and self-possessed, he is apt to make the improbable look like a piece of cake. The timing is matchless, the on-drives alone guaranteed to goose the hardiest pimple. Which probably explains why he has totted up 19 three-figure scores for his country in Tests and one-dayers but has yet to pass 140. All that said, in Port Elizabeth last month, he sealed South Africa's first reversal in a home rubber for thirty-two years with an innings of mature majesty. Though never less than serene or smooth, that self-denying 116 appeared to be the handiwork of a man waking up to the fact that his gifts demand more substance.

And then there's Heals. In the first Test against the West Indies at the Gabba, the hosts had slithered to 196 for 5 before the irrepressible Queenslander carved and slashed his way to an unbeaten 161, a career-best, his third Test century and comfortably the highest score ever made by an Australian stumper. In Sydney he was at it again, arriving at 131 for 5 and adding 93 with Blewie. The value of those contributions can be seen in the margins of victory: 123 runs and 124 runs. Yet take away that sturdy bat and he would still be an automatic choice. No pair of gloves are stickier, and none stealthier, no pair of heels springier. His partnership with Warney, moreover, verges on the telepathic. Aside, that is, from the ceaseless rat-tat-tat of encouragement – 'BAWL-ed Warney', 'Good BAWL, Shane'. Give him a pair of pom-poms and he could be the chief cheerleader at Notre Dame. Mind you, there are some, Desmond Haynes foremost among them, who maintain that those verbal mind games occasionally overstep the bounds of excess. While this may be akin to Ronnie Kray chiding Reggie for his homicidal tendencies, Heals was stripped of the vice-captaincy in South Africa, the image-conscious Australian Cricket Board taking a dim view when he was suspended for throwing his bat in a fit of pique during a one-day international. The fact that he made his debut during that fretful '88–89 tour of Pakistan cannot be discounted as a source of that infinite robustness. If Tugga is the soul of the side, here, indubitably, pounds its pulse.

'I *suppose* I did expect to be in.' Matthew's languid drawl is coming down the line from Melbourne. He tries to suppress his lack of surprise but there is no relief there, no sense of a weight lifted. Then again, a few weeks earlier, Trevor Hohns, the chairman of selectors, had tipped him a wink. A couple of weeks have meandered by since his return from South Africa. Not that he'd been idle. There were regular bedroom bike sessions, ideal for strengthening the knees. He'd also been swimming, going to the gym, attending stretching classes, keeping in trim. Now, at last, he was getting the scent. Was he familiar with the heritage he was about to embrace. 'I'm not as up on it as I'd like to be, as I know I should be. Being aware of that heritage makes it even more special, when you can walk out to bat knowing Bradman made 300 there, knowing what's been before. Guys tend to brush that sort of stuff off, although I know Tugga prides himself on his historical knowledge. But I want to know about it, too. I want to feel a part of it.'

He asks me to recommend some literature. The one must, I ventured, was *On Top Down Under*, Ray Robinson's deft, loving, twinkle-eyed portraits of Australia's Test captains, first consumed by yours truly in 1976 and on perpetual loan from a certain north London library service ever since. Late last year it had been repackaged and reissued here, complete with 'bonus' chapters by the estimable Gideon Haigh on Kim Hughes and Allan Border to bring us up to date on matters since Robbo's death. For this, Haigh was awarded equal billing, which was akin to one of *Granta*'s finest applying the finishing touches to *The Last Tycoon* and claiming a joint byline with F. Scott Fitzgerald. Heresy. Other suggestions blurted out. David Frith's *Pageant of Cricket*: a pictorial history nonpareil; the same author's *England versus Australia – A Pictorial History*; Haigh's rather more legitimate *One Summer Every Summer*, a vibrant diary of the most recent Ashes series. Matthew urges me to recommend something

40

from the thirties ('it sounds like a really exciting time, what with Bodyline and all those great players'). I propose *Australian Summer* by Cardus, his account of the 1936–37 rubber. The master on the mother of all Ashes series. I ask Matthew if he knows about it, about how our lot went two up whereupon Bradman led an uprising and his lot won the remaining three. 'Rings a bell. Vaguely.'

23 April, Alexandra Palace 'Labour lead collapses in new poll'

(*Daily Telegraph*)

Opening day of the championship campaign but my duty lies elsewhere. Anne is working at *Nursing Times*, so dressing, dropping off, picking up and filling up the kids is down to me. Ah, the trials and tribulations of the part-time househubbie. But what's this? In an interview with an Australian magazine, Junior has accused the Poms of lacking the mettle, the toughness or the selflessness to win Test matches. The nerve! 'They don't play as a team, they worry about themselves. Man for man they are not that far behind us but they lack hunger.' Ah, the first whiff of cordite.

2 May 'Labour win landslide'

(*Guardian*)

'She's German.' The pale lecturer from Liverpool sitting beside me on the couch points an accusing finger at the TV. Labour's first gain and the winner appears to have a distinct Bavarian twang (it might be South African, but I decline to press the point). 'Just shows what a forgiving society we live in,' I suggest, trying to console my distraught neighbour. She still looks uncomfortably like a sabre-toothed tiger in dire need of root-canal treatment.

Anne and I were attending an election-night party in Willesden Junction, in the same house where we'd endured all those dashed hopes five years ago. Labour (sorry, Labour

Nouveau) have just wrested Edgbaston from the Tories for the first time since 1922, the year its cricket ground hosted the most astonishing of all county matches when Warwickshire (223 and 158) somehow lost to Hampshire (15 and 521). An omen for the first Test? Myself apart, not one of the twenty-odd bodies clustered around the cathode tube has actually experienced employment under Labour. Our complexions may be uniformly pink and pale, but we're not a bad cross-section. Jocks, Paddys, Taffs, Tykes, Cockneys, Brummies and Scousers. Even, in Anne, a Woman of Kent. Which is why some of us have chosen to ignore all the predictions and stay steadfastly wary. Most bolt back their champagne after the first result. Others wait until Basildon falls. I hang on until that crotchety Eurosceptic Nicholas Budgen surrenders Wolverhampton South-West. 'Anthony Charles Lynton Blair' proclaims the returning officer at Sedgefield before confirming that the PM-in-waiting has successfully wooed his own constituents. A cry goes up from somewhere near the Twiglet bowl: 'One too many initials to be trustworthy.'

The departing PM will spend the first day of the rest of his life at his beloved Oval. One evening, sitting between Keith Miller and Alec Bedser at some black-tie do or other, our John bowled Alec what he fancied was a wrong 'un: 'When Surrey beat Warwickshire in a day – *in a day* – can you remember what your bowling analysis was?' 'Eight for 18 and 4 for 17,' rattled back Alec, quicker than you can say Srinivasaraghavan Venkataraghavan. 'Oh damn,' quoth our John. 'I thought I'd catch you out on that one.' The boy was never far from view.

5 May ' "Treacherous talk cost us Election" says Norma Major'

(Daily Telegraph)

'It was all about some very naive people who felt they could rip off cricketers for ever.' Pausing from his work at the

Sydney HQ of Consolidated Press, Tony Greig reflects on the revolution that shook cricket and English society to its foundations. His commentary duties for Channel Nine may be over for another winter but his pay cheque is still being monogrammed by Kerry Packer.

Kerry Francis Bullmore Packer, by his own admission, is wholly incapable of moderation. For that, cricket should be eternally grateful. But for that penchant for excess, after all, the world might never have seen a white ball smitten over a black sightscreen, let alone grown men in fluorescent flannels, or batsmen in crash helmets, or judgments by TV replay. For a sport yoked so firmly to the past, following this uncouth upstart's lead was the ultimate compromise. Without it, our national summer game would now be rugby league. As it is, the anachronistic splendours of Test cricket are not only alive but well (even if the record-breaking advance ticket sales for the Ashes series do disguise a distinct ailing further afield).

Twenty years ago next week, on the eve of another Ashes summer, the best-kept secret in cricket became public knowledge. Sheltering from the rain at Hove, Greig, fresh from leading England to their first victorious Test series in India for forty-four years, revealed to an apoplectic pack of pressmen that he had signed up for a series of unofficial matches in Australia organized by Packer, the media tycoon and noted polo player. Most of the game's foremost practitioners, he added, would be performing Down Under that winter. Before the week was out, he was an ex-England captain. It was war. One messy court case and a two-year separation later, cricket had lost its innocence and gained a future.

When did Tony meet Kerry? 'A day or two after the Centenary Test in Melbourne in March, at his home in Sydney. Apparently he wanted to see me. I didn't know what he had in mind but my mate Bruce Francis, the former Essex and Australia opener, had told me what he'd heard about World Series Cricket. Until that moment I was completely in the dark. There were players I drank with every night of that game – Marsh, the Chappells – and they didn't say a word. It turned out that they thought I was pretty establishment and wouldn't have gone for it. But, as I reminded them later, continuity of tenure among England captains is rather uncommon. I'd have expected to lead the side in that summer's Ashes series, but I was coming up for 32. And Australia appealed to me.'

Recollections of the venture flit between the proud and the piqued. 'I don't look back on it with a lot of joy,' he laughs, that Eastern Province lilt still discernible. 'We achieved something but it was a bloody hard battle. If I wasn't fighting a court case I was batting against Lillee. The marketing campaign portrayed me as the villain. I'd upset the very fabric of British sporting society. I have fond memories of the camaraderie, particularly with the Packers, but I regret the friendships broken. It was a very stressful time, seeing your mates in court, standing up against you. Donald Carr, the secretary of the TCCB, whose house I used to live in; Alec Bedser, then the chairman of selectors, who'd always been in my corner. I don't think they were in touch with reality.'

It was a struggle, as ever, betwixt barons and serfs. Packer lured Derek Underwood, the Poms' finest bowler, with a contract worth £12,000; since his debut in 1966, fees for home Tests had risen from £160 to £210. A month later, the Jubilee Test at Lord's would yield record takings of £220,384. Mind you, compared with their peers across the Commonwealth, the Poms were doing quite nicely. Only the 350 members of the county circuit, two dozen imports among them, could be termed full-time professionals. Overall, furthermore, Test crowds were in decline. Yet, for all the success of the maiden World Cup in 1975, the one-day hit-and-giggle was still regarded as an unsightly wart and hence concealed as often as humanly possible: only two had been staged in the winter of 1976–77. Sensing the possibilities for the small screen, Packer resolved to change all that.

He conceived WSC's outstanding contribution to the future well-being of the game, namely floodlit matches. ('It seems,' mused Greig slyly, 'that lights make it possible to play cricket and earn a living.') Here, all the same, was an accidental revolutionary. Rebuffed by the Australian Cricket Board over TV rights, he was hell-bent on revenge. If he couldn't come to the party, he was damned well going to throw his own. In Technicolor. In prime time.

Reactions, inevitably, veered between the hysterical and the histrionic. Some lamented the corruption of an ideal. 'Sir, will you please refrain from dignifying Mr Kerry Packer's commercial adventure with the title of such a traditional and honourable form of entertainment as the Circus,' snorted one letter to *The Times*. 'Sir,' retorted Dr E H Kronheimer, 'will you please refrain from dignifying Mr Packer's proposed activity as "cricket".' Others were strictly personal. Alan Knott, prince of wicketkeepers and national treasure, was accosted on his way out to bat at Chesterfield by an irate punter demanding to know how he could possibly be 'worth all that money'. Greig's daughter was ostracized by her friends' parents, persuading the family to flee the country.

Twenty Mays on and the aftertaste retains much of its bitterness. 'Johnny Woodcock made a comment about me not being "an Englishman through and through", on the front page of *The Times*. He'll have to live with that. Henry Blofeld wrote a book in which he made a connection between my epilepsy and my supposed erratic behaviour. I could have sued the pants off him. I was very grateful to England, but I made a decision for A W Greig and his family. Then I was asked to justify it, so I said it would benefit cricket. Even the Cricketers' Association couldn't see it. Test players were better off immediately: Cornhill came in the next summer and gave the England men £1,000 a game. And look at the salaries for capped county players these days! In my view, World Series Cricket gave the establishment a bit of a shake-up – and they needed it. Some people out there will never forgive us. I'm not losing sleep.'

Nor should he. That 'shake-up' bred an improved, more diverse product, capable of withstanding competition from less complex rivals while sustaining its traditional virtues. Without it, the Dirty Digger would have sold considerably fewer satellite dishes. And without those dishes, the game would not be expanding so freely in South-East Asia, let alone Europe or America. Yet the *Oxford Biographical Dictionary of World Cricketers*, an 820-page tome that purports to cover 'every notable player and influential personality', has the gall to omit Packer, airbrushing him out of existence. Talk about ingratitude.

8 May 'Diana: the truth about my bulimia'

(*Daily Mirror*)

'We may ask ourselves – ruefully, if we have any sense of proportion – when have so many people ever rhapsodized as extravagantly as in the case of Lord's about a theatre, a concert hall, a library, an art gallery, a museum or any other non-religious structure containing the mainsprings of civilization?' Not often, as Geoffrey Moorhouse rightly concluded. Being a nation, as John Arlott lamented, that takes its games rather too seriously, there has probably been very little rueing. For how long, though, will the rhapsodies continue? Judging by the response to the ground's gradual evolution into a lavishly appointed, state-of-the-art stadium, and by the backlash against its chauvinist membership policy, not that much longer.

That policy has already cost the MCC £4 million. In fairness, the refusal to open membership to women – fear of clacking knitting needles, wailing sprogs *et al.* – was held as merely a contributory factor in the decision not to award the club a Lottery grant. Colin Ingleby-Mackenzie, its breezy, hail-fellow president, believes the carpet should be lifted and the issue re-aired. There may even be a vote. Breaths, mind, should not be held. The secretary, Roger Knight, upper-lip rigid, stresses that these things take time. Why on earth the rush? Discard a cherished symbol of independence for the sake of a paltry £4 million? Perish the thought.

At Lord's, one suspects, it will forever be 1947. Or 1923. 'Sir,' harrumphed one missive to the secretary that year, 'I noticed one of the umpires today disgraced Lord's Ground by appearing with bicycle clips round his trousers during his work.' The letter, needless to add, was posted in the Pavilion. Nits will always be picked with relish, especially by those with too much time on their hands. The Long Room is a refuge, a boy's own world, untouched by time or trend. With one exception. Smoking has just been outlawed, the motion proposed and seconded by a couple of busybodies who don't even sit there.

Yet externally, as if to disguise this malaise, the ancient palace is currently in the throes of the latest in a series of largely impressive facelifts. Father Time has vacated the Grandstand and taken up residence atop the clock tower. A high-tech media centre, already christened 'The Gherkin', is taking shape between the Compton and Edrich stands. The Grandstand, venue for most of my A-level revision, is unrecognizable. Gone is the lower tier, that perennial refuge from the elements. Ditto the clock. Above the rows of shiny new white bucket seats towers a bulbous electronic scoreboard. Round the back, running the length of the concourse, a mass of grey tubing masks a brace of watering holes. The Nursery End, meanwhile, is festooned with breeze blocks and hard-hats, forklifts and Portakabins. 'THIS WAY ONLY' instructs the sign at the top of the car park. 'Thank-you MCC'. *Thank-you?* Gubby would have had a fit.

Those of us who enter at the Nursery End are personally escorted to the safe side of the ground by a steward. As we proceed past the Indoor School, we bump into a forlorn-looking chap bearing an uncomfortable resemblance to my late maternal grandfather. Play between Middlesex and Sussex has already begun. He sounds panic-stricken and appears to be utterly bewildered, a tardy first-former on the verge of missing his first lesson and unable to find the class-room. 'How the hell do I get to the Middlesex Room?' he blurts. He introduces himself as Ron Carter, newly retired and a Middlesex supporter for more than half a century. Some years ago he took charge of the British Eagle freight run to the Ministry of Defence's rocket range in Adelaide. Very hush-hush. 'We used two Britannias, and converted them into passenger freight lines. I spent a week out there. Tried Aussie Rules but they wouldn't pass to me. "LTPO," they'd say. Leave the Pom out. But I always liked the Aussies. Greg Ritchie [a tubby, hard-hitting member of the Cobbers' middle-order in 1985 and 1986–87] played for my local club, Hounslow. Grand lad. Enjoyed his food, and his beer. I'd played a bit in the RAF but I was umpiring by then. He'd purposely get himself out with what we called his "going away" shot. On one occasion, when he only needed three runs to break the club's record aggregate for a season, he played his "going away" shot and got bowled. "Why did you do that?" I asked him. "Because," he replied, "only an Englishman should have that record." Which I thought was rather sweet.'

Fresh from completing an arts degree, the cheery South African lass pulling our pints is spending the summer seeing these fair isles for the first time. Scotland and Ireland beckon, but, for now, having arrived nine days ago with the princely sum of £510 to her name, finance is the priority. 'I don't know anything about county cricket,' she confesses, 'but I know I prefer Test matches to the one-day stuff. Wickets are the essence in Test matches, and I love that explosion of energy whenever they're taken. No offence, but everyone knows English cricket is rubbish. Hansie Cronje's a nice guy, he loses graciously; Mike Atherton just seems sour. Back home in Cape Town we laugh about it. We see your cricket as very snobby, very exclusive, pompous. All that ceremony and cucumber sandwiches. It's quite ironic, really, what with England still being the centre of world cricket. We really laugh at the team when we see them on

TV. We want them to lose.' Cue sheepish grin. 'Sorry to say this, but it's almost vindictive. It's almost like, "damn the bastards".'

10 May 'Hughie Green's love life sparks row at funeral'
(Daily Telegraph)

Forget Middlesex's efforts to outwit the rain and achieve the immeasurably less demanding task of defeating poor, useless Sussex (they failed). Forget all those arguments over whether Fraser still has it in him to make the Aussies fidget and fret (on the evidence of his opening spell, not on your life). Or whether Gatting should step back into the ranks and allow Ramprakash to take the reins. The most urgent topic of discussion in the Lord's press box is Hughie Green, erstwhile compere of *Double Your Money* and *Opportunity Knocks*. According to the author and journalist Noel Botham (no relation), who gave the address at the funeral up the road at Golders Green, our hero had four 'capable' mistresses on the go, and a couple more on the bench (and, presumably, incapable). As if that were not enough, he has also left behind 'a daughter, a love-child', now a leading light in television. Why this should be in any way surprising is beyond me. How could you possibly trust a chap who ended every sentence with the assurance, 'I mean that most sincerely, folks'?

The other talking point is the Duckworth–Lewis system, the latest attempt to find an internationally acceptable method of determining the outcome in disrupted limited-overs games. By establishing mean scores for each and every stage of an innings (based on past performances worldwide), Messrs Duckworth and Lewis believe they have covered all possible scenarios. Unfortunately, there is one tiny flaw: a chasing side can surpass their opponents' total and still lose. Woe betide any game that allows itself to be dictated to by those responsible for keeping score.

12 May 'Paula Yates not Green's daughter says mother'
(Daily Telegraph)

'That Australia,' remarked my cabbie, a native of Islamabad and a dead ringer for Anil Kumble. 'They're a good team.' His eyes are full of pity. We are bound for Heathrow, Terminal 3, to greet Tubs and the gang. At 5 a.m. Sanity used to be a friend of mine.

The ECB delegation is all present and correct, headed by the Right-On Tim, who looks at me as if I really am a few arrows short of a quiverful. 'We got a mention in Sue Mott's *Heroes and Villains* column in the *Telegraph*,' he proudly reveals. 'We were the heroes, for coming down here at this an ungodly hour.' I mention something untoward about wanting to catch a glimpse of the invading hordes while they were at their feeblest. Having taken off from Sydney on Saturday, and stopped off en route for a one-dayer in Hong Kong, that traditional air of energetic menace will surely have bowed the knee to boredom and fatigue.

Instead, Tubs emerges from customs whistling (on his way to the scaffold, perchance?). Every man jack wears a prim grey suit. Ten of them are aged between 25 and 27, and two of the others are 22, but they all look so horribly . . . 'Mature,' proffers Richard Little, the ECB's Corporate Affairs Manager. (Where do they get these titles?) The sense of mutual pride, of unified purpose, is inescapable.

In 1989, lest we forget, Border conducted press conferences from his hotel bed. At the Waldorf Hotel in 1977, the absence of team blazers was noted with some dismay. Whenever Greg Chappell started to address the assembled ranks of the fourth estate, Doug Walters, cigarette stapled between his lips ('making him look,' according to Christopher Martin-Jenkins, 'like the original cartoonist's drunk'), would yell 'hear hear'. These, though, can be regarded as aberrataions. 'Australians *work* harder at being good ambassadors,' asserted Ian Johnson, the leader of the ill-fated 1956 expedition. 'Why should this be so? I can only suggest that, possibly, they appreciate more than the Englishman the propaganda value of cricket to the country of their birth.'

In the interests, one assumes, of colour-coordination, Junior shelters behind a pair of opaque grey shades. The unfamiliar disrobe themselves. Blewie is shorter than he looks on TV, and has a cleft chin; Punter sports a trim goatee; Pigeon looks a bit like Gary Cooper after a session on the rack. Applause rings out as a gleeful gaggle of girls spot him from the end of the walkway. The heartiest hurrahs are reserved for Tugga and Heals. 'Go on Steve,' exhorts a middle-aged compatriot clad in a pair of shiny blue sweat-pants not normally spotted outside Essex. The object of his acclaim permits a glimmer of a smile to sully those impene-trable features: Ol' Stoneface is back. Warney seems preoc-cupied. Leaving Simone had not been easy. 'She just said, "go over and do your job",' he had told a reporter from *TNT*, one of a sheaf of weekly magazines aimed at London's Antipodeans. We may not see the best of him until after the birth.

The press conference in the Westbury Hotel is prefaced by video highlights of the 1994–95 series, accompanied by the soporific strains of Dire Straits. Up on the stage, Tubs watches the screen intently as Pom after Pom shuffles back to the pavilion. Warney's eyes light up at the footage of his Melbourne hat-trick. 'Follow that,' chirps one of the visiting journos as the lights go up. The MC is that formidable writer and chat-show maestro, Michael Parkinson, whose renown in both lands, coupled with a genuine affection for Australians (in particular 'Nugget' Miller), makes him just about the most neutral choice for such a role outside Dame Edna. 'We wish them success,' declares Parky, 'but not too much success.' Matthew, who strikes me as wise beyond his years, is none too impressed by this. 'Why wish us luck,' he later reasons, 'if you don't really mean it?' Stinger warned me about the Victorians' affinity for grumbling.

The questions, virtually without exception, are aimed

squarely at Taylor. Each and every one is batted back with patience, dignity and grace. Even when the same enquiry is trotted out for the umpteenth time (in short, did he really believe he could remember which way up to hold a bat?) there is no outward sign of agitation. Of course he was confident of making it five series in a row. Of course he was confident of being reappointed captain. His form, he admitted, had been 'terrible', but this was 'the best country in the world' to rediscover it. 'And one thing about being in or out of form', he reckoned, 'is that you're only one innings from either.' Had he really given himself a month to justify his place in the side? 'I have to prove myself to myself,' he parried. 'I'll be captain until the selectors decide otherwise.' What did he think of the opposition? Well, in all honesty, he hadn't spent much time studying them, if only because 'we have the talent to beat any side in the world'. Did he not think the slimness of the itinerary before the first Test (two first-class fixtures and various biff-bangers) might prove misguided? In the past, yes, but times had changed. 'Two or three net sessions and a couple of trips to the middle' should suffice. After half an hour, the inquisition is over. Among the scribblers, admiration is unconfined. Atherton, it is suggested, would have skulked off after five minutes. Still, it could have been worse. In 1956 'Slasher' Mackay was asked how much gum he chewed during the course of a match.

14 May 'Why England loves to hate us'
(Sydney Daily Telegraph)

'Australia stands for something we have lost,' opined Simon Barnes in the *Spectator* the other week. 'No wonder we love them. No wonder we hate the bastards.' Speak for yourself, Simon. Bruce Wilson, the burly London correspondent for the *Sydney Daily Telegraph*, noted the depth of pessimism: 'As an indication of just how elusive optimism has become, one national newspaper published an Australian XI of expatriates playing here this season that would probably beat England: Matthew Hayden, Darren Lehmann, David Boon, Dean Jones, Stuart Law, Tom Moody, Shaun Young, Shane Lee, Geoff Foley, Don Nash and Shane Jurgensen.' Shane Jurgensen?

To The Oval, for any number of reasons. To doff the cap to Syd Lawrence, that gregarious linebacker of a fast bowler whose career should by all rights have ended with that excruciating howl of agony in Christchurch five winters ago. Knee repaired, optimism restored, he has just made a remarkable comeback for the unexpected championship leaders, Gloucestershire, the only side with a win after the first two sodden rounds. And to his teammate Monte Lynch, once of this parish and still smirking like a mischievous fifth-former (and still catching flies at slip). Then there's Surrey's Alex Tudor, the rangy quick from West Brompton who made such a resounding impression for the England Under-19s in Pakistan. Devon Malcolm with radar, so they say.

I'm also here to impart some dubious pearls for the even more questionable benefit of a few journalism students from City University. They are in the press box (sorry, Media Centre) under the auspices of Steve Pinder, one of my very favourite earthlings, the man who gave me my break as a scribbler in his former capacity as sports editor at *City Limits*, the now-defunct listings magazine for the politically correct. He has asked five of his brood, including a couple of charming Grecians, to take a stab at reporting the pre-lunch session as if they were working for the *Standard*. I'm there for moral support and technical advice. For a Yorkshireman – and he would readily concede as much himself – Steve's knowledge of the sward is endearingly modest.

Above all, though, I have come to watch the Hollioakes. If John Major can be said to have performed one invaluable service for his country – aside, that is, from proving that decent chaps have no place in politics – then it was the discreet push he gave to Adam's passport application. He

53

may not have been able to see his Cabinet for the disloyal charlatans they were, but he can obviously spot a cricketer. (It is to be sincerely hoped, in his final Honours List, that he also recognizes comic talent; Bob Hope is 93 but still awaits a knighthood. 'Why don't you retire and go fishing?' the ageless quipmeister was recently asked. 'Fish', he darted back, 'don't applaud.' Gooch must be cut from similar cloth.)

The competition between the Melbourne-born Hollioakes goes well past keen. 'We used to have a Sega Megadrive computer game,' recalled Adam, at 25 the elder by six years, 'and that turned into World War Three.' Ben amplified the point: 'We never finished a game of table tennis – it got to nineteen-all and the bats were thrown down and we accused each other of cheating.' If they went to the toilet together, chuckled Adam, 'I suppose we would see who could get it further up the wall.'

The bond, for all that, is strong. Strong enough for them to have cohabited in Wandsworth ever since their parents, Daria and John, who used to play for Victoria, returned to Australia four years ago. Strong enough for Adam to repay Alan Wells with interest last summer after the then Sussex captain had availed Ben of a few choice verbals. 'I do feel fiercely protective towards him,' Adam conceded to me at The Oval last October while balancing precariously on a rail high in the Bedser Stand, thirst for danger at least partially quenched. He was preparing to jet off Down Under at the head of an England A party widely expected to succumb to the states without much ado. Was he not piqued by the absence of representative fixtures? Not in the slightest. 'Winning', he asserted, 'is all I'm interested in.'

As it transpired, even though the states were seldom able – or inclined – to field their first-choice XIs, the tour went swimmingly. As a leader, moreover, Adam impressed all and sundry with his personable touch and energetic mind, albeit not his temper (given the obligatory accusations of treachery he was forced to grin and bear, this was surely excusable). As a consequence, the stock of this middle-order marauder and handy seamer has soared. Hailed as the latest FEC – helpfully, the management comprised David Graveney, now the chairman of selectors, and Gatting, now a selector – he promptly found himself appointed captain of Surrey when Alec Stewart decided, rather sensibly, to hive off some of his oppressive workload. A berth in the Texaco squad is the very least he can expect.

Benjamin Caine Hollioake is taller, a veritable Adonis. And, in Adam's estimation, much the more talented. Hence the growing hope that this Millfield graduate could yet become the first teenager to represent England since Brian Close in 1949. 'He has huge self-belief and no fear of failing,' warranted big brother, 'but he can be too laid-back and underestimate opponents.' Not that Ben lacks excuses for that cocky prowl. My first glimpse of him came last August, playing for the England Under-19s against New Zealand. Lust at first sight. As a bowler, his casual, easeful approach to the crease, as if transported by surfboard, kindled visions of Holding. Too chest-on for the purist but useful nonetheless. Yet it was with the bat that he enthralled and enchanted, as he does again now.

At lunch, Surrey are 83 for 7, undone by some spiteful swing, notably from Mike Smith, a chunky left-armer in the very thick of his prime. Mind you, Dickie Bird has certainly done his bit, twice awarding iffy leg-befores with a strident neo-Nazi salute. Syd looks fit and fast, and richly deserves his pickings. Uncowed, Hollioake Minor sheds his initial introspection and goes in search of big game. As Syd stampedes in like some overenthusiastic wildebeest, he plants a fearless foot down the wicket and flicks the resulting full-toss through midwicket. Talk about arrogant. Ignore the top-edged hook; the orthodox and genuine easily outscore the swishes and flukes. Smith, who almost gave up the game a few years back but is now, at 29, a chap with legitimate Test pretensions, sees a perfectly reasonable delivery clipped off the hip for a haughty six. The backlift is minimal, the head still, the timing exquisite. Had he hailed from Karachi or Kanpur, those bright, certain eyes would already be an object of schoolgirl fixation. A leading edge to mid-off finally calls a halt to the frolics, leaving Hollioake Minor with a top score of 29, out of a piffling 115. As Monte waddles off, his efforts to suppress his mirth prove entirely unsuccessful.

I don't know whether I was much help to the students. I did point out that Gloucestershire's thick-set all-rounder Mark Alleyne happens to be the first homegrown black player to captain a county, a fact of interest to *Standard* readers since he hails from Tottenham and graduated from the Haringey Cricket College. In return for such gems, they consent to volunteer their opinions on all things cricketing. The results are much as feared.

'You have a morning culture,' chuckled Chris Kaklamanis, an affable Athenian. 'We wouldn't dream of starting a game in the morning.' That said, he'd taken to cricket while watching the South Africa–Australia series on Sky ('it looks a very good game the way the Australians play it; England are in awe of them, I understand'). This, though, was his first close encounter. 'I enjoy watching the guys persevere so much. The strategy attracts me too. I don't understand it, but you can tell they're thinking hard. I also like the fact that it's so unpredictable. You can be down in the gutter, 20–nil down, and still come back. In Greece I don't think we have the patience. It's football first, basketball second. Mind you, it's much better than rugby. Rugby stinks.'

Noam Friedlander, a London-born sports 'nut' who follows 'everything but cricket', had a dire warning. 'You wait,' she predicted. 'Tim Henman will push cricket off the back pages this summer. I used to watch Lamb and Botham when I was about 8. I took an interest in colourful characters. But when they left the scene, I did, too. I want to learn about the game for professional reasons; it would give me something to cover outside the football season. But I'm interested in personalities, not games. At college, there are thirty students in the class, three or four of whom are into cricket. Football's at the top, just above badminton. A few pretty boys might raise the profile, build up a younger fan base, help the game become more contemporary. Having a winning Test side *would* make a difference. I'm certainly enough of an Anglophile to develop more interest but English cricket is perceived as elitist, traditional, archaic. How many blacks are playing at county level, let alone in the England team?'

Roz Isaacs was more encouraging. 'I like the sound of bat on ball. When I was with the Air Training Corps in Kent I used to play in the inter-squadron matches. I enjoyed that. My uncle followed Sussex. He was a real enthusiast, and I used to go to Hove with him when I was young. But if you put "cricket" and "England" in the same phrase you get losers. The only young boys I know want to be footballers. I prefer a more energetic, dynamic game, like hockey.'

Thank heavens, then, for Alison Kirkham. 'I used to watch the Tests by myself during the summer holidays when I was young. I was captivated. My best memory is Alec Stewart's catch off Lara at Lord's in 1995. I put £2 on England to win. It was the *Bodyline* TV series that got me into it. Bradman became a hero. And Jardine. He was so debonair. I love Jack Russell's doggedness. I used to spend quite a lot of time at The Parks when I was up at Oxford. I played for Wadham College, and once achieved a stumping. The Aussies came one year and caused havoc. Drank everyone under the table. I met Merv Hughes and had a nice chat.

'The biggest problem with English cricket is ill-discipline. It's a professional sport, yet how many players look as if they've trained, let alone as if they're on a proper diet? The Test team look like they expect to lose. The rest of the world are more competitive, and that competitiveness is nurtured from a younger age. I admire the Aussies because they retain their sense of humour while taking it seriously. Although I'm keen on keeping certain traditions – cricketers should always play in white – we need to make progress. The

Commonwealth countries are superseding us in many spheres. We still do everything the old way, especially in cricket.'

Fears amply confirmed, I thank my chastening respondents for their time and pop out to Henri's deli for some liver pâté sandwiches. On my return, Martin Bicknell, this season's Oval beneficiary at the tender age of 28, is operating off a shorter run than hitherto, and looking a good yard faster. Here is one of English cricket's more grievous casualties. But for the unfeasible demands on his body (one season he racked up 1,000 deliveries well before the end of May), he would surely have earned far more caps than the two he gleaned during the 1993 Ashes series. When it comes to foot-shooting, our aim is certainly unerring. Tudor, disappointingly, does not share the new ball. Joey Benjamin, that delightful ageing workhorse, is accorded that honour, and Hollioake Minor coasts on as first change. After an hour, the guilt begins to gnaw. Resistance is low, as ever, so I set off home, arriving at bathtime. Noddy and Big-Ears get an airing then it's back off downstairs, to call up the close-of-plays. Tudor, I discover, wound up bowling the hastiest spell of the day, scalping three. Buggeration.

18 May 'Government to outlaw fox hunting'
(*Sunday Telegraph*)

'Technique alone is never enough.' Botham? Casanova? Eddie Edwards? No, Raymond Chandler. Which rather suggests the Maltese Falconer would be patting the selectors on the back right now. Messrs Graveney, Gooch and Gatting have reeled in the years in assembling their Texaco squad, recalling Phil DeFreitas. (As the only suitable candidate to have emerged from an Ashes series on the winning side, he might prove a lucky mascot; the Poms, after all, have not beaten the Cobbers in a home one-day series since 1981.) Still, they've also summoned Hollioake Minor. With big brother also nominated, the Poms could field their first pair of brothers since the Richardsons forty summers ago.

Dominic Cork, a national hero two summers ago, is missing, injured, as he probably will be for most of the summer. Even if he had been raring to go, his inclusion would have been anything but certain. The story is a sad one, a parable for these celebrity-obsessed times, if not exactly unfamiliar, nor, in some ways, inevitable. Last winter, the highly strung Derbyshire seamer had been granted leave of absence from the trip to Zimbabwe to sort out his troubled private life. A broken marriage, exceedingly bitter and extremely public, had sent him scurrying into his shell, convinced he was being persecuted (which, to an extent, he was; even his parents found themselves besieged by tabloid lenses and tape-recorders, or so he has claimed). 'They used to say I was paranoid,' observed an exasperated Botham, who appears to have given up on him, 'but this bloke is something else.' In New Zealand, where his action appeared to have disintegrated along with that once brimming confidence, came close to being sent home by Lord Tesco. Less for his own benefit, it seems, than that of his colleagues, whose patience had worn thinner than an After Eight mint. Sudden fame is the bane of the immature.

Some crunchy numbers from the *Sunday Telegraph* magazine. The number of pieces of chocolate required to increase clear-headedness by one-third – according to findings by some eminently sensible researchers at Reading University – is just four. Which means, presumably, that if I eat a half-pound slab of Galaxy a day, I could develop into Archimedes or Aristotle. Meanwhile, in the esteemed view of Mr William Hill Esq., the odds on every day of the first Test being washed out are 500–1, which seems a mite mean. More intriguingly, the number of Britons emigrating Down Under last year was fourteen times the number making the opposite journey (11,300 to 838, according to Australian Office of Statistics/Home Office records). What was that about hating the bastards?

*

19 May 'Police quiz Labour MP over "bribe"'

(*Daily Telegraph*)

They buried Laurie Lee today. *Cider with Rosie* being the first book of my acquaintance to allude to sex, the author will always occupy a lofty place in my affections. Who else could have conceived an Army XI numbering the likes of Col. 'Tigger' Ffoulkes-Whyte and Maj. T W G Staggerton-Hake? Or embroidered the game with such lustrous imagery. To wit: 'I can picture that squat little whizzing man knocking the cricket ball out of the ground, his face congested with brick-red fury, his shoulders bursting out of his braces. I can see him crouch for the next delivery, then spin on his short bowed legs, and clout it again halfway to Johannesburg while heard far-off Sheepscombe cheer.' On the adjacent page to this extract in *Famous Writers on Cricket*, Roger Adams's slim yet compelling compendium, lurks a shot of Gatting cutting: teeth grinding, chin jutting. Nice touch.

The *Guardian* has a splendid new stats page on Mondays. Some, mind, will take exception to the comprehensiveness. Mark Ealham is hardly likely to wish it to be common knowledge that he is currently in possession of the highest bowling average (178). Nor Gloucestershire's promising Robert Dawson that he boasts the lowest batting average (5), let alone that 5 of his 7 innings have resulted in ducks. The expanded championship table shows John Stephenson to have won the toss in all three of Hampshire's fixtures without recording a (more meaningful) victory. Which infers (a) the toss is meaningless, and/or (b) Hampshire are crap. Either way, in the interests of equitability, why not dispense with such a manifestly redundant ritual and give the visiting team the choice? That way, at least, we could call a halt to the nefarious practice of preparing wickets to suit the home team (not, I am proud to say, an English trait, albeit only because the weather is so bloody unhelpful and the groundsmen tend to get a tad bolshie when given orders by strangers in suits; that said, I fear this summer could be different).

The papers are brimming with blue. Chelsea's FA Cup triumph, on the eve of the Flower Show, has prompted an outbreak of paens to south-west London. Even though I have supported the Blues since I learned that an uncle had sustained a fatal coronary celebrating a goal against Arsenal, Saturday's triumph against Middlesbrough left me cold. Feeling as if I'm missing out on something, I console myself with a list.

Twelve Reasons Why Cricket Is Better Than Football

1 Cricket is summer, bright mornings and contemplation; football is winter, dark afternoons and a quick fix.
2 Football is a game of two halves; cricket is a game of forty innings.
3 Cricket reflects its traditions; football mirrors advances in the coiffure trade.
4 Cricket didn't need a Hillsborough to shame it into treating its customers as something other than dirt.
5 Football fans go to see goals, and since the average match contains three, they spend 99 per cent of their time being shortchanged. Cricket fans go to see runs and/or wickets. On an average Test day, roughly speaking, runs come every 80 seconds (i.e. 75 per cent of the time) and wickets every 40 minutes (i.e. 11 per cent). It therefore seems reasonable to propose that its audience derives appreciably more pleasure and substantially less pain.
6 Football's most impressive scoreline is Arbroath 36 Bon Accord 0; cricket's most impressive scoreline is England 903 for 7 declared, Australia 201 and 123.
7 The 1995–96 *Rothman's Football Yearbook* squeezed a year's worth of happenings in South America, Asia and Africa into 2 of its 960 pages. The 1997 *Wisden* devotes nearly 20 per cent of its acreage to events with no British interest whatsoever.
8 When a batsman walks, even now, we aren't that shocked. When a centre-forward owns up to the fact that

the penalty he has just earned was not wholly deserved, as Robbie Fowler recently had the balls to do, gobs are not so much smacked as electrocuted. And the England coach, a purported born-again Christian, tuts.

9 In the space of less than five sessions at Leeds in 1965, John Edrich purloined 52 fours and 5 sixes in addition to 72 runs of assorted other denominations. In one over of a Ranji Trophy match at Bombay in 1984–85, Ravi Shastri, fresh from spending an hour in the 90s en route to a seven-hour 111 in the Calcutta Test against England, hoisted 6 sixes. Even at the very zenith of his powers, the best Pelé could expect from a week's work would have been a hat-trick, a couple of 'assists' and twenty telling passes that led to naught.

10 Football is 10 per cent artistry and 90 per cent perspiration; cricket is 20 per cent artistry and 80 per cent universal contemplation.

11 In footballspeak 'stylish' means lazy and selfish; in cricketspeak, 'stylish' can mean Holding as well as Gower.

12 Football is *Star Wars* without the special effects; cricket is *The Sound of Music* without Eleanor Parker.

Anne returns home after helping out at Laura's nursery. Lotto, and lots of it. I tell her I've been listing all the ways in which cricket is better than football. 'That sounds *really* interesting,' she says without a shred of conviction. I'm sure I detected a hint of pity. Off she trots to the zoo with Laura, Josef and Maia, Laura's best friend. When they return, Anne informs me that Julius, Maia's father, would consider having another sprog. As she hears this, Laura turns a purple shade of pale. 'I want them to keep Maia,' she implores, berry-brown eyes welling up with tears. Anne and I both crack up. 'Who said anything about getting rid of her?' asks Anne, wiping her own eyes and trying like buggery to keep a plausibly straight face. 'You did,' insists Laura, accusingly. 'If Bernadette has another baby, where will Maia go?' I ponder

availing her of a cricketing analogy: just because a new batsman is in, doesn't mean his predecessor's score is erased. In
the end, I think better of it.

That said, Laura is responding to my promptings and
developing a fondness for sport. ('You know something
Daddy,' she explained while we were walking Woody in
Highgate Woods on Sunday, 'I *love* balls.') Josef, though, is
leaping ahead. 'Say goodnight to Bobby and Herbert,' I
prompt him as Anne carries him to bed past the Spy prints
in the hall ('The Flannelled Fool' looks the dead spit of
Bobby Abel and Herbert Strudwick is the only pre-World
War I keeper I could think of the day introductions were
made). Given that, at present, Anne and I are both 'Dada',
my prodding seems somewhat optimistic, yet Joe goes one
better: Bobby and Herbert each receive a kiss. And to think
I never wanted a son because I was fearful of indoctrinating
him.

20 May 'Sports millions go up in smoke'

(*Daily Express*)

It's official. Tobacco firms will no longer be able to tout their
wares under the banner of athletic prowess. What a convenient way of stubbing out the B&H Cup, and hence easing
our cricketers' burden. On the other hand, as a willing and
occasionally ardent inhaler, I find myself in accord with an
editorial in the *Express*, which is definitely a first: 'It seems
more likely that people will take up the sport they are
watching rather than rush out to buy a packet of 20 because
the name of a brand flashes by on the side of a racing car.
What about sponsorship by the alcohol manufacturers?'

Ever the oddball, Jack Russell has secured himself a novel
form of sponsorship. The launch of *Jack Russell – Barking?*,
his much-scrutinized but almost entirely inoffensive autobiography, was bankrolled by McVitie's. In the book, rather
fortuitously, he had revealed his complete and utter inability to get through a day without consuming an entire

packet of Jaffa Cakes (or, for that matter, Milk Homewheats). McVitie's marketing bods seized the day, persuading their bosses to donate a pack of biscuits for every copy signed during the course of Russell's fifteen-date nationwide tour of the nation's literary supermarkets. Tetley's, the outgoing sponsors of the England team, have also been rather enterprising. The principal reason for withdrawal at the end of the summer, the brewery has made a point of remarking, is not that the sponsorees are such an embarrassment, as was widely supposed, but because five of the Test venues have barred their foamy wares. To circumvent this, a Tetley promotional bus will ferry fans to and from stations and car parks at the one-dayers and Tests, and supply a free can of beer to every passenger. How very considerate.

The evening brings the first in a new series of *David Gower's Cricket Monthly*, and with it a bit of a shock. 'I very much hope we will be at least prepared to consider radical change, and we can implement those changes as soon as possible.' It was a statement one never expected to hear uttered on the BBC prior to the watershed hour. Yet there was the Right-On Tim, brazenly dropping the words 'change', 'radical' and 'soon' into the same sentence. Give that man a knighthood.

21 May 'MP Sarwar admits he gave money to opponent'
(*Guardian*)

Paul Filer, who lent me my first cricket book thirty-odd summers ago, and struck my very first off-break through the Stonegrove Park shrubbery for four, rings up with some apparently hot news. 'Did you hear what's going on at Phillips tomorrow? Thomas Boxhall's *Rules and Instructions for Playing at the Game of Cricket* is coming under the hammer. 1804 edition. Estimated price two to three thousand. If it goes for much under five, it should be cheap.' He reads me the comments in A D Taylor's *Bibliography of*

Cricket: 'Perhaps the most rare and coveted of the very few contributions to the literature of the early game . . . probably worth its weight in gold . . . worth what it can fetch.' He wishes he could buy it, 'but it's a bit extravagant, don't you think?' Um, well, yes.

Stinger faxes me a clipping from today's Sydney *Daily Telegraph* headlined 'Poms not in the race'. The word 'Pom', it would seem, is not a racial epithet but a colloquialism used merely to describe a person's origins. A complaint brought against a Queensland paper, elaborated the report, 'has been dismissed in a Human Rights and Equal Opportunity Commission ruling to be released today. Commission president Sir Ronald Wilson said publication of the words "pom" or "pommie" was not likely to "offend, insult, humiliate or intimidate" people of English origin.' Don't know about the first three, but I'd definitely challenge them on the intimidation.

Limbering up for tomorrow's first one-dayer at Leeds, *The Pavilion End*, Sky Sports' weekly magazine programme, stirred the pot with a will. Having quoted Malcolm Conn's jibes in *The Australian* about playing 'the beleaguered Poms' being 'cheap and unfulfilling', Charles Colvile tackled the blackguard head-on. 'That's not very nice,' he asserted. Conn, an amiable cove, hammed it up for all he was worth. Nothing, not even a Sherwood Forest of a moustache, could disguise that glued-on smirk. 'This is like an end-of-season football tour. See a few castles, play a bit of cricket. A few cheap runs, a few cheap wickets. A bit of a doddle.' Colvile did his country proud, responding with the lowest of blows. What about David Leatherdale, the part-time seamer who'd just bowled Worcestershire to victory over the tourists in a one-dayer? Conn muttered something suitably disparaging. 'We've got better bowlers than that,' barked Colvile, clearly ruffled. 'Where are they?' wondered Conn, bottom lip quivering, sides on the verge of going their separate ways. 'I'm not telling you,' taunted Colvile, regressing by the second. 'I can't give away secrets.' So yah boo sucks.

22 May 'Old devil poised to haunt theatre'

(Guardian)

The Nutty Professor Is Back! Jerry Lewis, one of the few men ever to tickle British and French funnybones with the same act, is in town to play the devil in *Damn Yankees*, which is about to transfer from Broadway to the Adelphi. At 71, explains the venerable gagmeister, he has returned to the stage to 'stay young'. Dean Martin passed on a year and half ago but Lewis is still in mourning: 'It's like losing a limb. Or losing a child.' Whether it can be compared to losing the first instalment of the Texaco Trophy by a street and a half is something only Tubs could tell him. Judging by the Australian distaste for defeat, it might well be a close-run thing.

The omens for the new era, it must be confessed, had been some way short of auspicious. Following their recent three-day get-together at Upper Heythrop in deepest Gloucestershire – variously reported as 'charm school', 'seminar' and 'fashion show' – Atherton and co. have been issued with a twenty-eight-page guidebook designed to enhance, not performance levels, but public profile (as if the two could ever be mutually exclusive). On page seven, indeed, they are urged to present a more positive image to the media, which really would take some doing. Whereupon the Beeb are snubbed.

When Cork dropped out of Radio 5 Live's *Any Sporting Questions*, citing a pressing appointment with his physio, Richard Little, fully living up to his 'Precious' tag, denied access to any of the other members of the Texaco squad, even though John Crawley and Croftie, neither of whom needs much prodding in such matters, were both understood to have been ready and willing to oblige. Too close to the opening game, apparently. And this in the very week that the board have enlisted the services of the PR consultancy run by Sir Tim Bell, erstwhile adviser to Her

Thatcherness. One wonders whether Sir Tim comprehends the size of the task ahead.

Among the other directives in the ECB booklet is an insistence on royal-blue headgear and three-lion crest. Which means Stewart's 'lucky' white helmet has to go. Ditto – should its owner win a recall – Russell's beloved 'Floppy', the creased and crumpled sunhat that is as inextricable and endearing a part of his public persona as was Chaplin's bowler. Creating an impression of unity is all very well, but I can't help feeling this is stretching things a tad far. Next thing you know, they'll be insisting on a team aftershave (Old Spice rather than Brut). New Lord's, old rot.

Come Headingley, happily, deeds speak louder than words. For five hours, in fact, we are regaled with a limited-overs contest of epic proportions. On a pitch that might conceivably have outpaced a slug, each and every run has to be chiselled out, every quarter disputed. The Poms, chasing 170-odd, are down for 40 as Hollioake Major enters. Warney promptly befuddles him with googly, then flipper, whereupon Dizzy fetches him a horrid blow on the forearm, just below the elbow. He doesn't even give them the satisfaction of a curse. It brought to mind something Essex's estimable Queenslander, Stuart Law, said about Surrey prior to last season's NatWest semi-final: 'You can see they have what we call a bit of "mongrel" in them. Hollioake knows what it is like to be brought up playing the Australian way and it's creeping into their cricket now.' And not before time.

Hollioake's bravado alters the whole complexion. Not another wicket is lost as he and Thorpe, Surrey united, sweep the Poms home with ten overs and several furlongs to spare. Hollioake applies the *coup de grâce* with a six into the Western Terrace as his parents beam on from the stalls. John and Daria had landed at Heathrow this morning, and lost their baggage in transit: the Lord taketh, and the Lord giveth.

*

25 May 'Last Supper is a Gospel myth, says churchman'
(Sunday Telegraph)

Ever game for a lark, Oscar Wilde filled out a questionnaire during his days as an Oxford undergrad entitled 'Album for Confessions or Tastes, Habits and Convictions'. Misery, he wrote in the document, due to be offered at Christie's next month, was 'living a poor and respectable life in an obscure village'. Asked to nominate 'the saddest word in the world', his reply was more succinct: 'Failure'. There seems scant danger of Hollioake Minor suffering unduly from either of these fates.

To sit in the Warner Stand watching him thwack Australia's finest the length and breadth of Lord's in the third one-dayer was to feast on the splendours of unfettered, uncluttered youth, uncowed by man or beast. When invited to partake of their first pint in the St John's Wood saloon, most mortals tend to experience at least the odd collywobble; this lad drank the place dry and savoured every last dram. Not since Gower has a Pom's opening gambit stirred as many imaginations as Hollioake Minor's contemptuous off-drive against Pigeon. The riposte was a snorting bouncer, evaded with a sway of the head that bordered on the sniffy. Balls as well as talent. Nor was it an adrenalin-induced fluke, as his eventual 63 off 48 balls proved. Pride of place went to the six over square-leg off Warney. Bellylaughs at Lord's? How unseemly. Not since Dustin Hoffman swept Katharine Ross off the altar in *The Graduate* has a Benjamin stolen so many hearts.

Matthew and Croftie will have less cause to cherish the memory of their first international at HQ. Discomfited by the slope, Matthew lasts four balls before slicing an intemperate drive, swelling his total of deliveries faced on tour to eight. Croftie's ten-over stint yields 51 runs, a far cry from his strangling displays in the first two games. For Hollioakes Major and Minor, conversely, all is rosy. Once again, Major collects the winning runs, just as at Leeds and The Oval, and deservedly takes the Man of the Series award, which ought to preface a Test debut at Edgbaston. The Poms, even more uncannily, have taken all three games by six wickets. I nearly forgot how irrelevant these matches are supposed to be.

28 May 'Family may relent on beheading'

(*Guardian*)

The kith and kin of Yvonne Gilford, the South Australian nurse allegedly murdered by two Britons in a Saudi Arabian medical complex, made no bones about it. If found guilty, Lucille McLauchlan, from Dundee, and Deborah Parry, from Alton, Hampshire, should be beheaded. The accused, for their part, insisted that police officers secured their confessions by stripping them and threatening rape. Following an entreaty from the judges, happily, Frank, the deceased's brother, says he is prepared to consider alternative punishments. Under Sharia law, a victim's relatives may revoke the death penalty in favour of financial compensation from the perpetrators, i.e. 'blood money'. 'There are more options than just the blood money or the beheading,' added Frank. 'Apparently, there is imprisonment as well.' Who said Cobbers lack compassion?

Tubs hasn't murdered anyone. All he has done is mislay his capacity to hit a ball. Given the extensive nature of his services to team and country, one would have imagined that he, too, deserves a bit of compassion. Not according to Tugga. 'I can't be bothered worrying about Mark Taylor's game,' he snapped amid the aftershock of the Texacos. 'He's got to be concerned with getting his own form up. Likewise myself. We all put ourselves on the line. We're playing for our country. That's the way it is.' Cue yesterday's duck for Tubs at Bristol. The merde really is beginning to fly.

Speaking from Queensland, Trevor Hohns, the chairman of selectors, said he would willingly fire the pistol himself should Tubs refuse to do the decent thing. 'He is the sort of person who, if he is not travelling all that well as a player, would probably make the decision himself. But occasionally, difficult decisions have to be made regarding team selection. I am happy to make such decisions.' Before leaving Mayfair for Bristol, Tubs had been adamant. He was striking the ball every bit as well as the Waughs. A substantial score was just around the corner. The travelling press corps seem to feel he could teach Walter Mitty a thing or two about self-deception. 'The Mark Taylor case is becoming heart-breaking for all concerned,' wrote Greg Baum, the thoughtful Melbournian temporarily based in Birmingham – his wife works at the local university – and saddled with the unenviable task of filing acres of copy on a daily basis for both the Melbourne *Age* and the *Sydney Morning Herald*. Having conquered cancer a few years back, Baum himself is scarcely unfamiliar with adversity, hence his empathetic tone. But even his tolerance has limits. 'Self-belief has been [Taylor's] hallmark, but slowly it is turning into the poison of self-delusion.'

Much the same, mind, might justly be said of Australia herself. The drug-infested ghettoes around Sydney are about to be given a thorough wash and brush-up in preparation for the Olympics, but no end of interior decorating, it is said, can disguise the stench of decay. Trenchant columns are being written. Of late, the disillusioned and disappointed have been intent on finding scapegoats. Last March the electorate rejected political correctness and Paul Keating's 'big picture', ditching Labour. The dole queues had spoken. Sod the future: the people wanted their jam today. Under the Liberals, privatization and political incorrectness are all the rage, Asian migrants, who constitute some 5 per cent of the population, are increasingly regarded as the enemy within. Lurking in the background, as ever, are the Aboriginals, whose treatment continues to infringe the most basic ground rules of humanitarian behaviour.

This week Melbourne has been hosting a reconciliation conference organized by this persistently oppressed minority (roughly 10 per cent of the population). 'Bringing Them Home', a 700-page report by the Human Rights and Equal

70

Opportunities Commission, has revealed that, over the past twenty-five years, Aboriginal children have been hunted down in their thousands and dragged away from their families, never to return. Relating the report's accounts of sexual, physical and emotional abuse, Kim Beazley, the leader of the Labour Party, wept openly in Parliament. Sir William Deane, the Governor-General, has been equally supportive. Yet, while the Prime Minister made a personal apology, his refusal to do so on behalf of his party did not go unnoticed. As he spoke, delegates' backs turned in unison. Senator Ross Lightfoot, a member of the Parliamentary Liberal Party who once advocated that his state, West Australia, should secede from the Commonwealth, did precious little to alleviate matters, describing the Aboriginals as 'the bottom colour of the civilized spectrum'.

The Aboriginals could have given Martin Luther King lessons in cheek-turning, which is why the likes of Pauline Hanson can prosper. Once the proud owner of a chip shop, she was reportedly kicked out of the Liberal Party because of her arch right-wing leanings, whereupon she resurfaced as an independent candidate and swanned to victory in a traditionally safe-as-houses Labour seat. Asked in a recent interview whether she might be guilty of xenophobia, she stumbled: she didn't have the foggiest what the word meant. More recently, in her maiden speech, she not only accused the Aboriginals of whingeing but insisted there was no need whatsoever for her compatriots to feel the teeniest bit ashamed for past atrocities. What's gone is gone. Forgotten. Might as well not have happened. Which pretty much sums up the federal stance. Empowered by the 'race power' in the constitution, which overrides the Racial Discrimination Act, Mr Howard has drawn up the ten-point Wik plan which, if enacted, would effectively nullify all native land rights. To strive to rectify injustice, the PM and his underlings believe, is to hold a 'black armband' view of politics. What was that about compassion?

*

29 May 'MP's tears flow as report on stolen children is rejected'

(*The Australian*)

The black armbands are out in force. In the West Australian Legislative Assembly yesterday, Dr Geoff Gallop, the leader of the opposition, moved that the House apologize 'for the past policies under which Aboriginal children were removed from their families'. The state Premier, Mr Court, supported the motion, expressing 'deep regret at the hurt and distress that this caused'. Applauded heartily, Ernie Bridge, the only Aboriginal member of the Assembly, expressed his sadness that Mr Howard had qualified his apology to his people, adding that this showed 'a tendency of being mean . . . and of being a little man'. The South Australian Parliament passed a bipartisan motion of 'deep and sincere regret' and affirmed its support 'for reconciliation between all Australians'. The state's Catholic Church sent an apology to Pat Dodson, the chairman of the Reconciliation Conference, 'for the part our Church has played in the hurt and dispossession experienced by our Aboriginal brothers and sisters'.

Yet still the Federal Government refused to budge. The central recommendations of 'Bringing Them Home', that legislation be passed to regulate police, judicial and/or departmental functions with regard to adoption, child welfare and juvenile justice, have been rejected. Senator Herron, the Minister for Aboriginal and Torres Strait Islander Affairs, insisted such measures would constitute 'significant interference' on the part of the Commonwealth in State and Territory affairs. He also reiterated the Federal Government's view that financial compensation was not 'equitable or practical', and stressed that Parliament would only apologise if it was 'warranted' and the nation supported it. The opposition tabled a motion citing the decision to ignore the main proposals as 'a national shame'. 'Ms Pearl Gibbs, the old campaigner for Aboriginal rights, accurately summed up this unhappy business years ago,' wrote Tony Stephens in

The Australian. ' "You mightn't be one of us," she told Dr Faith Bandler, a South Sea Islander, "but you won't be free until we are." All Australians, it seemed yesterday, would not be free until the Aborigines are themselves free. And this would not be until the land rights issue was sorted out.'

Mr Dodson, whose long, white, wispy beard lends him the air of an Old Testament prophet, closed the conference with an emotional speech, tearful but far from vengeful. His country's lamentable human rights record would, he said, 'go up like a blimp' for the rest of humanity to see, but both tone and content were conciliatory. 'All the wisdom and love here will provide tools in the fight for true reconciliation. We together have shown over these three days that no barrier of hatred will provide such adversity that we will be unable to pull it asunder ... all the pains in the battle are nothing when the goal is just and honourable.'

Tubs would do well to take heart from such sentiments. Not that he needs any lessons in cheek-turning. Chappelli had been his usual plain-speaking self in the Sydney *Daily Telegraph*: 'Australia have got to get two openers in form and haven't time to mess around with him anymore.' At Bristol this morning Captain Sensible stepped off the coach to be presented with the 'Duckbat', a slab of wood measuring three feet across. A *Daily Mirror* snapper hovered in the bushes, poised to record his reaction. True to form, the butt of this pathetic stunt took it with good grace, which is more than can be said of his livid countrymen. Crommo demanded that the snapper hand him the offending roll of film but subsequently discovered he had been handed a blank. This morning's *Mirror* had run a spoof story about Tubs and the Duckbat, calling it 'the biggest row since Bodyline'. Refusing to have anything to do with it, the rag's cricket correspondent, Chris Lander, had been accused by his sports editor of having a humour bypass.

Matthew was more shocked than angry: 'Things like that really open your eyes. We're lucky we don't have tabloids like that. I hardly read newspaper reports of games I play in.

What are you looking for? Kind words? An ego massage to help your insecurity? You don't get a false sense of right or wrong if you don't read them. We have media training, which teaches us to have a laid-back attitude. It's no good wrapping yourself in cotton wool, but you do have to be careful. People are so quick to make judgments, which is why I try not to turn down autograph hunters. I was shattered when Allan Border didn't sign for me. Mind you, I do think people here take all this too seriously. They seem to enjoy talking English cricket down, but there can't be too much wrong. England were fantastic in the one-dayers, made us look a lot worse than we are. The weather may be a factor, but the English seem to be a pretty pessimistic people. Mind you, I read somewhere that we've got the biggest youth suicide rate in the world.'

On the second day at Bristol Nick Trainor, a rangy red-headed Geordie previously rejected by Durham, had thrust three consecutive ducks behind him to register his maiden century for Gloucestershire, then proffered the view that the tourists were 'going through the motions'. The previous day Russell had been taken aback by their ethics. 'Four of them walked,' he had noted with a mixture of admiration and profound disbelief. Before resuming his innings this morning, Tubs immersed himself in slip-catching practice, gleaning reminders of what it felt like to be in control of his muse. Clasping one particularly tricky offering, he let out a cry of self-affirmation: 'Woah!' Every ball pouched safely in those fleshy palms was a platform on which to resurrect self-belief. In the nets he middled almost everything; then Warney beat him, unleashing a loud groan. 'How was that?' asked Tubs. 'Close,' warranted the bowler. 'Good,' asserted Tubs, ever mindful of the collective need. Though sticky in patches, his batting in the middle shows signs of regeneration: a full-toss clumped through mid-off's legs, a long-hop dispatched with a lack of ceremony verging on the derisive. One over from the off-spinner, Martyn Ball, yields 9 runs courtesy of a square-cut, an on-drive and a glance to fine-leg, but Ball has the last word, defeating a push to leg with Tubs on 30. He walks off to sympathetic applause, running fingers through a tousled mane, a man seemingly in the market for a new head.

For the rest of the morning and much of the afternoon, Matthew holds centre stage, upright, magisterial, hungry. Up to the start of play his crease duties on tour had comprised the princely sum of 19 deliveries; now it's 233. Overcoming a fidgety and streaky start (over-anxiousness?), he is soon punching drives through the V, pulling and cutting the seamers, attacking the spinners with deft foot-work. The timing, for the most part, is flawless. In South Africa, intriguingly enough, he had persuaded colleagues to strap pads on their hands and allow him to pound them with his fists, 'pumping myself up and improving my timing in one fell swoop'. Undeterred by the slow handclap that accompanies him on the final lap, he gathers his maiden hundred for his country in a shade over four hours. Up on the balcony in the Grace Stand, Tubs claps with gusto then resumes chewing his nails. Upon falling leg-before to the new ball for 124, playing across the line to Mike Smith, Matthew lopes back, practising the shot he should have played, then returns to the dressing room for Hooter to encase his knees in ice packs. When he re-emerges into the searing sunlight, half a dozen boys scamper over, clamour-ing for an autograph. Mission accomplished, one turns to another with a quizzical air: 'Matthew Who?'

'A good little kick in the pants,' is our anonymous hero's summary of the Texaco debacle. 'It made us realize things might not be as rosy as we thought. Subconsciously, we went into those games a bit complacent. Maybe only 5 per cent, but that's all you need. I felt low because I didn't have a good start, but I can keep these things in perspective. I don't self-combust. I struggled at first today, going at it a bit too hard, reaching too much. Eventually I waited for the ball to come on and things improved from then on. I wasn't fussed about the slow handclap. Some people want it all. Give us a chance!' Megan arrived at Heathrow yesterday; with a decent innings under his belt at last, the stocks are rising.

'He only gets 'em when he deserves it,' announced Hooter, referring to the ice packs. 'My reward for a long innings,' Matthew assured me. The eyes looked somewhat less convinced. And with good reason. The confession comes as Hooter withdraws. A couple of mornings before the party flew out, Matthew had seriously contemplated withdrawing. 'My knees were so sore. I'd made Megs's life a misery with my incessant worrying, and that morning felt like the last straw. I tried to run down to the corner shop, which is only a few hundred yards from where we live, and it was a real struggle. I told the specialist I didn't think I could go, but he said there wasn't much wrong and that I should try and cope with the soreness. Some days are better than others.'

2 June 'Blair apologises to Irish for Potato Famine'
(*Daily Telegraph*)

David Ligertwood, the Durham wicketkeeper, has some revealing thoughts on the thorny issue of dual nationality. A product of Grade cricket and a member of the South Australian squad since 1991, he joined Surrey in 1992, thereby qualifying as 'English'. 'In cricketing terms I consider myself English,' he writes in the *Telegraph*. 'I want "our" system to produce better cricketers, including myself, than the Australian one, culminating in an Ashes triumph. Having said that, I cannot say I'm "English" in general. But I believe cricketing allegiance to England is sufficient in our professional age when most sports people unfortunately play predominantly for themselves, secondly for their teammates and even less still for their roots and the people they represent.'

4 June 'Dateline founder "died a reclusive alcoholic" '
(*Daily Telegraph*)

'I'd rather face Dennis Lillee with a stick of rhubarb than go through all that again.' Thus, in 1981, spake a relieved Ian

Botham after being cleared of assault at Grimsby Crown Court. Steve Rouse will doubtless second that emotion once the first Test is done and dusted.

The Warwickshire groundsman, after all, has spent the last few weeks flitting between rocks and hard places. Called into question after three-day finishes against the West Indies in 1995 and India last June, Edgbaston's future as a Test venue is shaky, hence the club's insistence on a pitch built to last. However, the message from the ECB's inspector of pitches, Harry Brind, is said to have lacked nothing in clarity. Green seamers, runs the received wisdom, are to be *de rigueur* this summer, presumably to thwart Warney. The reasoning, one assumes, is that the visiting seamers are perceived as less of a threat, which ought to do wonders for Pigeon's motivation.

This may be unwise on another count. In Croftie and Tufnell, for the first time since Edmonds and Emburey enmeshed Border's battalion in 1986–87, the Poms have the edge in spin, in quantity if not necessarily quality. Nothing in Bev's form to date portends otherwise. Rouse's preparations have been closely observed by both Brind and Dennis Amiss, the Warwickshire chief executive, but Tufnell's early release from the squad has rather given the game away. Word is that Rouse has been guarding the square at night, kipping on a tarpaulin.

It seems unlikely that a story in this morning's *Telegraph* will improve his mood. At the ECB's behest, Dr Bill Adams, a member of the University of Wales's Soil Science Unit at Aberystwyth, and Dr Stephen Baker, of the Sports Turf Research Unit in Bingley, are busy trying to develop so-called 'designer' soils, using various unusual combinations of clays together with sand of a given particle size. Adding sand, reckons Adams, 'can affect the bite of the ball'; the granules, apparently, heighten friction. Personally speaking, the return of the customized surface, buried in Kerry Packer's hothouses, cannot come soon enough. In the pursuit of conditions that satisfy batsmen, pacemen, twirlers, treasurers and spectators alike, it seems the obvious step. Given the ramifications for his profession, Rouse would be fully entitled to disagree.

Anne drives Laura, Joe and Woody to her parents' house in Stratford-on-Avon while I catch the train to Birmingham New Street. Since Laura spilled out on to the lounge carpet four Mays ago I have been terrified of navigating motorways. A couple of days later, on my way home from a championship match at Chelmsford, I had dozed off for about four seconds on the M25. I was still shaking come bedtime. No more, I vowed, the new father suddenly, acutely, aware of his own mortality. Why take the risk when the number of people depending on you has just doubled? Anne is convinced it's a phobia, which it is, and urges me to 'see someone about it', which I have no intention of doing. Besides, I am deeply fond of trains. As someone who spurns mobile phones on the grounds of excessive intrusion, they provide an opportunity for relaxation as well as solitude. They also afford a sense of perpetuity. The seats may have been upholstered, the wheels may spin faster, the buffet car may even offer a moussaka, but it is still possible to imagine oneself clickety-clicking across the same country Bradman and co. traversed. Seeing the same fields and hedgerows, the same pylons and plumes, the same greens and greys. The downside of privatization, sadly, is becoming increasingly apparent, with unprofitable branch lines being shut down and towns cut off. If Labour truly are intent on improving the environment by reducing the number of cars on the road, and hence curbing the noxious emissions, now, one would have thought, is surely the time for re-nationalization. Intriguingly, the BBC recently unveiled *Oh, Dr Beeching*, a sitcom somewhat longer on sit than com. Based on the trials and endless tribulations of a modest-but-proud provincial station around the time of Beeching's report on the railways, it was more dewy-eyed than double-entendred, harking back to an era of stronger community spirit. The chances of us seeing its like again seem decidedly remote.

ACT 1

The main Edgbaston scoreboard is in patriotic mode: the slot for England's first innings reads 2,000. Malcolm and Caddick are strutting their stuff out in the middle, the target a single stump. Both uproot it, but whereas Malcolm greets success with a shrug, Caddick, the loner, has a bit of a cavort. Tongue-in-cheek perhaps, but might it also be self-affirmation at play? Ever since this son of Christchurch (New Zealand rather than Hampshire) took 96 wickets at 12.84 to run away with the 1991 Rapidline 2nd XI Player of the Year Award, expectation and infuriation have snapped at his heels without respite. In that respect he has much in common with poor old Graeme Hick, whose absence from this summer's frolics is all but taken as read. Thus far, Caddick has picked up 37 wickets at 37 during the course of a Test career that began with 'Warne's Match' at Old Trafford and has seen him selected eleven times, i.e. one in every four engagements. The overture to his debut should certainly have given him due warning about selectorial peccadillos. Alan Igglesden suffered a groin strain in the indoor school on the eve of the game, whereupon DeFreitas was summoned and picked ahead of Ilott, a member of the original twelve.

It would be wrong, though, to apportion more than a modicum of blame to the jury. Shin problems almost cost him his livelihood, but even when he has been firing on all cylinders Caddick's contributions have been erratic. If there were times during the winter when he appeared to have left every ounce of oomph in Taunton, there were occasions on his return to his native New Zealand when he looked the part, for all that his figures did scant justice to the frequency with which batsmen were left groping and grimacing. It was all there – control, rhythm, precision and icy menace, Hadlee incarnate. Which is why, with the exceptions of Chris Lewis and Mark Ramprakash, he remains English cricket's most perplexing enigma. Can this be attributed to a lack of belonging? The other week, one Somerset colleague, baffled like so many, suggested to me that Caddick's desire to be 'one of the boys' verged on the overbearing. If the need wasn't there, why on earth would he constantly avail the dressing room of so many puerile jokes? The question is straightforward: has he turned the corner, or did the determination to prove a point to his countrymen temporarily focus his mind? Of one thing we may be certain: more than any other member of Atherton's entourage, he must be made to feel valued, to feel wanted.

Then it's Croftie's turn, floating fizzers while Stewart minds the stumps. Alan Knott presides puckishly, the prince of English stumpers monitoring the incumbent's every glide and gather, scrutinizing feet and hands, nodding approval, forever encouraging. Can 'The Gaffer' keep riding two horses with one behind? He has certainly confounded the sceptics since last June, when Nick Knight's broken finger provided him with the speck of luck he required to resuscitate a career many assumed had expired with his non-existent footwork in South Africa. In the Tests of 1996 no runmaker in the world amassed more. Nor did he start 1997 badly, racking up 173 in Auckland to break Les Ames's sixty-seven-year-old record for an England keeper. The most astonishing aspect of that innings was that the author, having been in the field for a day and a half, had put his feet up for a few overs then re-entered at 18 for 1. Barring Tugga, is there any more dedicated follower of passion? He seems not so much to thrive on adrenalin as be impotent without it. With the gloves, there is little to choose between him and Russell; if the latter has marginally swifter hands, Stewart is more agile. His presence as principal all-rounder is doubly valuable because it also permits the inclusion of a quintet of bowlers. All the same, to keep him in the first three, should Pigeon locate the right length, might be asking too much.

Bump into Mark Butcher as he leaves the nets. He looks rather sheepish, as if uncertain he ought to be in such elevated company. I wish him luck then extend the same courtesy to a subdued Hollioake Major. He is not optimistic about making the final XI. The prevailing wind does indeed suggest that Ealham, twice the bowler but half the batsman, will get the nod in preference, which strikes me as downright dotty. Industrious and pugnacious as Ealham is, it is hard to avoid the conclusion that his particular mix of talents would be more desirable within the context of a stronger attack. In three innings against his erstwhile compatriots, the second most gifted Hollioake in Wandsworth had delivered the final dagger-thrusts, all but proving himself invincible: to drop him now might prove an injurious case of coitus interruptus.

The visiting journos are fuming. In response to my asking him whether he had seen Greg Chappell's comments about Tubs in the papers back home, Malcolm Conn poo-poohs such trivialities and asks me whether I'd read Bobby Simpson's scathing attack in the *Mail*. 'He's been giving it to Tubs with both barrels,' he growls. 'God, he's a bitter man.' Simpson's triumphs as the Cobbers' coach failed to ward off heavy criticism of his regime, not least among those who believed he saw the team solely as a vehicle for himself. The press conference finds Tubs in remarkably chipper mood. 'Bit short of people, aren't we?' he chirps, scanning the meagre throng. 'People have got sick of talkin' to me.' A radio reporter wonders if he felt he'd been 'to hell and back'. Tubs grins softly: 'I think hell is a lot worse.' Did the comments from Simpson and the Chappells bother him? Apparently not: 'It has got very personal. You have to handle the knocks, ride the bumps. But all those ex-players and captains – they're no longer in the team. The support of the players is paramount, and it's been excellent.' Tubs is more concerned with Warney ('hasn't given the ball as big a rip as I know he can') and the lack of time to find form ('to an extent, the team have suffered from the itinerary'). England, he conceded, 'definitely seem more buoyant'; there was a 'bit of apprehension' there. Not that any of this can deter our transatlantic guest, Bill Glauber of the *Baltimore Sun*: 'You lot haven't got a hope, have you?'

Don Shepherd perambulates the perimeter with BBC

Radio's man in Wales, the indefatigable and matey Eddie Bevan. Both have played parts in Croftie's rise: Bevan as informal agent and guide to the media whirlpool, 'Shep' as technical overseer and purveyor of wisdoms. Even though the latter's delight is transparent, he would prefer not to make too much of this: 'I probably first saw him at winter nets when he was in his mid-teens. Good action, good attitude. He *looked* like an off-spinner. Some work at this game with modest gifts, and you feel they're not going to get to the top, but Croftie had everything you wanted. Early on, he did a lot of bowling in conditions that weren't conducive to off-spin, which I think has helped him.'

Tony Smith, the tourists' baggageman, another hardy perennial, ambles by. 'Off to get some prescriptions,' he announces. Blond and ever so slightly batty, the king of fetchers and gofers has always reminded me of what Catweazle might have looked like after a decent scrub. This summer, he reveals proudly, marks his twenty-sixth consecutive stint with a touring team, and his eighth Ashes assignment. The sweater? A gift from Graeme Wood in 1981. The Waughs, I point out, fishing for some incriminating tittle-tattle, had turned 32 the previous day. 'I'm sure they celebrated in style,' he replies, resisting the bait with accustomed ease. Can any Englishman have a sterner test of loyalty amid such a summer?

The genesis of this oddest of couplings? 'Answered an ad in one of the Sunday papers, just before the start of the 1972 Ashes tour. The Australian Cricket Board had written to the MCC asking for a van and driver, so the MCC got on to Gillette, who put the ad in the *Sunday Mirror*. I'd been working in Twickenham with my dad in the building trade for twenty years. He ran a maintenance and repair business but he was about to retire and I was thinking about getting out. Three days later I got the job. I'd never been very good at cricket but I always enjoyed it. I saw every Test in England from about '59, when I first owned a car.

'All the Aussies have been pretty friendly, although it was

a bit nerve-racking in '72. The high points are always when the Aussies regain or retain the Ashes. The most dramatic tour was '81, of course. Three times I got the champagne out of the van; three times I had to put it back. This is probably the youngest party I can remember. You do get taken for granted a bit these days. Up to three or four years ago I looked after the whole team's gear, but now it's the personal stuff: fetching prescriptions, taking people to the local hospital, going on ahead to hotels, making sure the gear is all in the correct rooms, seeing to the laundry – twice a week, three times during Tests.' The oddest request? 'I was once asked if I had any young ladies' telephone numbers. Kim Hughes gave me a whole load but I suppose most of them will be out of date by now.'

The Cobbers practise after lunch. Warney plies his wares while Lancashire's young leggie, Chris Schofield, makes a distinctly favourable impression in the adjoining net. Matthew purveys a studious slow left-arm, giving the seam a fair old tweak but not obtaining as much turn as he would wish. When one delivery jostles timber, Warney pats him on the bum. Hurrying back towards the changing rooms in the hope of a quick word with Croftie, I notice a trim-looking Jeff Thomson outside the indoor school, resplendent in a T-shirt that reads, with some aptness, 'Raw Power'. Of all the ironies, he and Lillee have been hired by the *Daily Telegraph* to help find the Poms a matchwinning strike bowler. This is the first of three Assessment Days designed to whittle down the cream of 15–18-year-old Midlanders. Swathes of grey hair sprouting from beneath the rim of a jaunty baseball cap, Lillee spots Shep and offers salutations. 'My son's idol,' Shep whispers to me. 'He said some of those quickies were good.'

Matthew has asked if I can meet him at the team hotel, the Holiday Inn. When I arrive, Tubs is prowling the foyer in Bermuda shorts and T-shirt. Denis Rogers, the portly chairman of the ACB, has just arrived with his wife. As captain and boss chat, the humour seems healthy, the flow of banter liberal. But what was this item on the noticeboard? 'To all

Team Managers. Please be advised that several complaints of misbehaviour have been reported by hotel liasion officials, also venue cafeteria security staff. This will not be tolerated, any further incidents and offenders will be disciplined and if necessary sent home.' The mind boggled. Had the *Sun* heard about this? Had that notorious prankster Pigeon gone too far? Further investigation reveals the warning to have been aimed at those high-spirited young boxers who had come to town for the European Junior championships. Earlier in the week, a 15-year-old Moldovan had been caught stealing from the cosmetics counter at Marks & Spencer and a 16-year-old Lithuanian detained at the same store after attempting to smuggle out a pair of trainers. To them, at least, Birmingham must seem positively glamorous.

Atherton has been confronting the microphones and cameras with something approaching mild pleasure. Interviewed by Sky, he certainly appears more at ease than is his wont. Then again, he knows full well how much trickier it is to misquote a chap when you can actually sees his lips move. He is obliged to talk the talk, of course, but blowing trumpets has never been his style, so he settles for a low-key toot: 'I sense in the team and public at large a bit of optimism. The important thing is that we've got the public on our side, believing we've got an even chance.' Cut to David Lloyd, bullish and emphatic: 'It's not about players from 20, 30, 40 years ago. It's about these lads, NOW.' Back to Atherton: 'We feel the ghosts. We don't want to let them down.'

Writing in the *Telegraph*, Sir Tim Rice spells out his ideal outcome: 'Australia 150 (Taylor 125 not out) and 90 (Taylor 60), England 550 for 4 declared.' Barring a couple of fifties for Matthew, I wouldn't squabble with that for an instant. Nor, I suspect, would many other Poms. What a lot of soppy Hectors we are.

MATTHEW ELLIOTT

Even though we lost, it was good to see Tubs working his way through his bad trot at Derby. I don't think it's had too much of a negative effect, although a Test match might be different. I honestly don't know what I'd do in his position. I haven't experienced a protracted period of bad form since I started playing for Victoria. I don't think he's being selfish by hanging on. It's a really tough situation to be in, an unenviable one.

What I so admire about Tubs is his consistency. You'd never know what he's going through, the enormity of the pressures. His attitude, the way he's been to the guys, hasn't changed at all. That's his strength. That's why he's such a good captain. He's always the same. Even on the opening morning of a Test. He'll just say 'make sure you bowl off-stump', that sort of thing. He's not big on words, never complicates things. He's such an even-tempered bloke, such an even character. You look at him in the field and you know you can't let him down.

I'm glad I'll be opening. It's what I do best. I hate sitting around waiting. I'm a bit apprehensive about tomorrow, a bit nervous, but in a positive way. There are things I want to prove. I've only played five Test matches and I feel as if I haven't achieved as much as I wanted. Having only two first-class games before the Tests hasn't been ideal but I made that hundred at Bristol and a good 60 at Derby, and the knees have definitely improved. I'm happy with my form and I'd love to get in there first thing.

It's ironic, but if I'm letting the ball go well early on, the chances are I'll make runs. It tells me I'm really watching the ball, picking it up early, making decisions early, making the bowler bowl to me. I tend to be suspicious of those days when you bat like a million dollars, playing shots early; those are the days I tend to get out for 20. We watched some videos of Gough this morning. Good strike bowler, a few tricks up his sleeve, gets a lot of his wickets with reverse swing at the end of an innings. Croftie also looks a good bowler.

The pitch looks a bit green but dry, so I reckon it will be a good strip. Unless it's an absolute minefield, I'd bat first regardless. Putting the opposition in is negative. You want to bat, to set the tone. That's the way Tubs thinks. This morning he emphasized the importance of jumping out of the blocks, which would erase the disappointment of the one-dayers. We had a good team dinner at Bristol and one at Headingley before the one-dayers. We can't all be best friends but we all get on very well. Mind you, there was a bit of cheating when Pigeon and Bev played golf. Incorrect marking of cards, general skullduggery. They strike me as needing to be competitive in everything they do.

I don't think of myself as playing to uphold a tradition. What I do know is that if we win this series we'll have won five in a row, something neither country has achieved before. That's not to say I don't think about that tradition. It's there at every ground we play on. At the moment I feel as if we're being lulled into a false sense of security. Everywhere I go I hear people say things like, 'Oh, we're no good, you'll thrash us.' It almost feels as if we've got nothing to gain and everything to lose. It's a strange feeling, very odd.

ROBERT CROFT

Some of the older players may feel differently, but no one has to fire me up for this. Pulling on that England jumper for my first Test against the old enemy is enough. I can just about remember '81, Botham's Ashes. I was 11. I watched those marvellous hundreds at Headingley and Old Trafford, thrilled to them, albeit on TV. He had that belief, in himself and the team. He showed me the spirit you need to play a game.

I realize the majority of us spent four months together during the winter but I found the management training course at Upper Heythrop valuable and worthwhile, a good innovation. It was all about team-building, identifying a squad of players who are going to be in contention for places this summer and helping them get to know each other better. We talked about our different roles, did exercises, solved problems, physical and mental. It created a greater degree of respect, knowing what qualities each of us could bring to the collective effort.

The management gave us a clear picture of what was expected and what is needed. We want a successful English side, a successful British side. Run professionally, everyone going in the same direction. Not all the problems ailing our game have been solved but at least everybody is playing for each other. Making us dress smarter, making sure we all wear the same cap, means that people get the impression of unity, and sometimes it does feel as if we are a family. We're all behind each other, looking after each other. If somebody leaves the circle because he's not having a good day, we drag him back in.

The two forms of the game are so different, and offer such different challenges, but I'm sure the Aussies would have loved to be going into the Tests having beaten us three times. We couldn't have done any more in the Texacos; it may well give us a psychological advantage. What pleased me was that everybody chipped in. Look at Athers's hundred at The Oval, Thorpie and Adam Hollioake at Headingley, Ben taking to it like a duck to water at Lord's. There's no one out in the cold.

In contrast to the early part of the winter, when the mood would generally veer between the hyper and the flat and rarely achieve an even keel, the dressing room is a reasonably calm place. There used to be more music playing but one day somebody forgot the CD player and it seemed to be phased out. Which to me suggests minds are focused. The important thing is to go on to that field feeling better than your opposite number. You have to feel you're better than him, no matter what the statistics say. And I know we're talking about Shane Warne here, but I must feel I can compete with him, that I can beat him. People like Thorpie, Athers and Stewie are bursting with encouragement, as well as advice. Which only goes to emphasize how much we're playing for each other.

I remember having a good tussle with Matthew at Neath when he was touring with Australia A. I'm looking forward to resuming hostilities.

5 June 'What a shower! Aussies whinge at our plumbing'
(Daily Express)

According to the new *Lonely Planet Guide to Britain* (an Australian production, it bears mentioning), Englishmen 'don't understand that a good shower is one of life's basic essentials', are obsessed with hobbies and speak, further-more, in impenetrable accents. Coventry is 'dismal', Piccadilly Circus 'fume-choked and uninspiring', Wales 'England's unloved backyard . . . a suitable place for coal mines and nuclear power stations'. One shudders to think what Croftie would have made of that last contention.

Arrive at New Street station after a pleasant trek from Stratford through the Warwickshire countryside to be greeted by an anaconda of a taxi queue. A spot of earwigging reveals a wary mood. The Texaco result must be ignored. After ten minutes of inching forward, I give up and head for the underpass in the hope of flagging a cab on the other side of the roundabout. 'Who do you think will win?' a fiftysomething gent of Caribbean extraction asks a strapping twentysomething as we surface into the hazy sunlight. 'England,' comes the unhesitating reply. 'Really?' wonders the more experienced man, eyes riddled with scepticism.

Nevertheless, as my cab pulls into the ground at 10.59, you can almost taste the buzz. The Texaco result must be a factor, ditto the Lions' derring-do in South Africa, and the scarcity of clouds. Even the muddied oafs have been doing their bit, beating Italy last night for the first time in a competitive fixture since 1977. Whatever the causes, the effect is invigorating. In an attempt to persuade myself that I can retain a neutral outlook, I tug on the New South Wales cap Stinger sent me. Who am I kidding?

By the time I reach the press box, much to my chagrin, I've

missed the first two balls. All winter I'd promised myself I would be there for the off, imagining, somehow, that I could serve as a talisman. At Old Trafford four years ago, DeFreitas was entrusted with the honour and served up something horrid, which Slats duly clattered halfway to Didsbury, setting the tone for the series. Fortunately, David Lemmon apprises me of the good news: Gough's initial offering had swung lavishly in the muggy air and defeated Tubs's offside grope. Whew!

As is his custom, Tubs had called tails and opted to bat first on a pitch with a discernibly green sheen. A brave move but one entirely in keeping with this positive thinker's favoured modus operandi: two days of pillage then unleash Pigeon and Warney as the surface begins to show its age. Ladbrokes' odds reflect the natives' growing flight from pessimism: Poms 3–1, Cobbers 6–4, the draw 11–10. A couple of weeks ago, the odds against the hosts winning the rubber had been 16–1. In the esteemed opinion of the spread-betting fraternity at Sporting Index, the Cobbers will tot up between 335 and 355.

Tubs gets off the mark with a push into the covers, bringing Matthew toe-to-toe with a visibly pumped-up Gough. The field comprises three slips, a gully, short backward point, short midwicket, cover, mid-off and long-leg – aggressive but not foolhardy. Matthew digs out his first ball, a trademark inswinging yorker, leaves the next with a flourish – though television replays suggest he might have been lucky to survive the ensuing appeal – then eases through midwicket for 2. At the other end Malcolm is roared in with affection as well as belligerence, and rips a snorter past the captain's outside edge. Crawley brings off a fine left-handed stop at short-leg and instantly flicks the ball back at the stumps. It avails him naught, but the import is plain.

Matthew now endures a torrid examination. After padding up to the first ball of Gough's second over, the next is fuller and wider, inducing an inside edge that thuds into his pads. The third boomerangs back and misses off by a

couple of millimetres as Matthew lets it pass, judging it
almost too nicely. He leaves the fourth, too, but pays for
such temerity with ringing testicles. In the Yorkshireman's
third over, a controlled steer off the face of the bat earns a
four past third slip's forlorn dive, whereupon the following
offering swings in between bat and pad as Matthew, on the
walk, shapes to drive through mid-on: 11 for 1. The ejected
stump, split at the top, testifies to the one-sidedness of the
debate. Joy and sympathy mingle uneasily.

Anxious to assert, Tubs thumps a Malcolm half-volley to
the extra-cover boundary, on the up, but the next ball is
slightly fuller and he snicks towards Butcher's midriff at
second slip. After a heart-stopping bobble or two, Butcher –
sporting a pair of those wraparound shades which may or
may not impair vision – clings on: 15 for 2. Pop downstairs
for a coffee. A fetching catering assistant pops the question:
'How many innings do they have?'

Caddick replaces Malcolm for the tenth over but Gough
makes the next incision in the eleventh. Having broken his
duck with an unintended edge through the slips off the
ebullient Yorkie, Junior pushes forward to an absolute
corker that pitches a shade outside off, jags back and bowls
him through the gate. Tugga chugs in at 26 for 3. Wizened
hacks nod knowingly, wearily. The BBC boys underscore
their concern by posting up his Ashes average on Pommy
turf: 102.44. Not even Bradman managed that. For all that,
he is soon nicking Caddick just short of slip, much to the
undisguised pleasure of the raucous denizens of the Hollies
Stand. For those of us confined behind glass on such occasions, atmosphere is impossible to gauge. You feel anaes-
thetized. Fortunately, somebody kindly informs me that
there are a few spare seats in front of the press box so I rush
outside, eager to savour the moment.

The hubbub kindles memories of the Arab market in
Jerusalem. The air crackles, the voices trill and buzz. Lovers
and strangers exchange grins of disbelief. Toasts are made
with champagne flutes and plastic cups, scorecards filled in

with feverish assiduousness. The last time I experienced a commotion as exuberant as this was when I walked into Lord's two Junes ago, at the very instant Stewart was launching himself to grasp that gobsmacking catch off Lara, setting up England's first Test victory over the West Indies at HQ in my lifetime. The sense of something equally memorable unfolding is quite inescapable.

That much is affirmed in Gough's next over. The first ball bowls Blewie and 20,000 pairs of lungs explode, only for a cry of 'no-ball' to stifle the celebrations in their womb. Blewie hammers in the missing stump and back marches Gough, cursing the whims of fate. As he turns at the end of his run, however, he looks composed, settled, misfortune banished. Lo and behold, the next ball, a perfectly pitched outswinger, finds the edge and loops in a gentle parabola towards third slip, where Hussain swoops forward to clamp both mitts around the prize: 28 for 4, Gough in clover, Poms on cloud ten. Cheers cascade as a chap in a T-shirt strides along the bottom of the Hollies Stand waving a flag sporting red-white-and-blue favours. It may not be a Union Jack but purportedly provocative accessories of this order are officially barred from the premises. Unless, that is, you buy them here. What hypocritical tosh.

Caddick summons movement and lift to outwit Tugga outside off but gets his comeuppance with three boundaries in double-quick succession. Malcolm relieves Gough (3 for 18 from eight rip-snorting overs) then Caddick has the final say in his duel with Tugga, arrowing down a vicious leg-cutter that climbs and clips the shoulder of the bat. The appeal is long, hearty, doubt-free; Tugga withdraws the blade and refuses to budge until formally unfastened. The only time he walks is in his sleep.

A ball later, as Heals hangs out an unusually limp bat at another impeccable leg-cutter and Stewart snaffles the gift, 48 for 5 becomes 48 for 6. Caddick threatens to puncture more than a few eardrums as he jigs towards his colleagues' embrace, then turns back, just to make certain Steve

Bucknor's slow-burning forefinger has done its duty. A chant familiar from the soccer terraces wells up from the Hollies Stand: 'You're not singing anymore, you're not singing any more.' Quite who was singing in the first place is unclear, until you notice the smattering of drooping Southern Crosses.

Dizzy drops a glove as he pads out to the middle but recovers his poise and expends an eternity taking guard. The hat-trick ball beats everything. The crowd rises and applauds with gusto. Three overs later, Malcolm disposes of Bev with a brutish lifter that balloons off the shoulder of the bat and loops to gully. 'Oh, Jeesus,' laments one visiting reporter down the phone. 'Seven for forty-eight.' Back strides Caddick to glean a leg-before verdict as Dizzy retreats to one of fullish length: 54 for 8, the twentieth over still in progress. Hard as we might be pinching ourselves, whatever transpires from here will surely never dim the memory of such shamelessly parochial exhilaration. God knows we've waited long enough for the boot to switch feet. (Tut tut: all these we's and our's!)

Warney bustles in with businesslike gait, and proceeds to glance and drive the returning Gough for four fours in the space of six balls. Maintaining the same vigorous vein, he spirits the score to 92 for 8 by lunch, but the joy in the stands remains untrammelled. Mission accomplished, I pack my bags and head for the exit. Work beckons me back to London. 'See you on Sunday,' I chirp to Paul Newman of the *Sunday Telegraph* and Charles Frewin, the managing editor of *Inside Edge* magazine, for whom I write a column. 'If it goes that far,' quips Paul. 'C'mon,' I say, striving to be the fount of reason, 'let's not get too carried away.'

On the way out I meet Kevin Garside of the *Express*. 'That Warney's a boy, isn't he?' he marvels. 'After all that they go off feeling down. Typical.' Which makes me feel like volunteering my services as Richard Wilson's understudy on *One Foot in the Grave*. I can't believe what I'm hearing. At the start of play, how many wickets did he think they would have been happy with? Four? Three? 'Um, three,' he replies. The case rests.

Euphoria diminishes momentarily while reading Eric Hobsbawm's *Age of Extremes* on the train to Stratford. 'If I had to sum up the twentieth century,' the author quotes Yehudi Menhuin, 'I would say that it raised the greatest hopes ever conceived by humanity, and destroyed all illusions and ideals.' Oh, I don't know, Yehudi. On days as sublime as this, the world really can seem quite wondrous.

Aided by a car radio that declines to operate on long wave and an unslakeable thirst for suspense, I remain blissfully unaware of developments in the middle session. A score of 150 for 2 by stumps would be nice. By the time we reach Ally Pally and Richie's elongated vowels, it's 146 for 3, the lead 28, and Thorpe is flicking Dizzy nonchalantly off his hip. He and Hussain, it transpires, are hurtling towards a century stand at 4 an over. Replays suggest Atherton, Butcher and Stewart all played a part in their own demise with shots of untempered aggression; the fourth-wicket pair are evidently in no mood for subservience either.

Thorpe inches forward, luring Warney into dropping short, then leans back to puncture the covers. Nose and lips smothered in sun block, Warney pitches short once more and Thorpe repeats the dose. What on earth is going off out there? Warney's grunt at the point of release, normally such an accurate indicator of the great man's fettle, seems significantly muted. Standing impassively at slip, arms entwined across that barrel of a chest, Tubs masticates his chewing gum with increasing earnestness. The jaw movements intensify still further when Hussain, adjusting brilliantly, squeezes Bev's attempted yorker between captain and keeper and watches the ball hasten to the third-man boundary. 'Who's going to win at cricket today, Daddy?' asks Laura. 'Nobody,' I tell her gently, 'the game lasts five days.' Tom Stoppard once remarked that he could hardly be expected to take any game seriously that takes fewer than three days to reach its conclusion, but I resist the urge to complicate matters.

Gower advises us that Dizzy has pulled his left hamstring. 'We hope not too seriously,' he adds, sounding as if he means it. The 150 stand arrives in 158 minutes: breakneck stuff. 'When was the last time we won the Ashes here?' wonders Anne as I dart into the kitchen in search of a Diet Coke. 'Eighty-five. We didn't even know each other existed. I was going out with Maggie.' She recalls being in Kashmir, 'with that nutter Sian'. At the end of his final over of the day, Warney runs those thick-set fingers through that golden mane and gazes to the heavens for inspiration. Ever mindful of the element of surprise, Tubs entrusts the last six balls to Tugga, who thus doubles his first-class output for the tour, but the breakthrough is not forthcoming. 'They've had a most wonderful day,' exults Boycott as Thorpe and Hussain bounce off side by side, chums conjoined in heady harmony. 'It's what you dream about, if you're an Englishman,' adds Sir Geoffrey. 'The only thing that can stop them is rain. So stay away.'

Unsated, I wallow in the Sky highlights. Can't quite decide which was the more unlikely: Warney looking so human, Pigeon erring so frequently in length, Malcolm being England's most economical bowler, Croftie not getting a twirl or England leading by 82 at the end of Day One. Ever the gent, Tubs refuses to blame the pitch; Athers, indeed, confesses that he would have batted first. 'They're not going to slag us off after that,' smirks Gough, who seems less than 100 per cent confident.

Time to sober up. The Right-On Tim's comments in this morning's *Telegraph* do the trick handsomely: 'Even if we have a wonderful summer, it must not deflect us from looking at our whole game. Fundamental structural changes are needed to rekindle enthusiasm and improve the quality of cricket in this country . . .' In the wake of today's events, one can only trust he and his colleagues retain such a firm hold on reality.

Daily Accumulator (out of 10): Poms 10 Cobbers 0

6 June 'Don't you just feel Great to be British?'

(Daily Mirror)

Gough needn't have fretted. The Great British media beat the drum with a vengeance. 'This is the ansaphone for the Australian cricket team,' intones a disembodied voice in a radio ad. 'Sorry – we're all out.' Boom and, furthermore, boom. The front page of the *Mirror* is dominated by a photo of Caddick, head flung back, arms at five-to-one. Did the news desk not realize where he was born and bred, or did they decide, in their glee, that this was immaterial? It certainly won't have done his sense of belonging any harm.

Packer, albeit unwittingly, had done his bit for morale Down Under: Channel 9 had held fast to their stated intention not to beam over the first session of any of the Tests (which reminds me: the Australian Broadcasting Corporation did not start televising cricket until late 1956, conveniently sparing the nation the pain of Jim Laker's n-n-n-n-nineteen). This has fuelled no end of harrumphing. In some quarters it is even being proposed that terrestrial broadcasters be legally obliged to screen major sporting events of national interest in their entirety. The absence of visual evidence, needless to add, makes scant difference to the press there. 'Taylor fails again as Australia collapses,' mourns the headline in the *Sydney Morning Herald* under a rather pointed photo, taken before the start of yesterday's play, of Tubs exercising in a prone position. The most discussed issues of the week in New South Wales have been, in order: a riot at one of Rupert Murdoch's Super League rugby league games, the possibility of a poker tax, the possibility of a hotel-bed tax, and the Oklahoma bomb trial; according to inspections of the *SMH*, *The Australian* and the Sydney *Daily Telegraph*, there have been more mentions of Tubs than anybody bar John Howard. That said, one former Test batsman has been even more maligned. Greg Ritchie has lost his job as a pundit on Channel 9's *Footy Show*, hours after apologizing for making racial slurs in front of an

Aboriginal while awaiting a flight from Perth. He is alleged to have spat food at Michael Jauncey, an airline employee, and called him 'a coon'.

Spend the day sub-editing at the *Sunday Times*, catching the fleetest of glimpses of Hussain and Thorpe as they extend their liaison to 288, a fourth-wicket record for the Poms in pursuit of the urn, comfortably outstripping Hammond and Paynter's 222 at HQ in '38. Border is contributing a column to the paper this summer and his ghost, Martin Searby, ever the pro, files it a day ahead of schedule. Border takes his countrymen to task for their body language in the field, suggesting this indicates a lack of support for the captain. Towards the close, with Hussain finally removed for 208, his highest score in any form of cricket, Croftie biffs merrily in consort with Ealham – 331 on, four wickets intact. Head off to Paris to do a piece on the television coverage of the French Open women's tennis final, smug as hell.

Daily Accumulator: Poms 9 Cobbers 1

7 June 'Hosepipe bans as rivers run dry'

(Daily Telegraph)

Unchecked, Tubs's smile would have reached Wagga Wagga. To hear Chappelli sing his praises over the air, one might be forgiven for thinking he had never cast so much as a single aspersion about Captain Sensible's suitability to remain in office. 'Ton 'o guts,' asserts Swampy, lost in admiration for the man with whom, one equally fine day eight summers previously, on the very same ground, he had occupied the crease from first ball to last. Not that the Cobbers are alone in their undiluted delight. Has a century by an opposition skipper ever goosed so many jaundiced pimples?

Get back from Roland Garros in time to see Day Three in précis, and rejoice wholeheartedly in Tubs's renaissance. Admittedly, keeping tabs on the score in the land of boules had been no easy matter. The only hint of developments came an hour or so into the morning session when, courtesy of a sneaky feed to Sky Sports from the Eurosport studios, I learned that the declaration had come at 478 for 9 and the Cobbers were 10 without loss. Not until late afternoon did Simon Reed, Eurosport's chief tennis commentator, prod me to ring up the *Sunday Times* and ascertain the state of play. By then it was 175 for 1, which pleased us both. Where's the fun in beating supine Cobbers?

Matthew, the highlights reveal, batted like a dream. Authoritative, assertive but never reckless, at times dashing, even elegant. Gower approves heartily, and so he should. Matthew looked distinctly fortunate to survive an early shout for a catch behind against Croftie, who ultimately bowls him for 66 when Matthew props forward, turns the bat face 90 degrees as if aiming to glide, and has his off-stump pranged. Richie gently chides Croftie (1 for 70 off 22 overs) for giving the ball too much width. Details, schmetails.

By the close, the Cobbers are 104 behind with 9 wickets standing. Blewie, graceful and forceful, is motoring along as if at the wheel of a Bugatti, Chappell Minor incarnate; Tubs, who could probably earn himself a decent living giving seminars in resolve to the Foreign Legion, is still entrenched. Among the videos Lloyd deploys to fire up Team England is a mélange of boundaries and wickets set to Sid Vicious's version of 'My Way'. Tubs, one imagines, can recite the song backwards. Houston, I think we may have a teensy weensy bit of a problem.

Daily Accumulator: Poms 2 Cobbers 8

8 June 'Scientists say PMT is all in the female mind'
(Sunday Times)

The humiliations of Edgbaston pale beside the other current source of shame Down Under. On jetting in for a brace of concerts at Melbourne's Crown Casino, Stevie Wonder assailed Pauline Hanson for being 'on the wrong side in the battle of spiritual warfare'. Urging his hosts to take a stand against Hanson's stance on immigration and aid to Aboriginals, he likened the situation to that in America: '[We] have ignorant people saying of minorities "Kill them all because they're diffferent." It's this kind of thing that has led to the wholesale slaughter of the American Indians, the African Americans, the Jews and lots of other peoples.' Opening a London exhibition of paintings by the Aboriginal artist Clifford Possum, Germaine Greer, clad in a T-shirt emblazoned with the Aboriginal flag, referred to Hanson as 'that Pauline person' and lashed out at her homeland's 'system of successful apartheid'.

Fatigue convinces me to monitor the day's proceedings from the sofa. Before play resumes I put in a call to Stinger. He is still aggrieved that Packer's puppets had opted to screen Pat Rafter's French Open semi-final on Friday in preference to the flannelled tomfoolery. 'Tennis', he rightly scoffs, 'is not worthy of that.' Much as some might like to think the decision was at least partially prompted by the balance of power in Birmingham, that it reflected the Australian distaste for humility, had our Mr Henman been in a similar position the BBC would have done precisely the same.

According to research conducted at Bristol University, while 53 per cent of French schoolchildren say they are proud to be French, only 33 per cent of their counterparts in the UK claim to be proud to be British. It pays not to take these things too seriously, of course, not least since the sample size is seldom large enough to justify unequivocal conclusions, but the message is still painful. Can success on the field of play make any difference? Given that it unites the population in a way no other aspect of our cultural life can remotely approach, why not?

The Cobbers' quest receives an early lift when Junior, who had gone to hospital the previous day suffering from nausea and suspected appendicitis, declares himself fit to come in at number six. That said, he might not be required, so smoothly do Tubs and Blewie pick up from where they left off. Shortly before midday, Blewie, hindered by a painful right knee and dealing almost exclusively in boundaries, square drives Caddick to register his eighth four of the morning and thus become the first Cobber to reach three figures in each of his first three Ashes Tests. 'I think he's sick and tired of being bounced up and down the order,' notes Chappelli.

Croftie comes on for the next over and immediately pitches well outside Tubs's off-stump then blows on his right fist. Tubs essays a risky sweep and gets away with it. Richie informs us that one visiting journalist put £200 at 25–1 on the captain making a hundred then backed Benny the Dip in the Derby: 'It's enough to make you want to give up punting.' Having survived a close call for leg-before earlier in the over, Tubs clips through midwicket as Croftie pitches on middle-and-leg. 'Not there,' scolds an exasperated Boycott. 'Get it up there, make 'im drive.'

Stinger calls to tell me about the story he has filed for the *Sunday Age*. During the tour of South Africa, he has it on reliable authority, some of the Cobbers had contemplated strike action. Taking their cue from the newly formed players' union and its embittered chief executive, Graham Halbish, the gamekeeper turned poacher sacked by the ACB after fifteen years, they had been unhappy, quite understandably, about the relentless demands of their claustrophobic itinerary. A share of TV receipts might do the trick, but would the board really contemplate such an unprecedented gesture? Hold on to your seatbelts: another Packer-type revolt could conceivably be in the offing.

Suddenly, a surge of volume from the TV spurs me to leave Stinger hanging on while I dash from hall to lounge. Drawn forward and beaten in the flight, Tubs has mistimed a drive and popped it straight back to Croftie. 'Sorry to be the bearer of bad tidings,' I tell Stinger, summoning as much sympathy as I can muster, 'but you've just lost a wicket.' He reckons the footmarks are too far from the stumps for Croftie but not Warney, that 500 will therefore be enough; I suggest 600. 'I have a feeling', he muses, 'that I'm missing the great Test of the series.'

A phalanx of fellows in Viking helmets sings 'God Save the Queen' as Blewie skips through the pavilion gate at lunch, the deficit now down to 8 runs, local confidence wavering. Pop out for a Chinese with Anne and the kids, and return, amid a downpour, to behold a rather healthier sight in the top right-hand corner of the screen: 403 for 5. Replays fill in the blanks. Croftie claimed Blewie via a catch at silly point, possibly off the back of the bat, whereupon Gough struck twice in successive overs. Undone by bounce once more, Bev had fended to gully while Junior, beaten for pace, had been gloved. Hussain's catching of the former brings to mind an item in Paul Newman's *Sunday Telegraph* diary. Hussain and Mark Ramprakash, due to be married on the same day a couple of years ago, each invited Thorpe to be best man. Not wanting to let down either, he declined both. What a sensitive soul.

The torrents in the capital reach Birmingham around 3 p.m., enforcing the best part of an hour's delay. Tugga and Heals resume with a stream of vibrant strokes but with the lead a flimsy 71. Gough, bowling with pace and no little fire, pins Tugga back with one that cuts in deviously to defeat a swish to leg and elicit a leg-before verdict. The final nail? Not if Warney has anything to do with it. Defeated by a lifter first ball, he uppercuts Gough to the third-man boundary, finds Bucknor in his corner when Croftie unleashes a vehement appeal for leg-before, sees Butcher narrowly fail to cling on to a bat-pad offering in the same over, pulls Gough high over midwicket then eases a yorker through extra cover for 3 with something approaching nonchalance. At the end of the over, Gough, pink-cheeked and puffing, smiles wanly, plainly tuckered.

Atherton replaces Croftie and turns to Ealham, and not

before time, but the pattern continues. Warney swats his first ball over midwicket as the stocky son of Kent brushes the bails off in his delivery stride, then pulls another short 'un for 4 to extend the advantage past 100. 'England really are looking ragged,' laments Tony Lewis. Caddick relieves Gough and quickly slips into a niggardly groove, clearly more at ease against right-handers than left. Then fortune bestows its favours. The first ball of Ealham's next over, short and wide, sits up invitingly but Heals, knees bending, can only slap it to deepish gully, where Atherton swallows a stinger. Heals mutters agitatedly as he slinks back to the dressing room. Two balls later, Kasper edges a riser to second slip and Butcher, moving to his left, engulfs it with both hands as if rocking a baby. Cries of 'Enger-land, Enger-land' and 'Ashes coming home' rent the air as Dizzy, whose hamstring had restricted him to ten overs on Thursday and Friday, comes in with Bev as his runner. The cameras pick out Tugga at the back of the players' viewing area, looking decidedly pig-sick.

Warney persists with the bravura approach, taking due toll of a wayward Caddick. Then Dizzy plays Ealham to leg, Bev fails to respond with sufficient alacrity and confusion sets in. Crawley dashes back from short-leg, picks up near the umpire, then turns and shies in one movement. He misses the non-striker's stumps but Gough, running from mid-on, gathers, dives and completes the job. Dizzy and Bev exchange words as they trudge away. 'Rule Britannia' pipes up from the Hollies Stand.

Warney drills the next ball straight back at Ealham and the deed is done. The last three wickets have slipped away for a dozen runs, leaving the Poms almost four sessions to glean the required 117. Between them, Atherton, Butcher and Stewart, adrenalin at full throttle, complete the task in less than an hour and a half. Scampering a single shortly after reaching his 50, Atherton pushes back the beak of his helmet much as Gary Cooper did at the end of *High Noon*. At 6.51 Stewart leans back, drops on one knee and dispatches

Warney through the covers for the conclusive boundary, then flings his arms skywards. The snarl soon dissolves into a beam. 'Well done, mate,' says Tubs, nodding to Atherton. Face daubed in red and white, one member of the onrushing throng grabs Atherton and yells his felicitations. As they gambol up the pavilion steps, Atherton drapes an arm around Stewart, who slaps his skipper's helmet. Boycott is overjoyed: 'They've stuck it up Australia.'

As we await the ceremonies, Richie reiterates his fears about the tourists' attack. The camera pans to a drop-dead blonde wrapped in a Union Jack. A gap-toothed boy in an England one-day shirt perches on his father's shoulders, arms upraised. A lass with close-cropped hair sings her heart out: 'Enger-land, Enger-land'. As MC Gower struggles to make himself heard above the almighty din, Croftie raises a can of Diet Coke to the massed ranks below and claps it with his free hand, acknowledging the debt to the 20,000 twelfth men. Atherton goes up to collect the £17,000 winners' cheque then digs out a dob of wax from his ear as the tumult reaches fever pitch. Rouse shuffles forward to receive his medal, wreathed in a smile of vindication. Bob Willis, hair verging precariously on the bouffant, hails the groundsman's handiwork as 'magnificent'.

Hussain, rather than Gough, claims the Man of the Match citation, for what Willis describes as 'the best innings I've ever seen at Edgbaston'. 'He's got funny eyes,' notes Anne as Hussain accepts the magnum of champers and raises his arms like some newly crowned heavyweight champion. I point out that this may have something to do with the fact that he wears a contact lens in his left eye while batting. Tubs, who insists, typically, that he would have preferred a duck and victory to a century and defeat, informs Gower that his attack had functioned well below par. The silver-haired maestro offers 'personal congratulations' on his indomitable creasemanship, 'after all the struggles over the past year'. 'Six months,' corrects a slighted Tubs.

The positive thinking is approaching epidemic proportions. Syd Lawrence has apparently laid a sizeable bet that he will be bounding in with the new ball in the final Test. From here on in, there is only one certainty: from the host country's point of view, the summer can only go downhill. Which is a shining example, I suppose, of what Matthew meant by the native pessimism.

Daily Accumulator: Poms 8 Cobbers 2
Match score: Poms 29 Cobbers 11

ROBERT CROFT

The crowd were incredible. Every time we took a wicket it was as if we'd won the World Cup. I've never played in an atmosphere like that. Goughie would be at the end of his mark and he couldn't hear what anyone was saying to him because of the sheer noise. Mind you, with that sort of spirit behind you, you don't exactly need much encouragement from your colleagues. It was like watching an international at the Arms Park and suddenly finding yourself on the field. Some of the lads said they felt as if it was a football match. To get a start like that was tremendous, and the crowd played a major part in that.

We had to show the Aussies that we weren't going to lay down and die, which is why that first ball from Goughie was so important. I think we would have been satisfied if we'd taken three wickets that morning. It was just one of those days. We swung the ball quite a bit and caught everything. The highlight for me was when Goughie got Blewett the ball after bowling him with a no-ball. 'Oh shit,' I thought when the no-ball was called, but to come back like that showed real determination, true professionalism.

I watched the stand between Thorpie and Naz from the manager's room, which was not what I would call spacious. We're a superstitious lot, us cricketers, and I wouldn't budge, not even when I was dying for the toilet. You always imagine a wicket will go if you move. Bob Willis had a tricky decision to make in nominating his man of the match, but the ball dominated the bat for the first two or three days and to bat the way Naz did, to dominate the way he did, was exceptional. Unfortunately, I can't say that I enjoyed watching him as much as I would have wished. When I'm waiting to bat I'm always thinking, 'a couple of wickets and I'm in'. Even at number eight, I find myself thinking 'all it'll take is six good balls and I'm in'. I was desperate to succeed. I didn't pick up the first two balls that well because the sightscreen is a bit low, but I was fairly happy with the 24 I made. It was good to bat against Warne. He's been a breath of fresh air for spin bowlers. He's put us back on the map, made us fashionable again.

We were prepared for them to fight back. Rarely, even in county cricket, do you bowl out a side cheaply twice. There was a tendency to worry a little after they batted so well on the Saturday and Sunday morning but you still have to have that inner belief that it only takes one ball to change things. Then, all of a sudden, I nipped out Taylor. Then, after lunch, I nipped out Blewett, which meant there were two new men at the crease and Mark Waugh wasn't fit to come in at four. You had to fancy that. But what summed it up for me was the final run-out. Crawley had hardly been in the game but the way he and Goughie brought that off demonstrated the intensity we maintained throughout, particularly in the field.

The wind was difficult to handle on the Saturday. One moment it would be blowing straight at you, the next it would swirl. It was changing direction all the time. The coach phoned me on Sunday morning and said I was bowling from too close to the stumps, which is probably why I'd bowled too straight at Taylor. So I decided to bowl a bit wider, make him play on my side of the wicket. There was a spell of three overs when I thought I could get him out at any stage. Then he came down the wicket, the ball held up a bit and he clipped it back to me. I think I threw it out of Edgbaston. I didn't bowl so well at Matthew either. I dropped quite a few short and he put them away, but by the same token I thought I'd had him caught behind, so bowling him gave me quite a bit of pleasure. He's a top-class player but I trust I can make him work harder for his runs next time.

I was pleased for Taylor. After all, we are all fellow professionals and to have read some of the stick he's been given in the press has been incredible. I'm relieved for him that he's been able to silence his critics. He's still a very fine player. Would I be saying all this if we hadn't won? Quite possibly not. It's not often you get to have your cake and eat it.

To recognize the faces in the crowd at the end was really moving. Friends, family, supporters who'd been in Zimbabwe and New Zealand. In Zimbabwe, some of them had seen English cricket at one of its lowest ebbs, at least in one-day terms; this was their reward. My father was there; he told me he was very proud. We stayed behind for a few beers, with Marie and some of the other wives, but it was a Sunday night, everything was closed early, so we didn't make as big a night of it as we otherwise might. But that didn't matter. It was one of the best matches I've ever played in. They fought back and we stuck to our guns, kept that belief going, and finished them off again. It would be fair to say that it all went about as smoothly as we could possibly have wished.

MATTHEW ELLIOTT

When we lost those eight wickets in the first hour and a half our dressing room was in a state of bewilderment. I realize this is coming from a batsman's perspective but these things can happen when you bat first and there's life in the pitch. What bothered me was our performance on the second day, which may have been a legacy of those shock waves. We let ourselves down big time. We didn't bowl well, didn't hassle in the field, didn't make them fight, didn't make them earn every run. It was almost a case of 'Oh shit, we're behind' and then just allowing Thorpe and Hussain to take the game

105

away. Mind you, if I'd been fielding in the same position for the left-hander as I was for Stewart and Atherton, that edge from Thorpe before he'd broken his duck would have gone straight down my throat.

On the Saturday evening I felt we had clawed back a lot of the ground, and by the end of Sunday morning I even thought we had a sniff of a win, but we lost the initiative after lunch. If Junior had been able to bat at four, it might have made a difference because I'm sure he would have contributed the quick runs we needed.

I was a bit nervous in the first innings. I was letting the ball go pretty well. I misjudged a couple early on, survived a shout for leg-before and edged a four, but I felt I was getting my front foot out in time, making the bowlers bowl to me. I couldn't believe the way I got out. I probably got too far down the wicket and the ball dropped between bat and pad. I sat in the dressing room in complete shock. To Gough's credit, he bowled well. There was a bit in the wicket for him and he put it on the right spot. He was as sharp as any bowler in the match. In terms of the challenge, I thoroughly enjoyed batting against Croftie. He wasn't spinning the ball a great deal but he was making it drift, using the breeze well. That took a while to get used to, but then I cut a couple of fours and they took him off, so I thought, 'that's good'. That's why I was so disappointed to get out the way I did. I'd become a bit defensive. I should have carried on attacking. I'll learn from that.

Tubs's century was fantastic. We were all on our feet in the dressing room when he got it, roaring our heads off. We all realized how important it was. It means we have an opening pair in form and a captain who's comfortable with his position. He just got back to basics. He was more patient, letting a lot more balls go, not trying to drive as much, playing straight, trying to get his front leg moving towards the ball more. He had one difficult spell but then he top-edged a bouncer for six and that broke the shackles a bit. Before you knew it he had 40. To be honest, I couldn't see him playing that sort of innings. I couldn't see him getting out of his slump. Apart from that 60 at Derby there had been no indication that he would. But once he got that start, the change was almost instantaneous. He really looked solid. I think he was aware of how many people here wanted him to succeed. I know we lost the match, but to see him come through his ordeal has given the whole side a real lift.

Unfortunately, I had a decidedly unpleasant experience when we were coming off at the end of the match. A bloke came up to me, grabbed my cap and ran off with it. I asked him to give it back but he wouldn't so I charged after him. When I caught him, I tackled him to the ground and retrieved it. It's the only cap you're ever given. They're all numbered individually, which is why I never forget I'm the 368th player to be capped by my country. 'Thanks mate,' I said, a bit gruffly. Then, as I walked away, he and his mates kicked and punched me all the way back to the pavilion. It was disgraceful. I've reported the incident to the management but they're wary that there might be a legal problem because the bloke who stole my cap might say I caused him damage when I tackled him. The point is that the authorities can't just let people walk on to the ground willy-nilly. It doesn't happen at home.

It was just like that scene from the movie *Braveheart*, when William Wallace leads the Scots on the charge and they take the castle down, brick by brick. People here have been waiting a decade to beat us. Hitting me showed how much it means to them. They really want to beat us big time. That's healthy but it can get out of hand. Most of the guys are pretty laid-back but I think this will get backs up a bit. Tugga is the only one of us who has experienced losing an Ashes series; he has made it quite clear that it is something you want to avoid if you can possibly help it.

ACT 2

9 June 'Teenagers rate Charles a bad dad'

(Guardian)

Beflannelled Fools 1 Muddied Oafs 0. Even though the footy boys win Le Tournoir in France, cricket dominates the front pages of the Monday sports supplements. William Hill have slashed the odds on a 6–0 home whitewash from 400–1 to 40–1. Now, now, boys, let's not get too cocky.

Not every Cobber is in high dudgeon. Swan Richards, the man who convinced Matthew he would be better off honing his skills in Eastcote than at the Academy – and who has persuaded Stinger to come out of retirement and play for his Crusaders side on their impending tour of the shires – admitted to his left-arm spinner that the Edgbaston denouement afforded him a considerable degree of satisfaction. Not least the fact that the Cobbers' chief runmakers were Tubs, Blewie and Matthew, 'the three good guys'. He, too, is aware of the rumblings from South Africa. Stinger sounded a little low when I rang. He fell asleep during the latter stages last night and was unaware of the course of events, but defeat was not the cause. Tugga wants to see him when he arrives on Friday, having apparently taken umbrage at his story about the supposed unrest in the Republic, causing Stinger to question his sources. Has he been set up?

Croftie dashed home first thing, eager to make the most of an unexpected day off (a riverbank doubtless beckons). Matthew remains in Birmingham, and spends the morning practising. Naughty boy nets? Only for the bowlers, whose errors in length – too short or too full – are deemed to be the root of the side's ills. Call Croftie to congratulate him. 'Brilliant game, wasn't it?' he chirps. We arrange to meet in London prior to the Lord's Test. 'If I'm picked,' comes the rider. I tell him not to be so silly. Never, he reiterates, will he take these things for granted. I avail him of some pertinent statistics: not since 1968–69, against the West Indies, have the Cobbers lost an opening Test and recovered to take the series; not since 1936–37, moreover, have they done so in an Ashes rubber. He sounds vaguely encouraged.

11 June 'Bones point the way to new human ancestor'

(USA Today)

The first day of the tourists' match against Nottinghamshire is washed out. Matthew is far from dismayed. 'You only have to train if you're not playing,' he reasons, 'but I am, so I can put my feet up.'

Sky's *Pavilion End* show features the so-called Barmy Army in a recording studio. 'We're rising from the Ashes,' sing a batch of remarkably unthuggish young things, 'there's no other team on earth we need to beat.'

12 June 'Blair wins Ashes'

(Private Eye)

Arrive at Trent Bridge in mid-afternoon to be greeted by glowering clouds and the news that Dean Jones has left Derbyshire in a huff and stomped back to Melbourne, claiming lack of dressing-room support. Remembering his acrimonious exit as captain of Victoria under similar circumstances, none of the visiting journos seem the vaguest bit surprised.

The first ball I see yields a second wicket for Pistol, who has been flown in to replace the unfortunate Bick, homeward bound after suffering a stress reaction to his lower back. At a Variety Club function a month ago, the quietly spoken Victorian was driving a hearse: an apt metaphor, or so it seemed to onlookers, for his international career. 'This bloke should have been here all along,' proclaims Ken Casellas, the amiable veteran hack from Perth, echoing the general consensus.

Pistol, however, does not have things all his own way. Galvanized, presumably, by the sight of the baggy green, Nathan Astle, the New Zealander recently signed by Nottinghamshire to replace Mohammad Zahid, their injury-plagued Pakistani paceman, reels off a string of sweetly timed drives. Not until Pigeon provokes a slice to slip just before tea does he bid adieu, having blazed to 99 off 109 balls. Greg Baum looks as if his crest is about to fall through the floor.

Teletext keeps us up to date with happenings elsewhere. At Cardiff, Croftie has dragged Glamorgan from a trough of 64 for 4 against Middlesex with an unbeaten 62; at The Oval, Hollioake Minor is 45 not out against Yorkshire; at Edgbaston, Dougie Brown has taken the first four Derbyshire wickets. David Lloyd of the *Standard*, one of the circuit's true gents, predicts that Brown, who turned down a chance to represent his native Scotland in the ICC Trophy because it might scupper his prospects of playing for the Sassenachs, could be a serious contender for England's next World Cup squad. 'We could do with him by then,' warrants a grumpy Baum. 'Oh, come now Greg,' says Lloyd, 'you've just had a minor hiccup.' Baum cracks a smile: 'More like a big belch, really.'

Wind billowing his flannels, length a good foot fuller than at Edgbaston, Pigeon rattles through the tail, wrapping up the innings for 239 and leaving Matthew to see out the last hour in company with Slats. Matthew's back foot is moving more freely than hitherto: the knees are obviously having one of their better days. In his first knock since 22 May, when he was run out in the opening Texaco match, Slats goes for 14, unhinged by that redoubtable trouper Kevin

Evans, leg-before pulling impetuously, undone by moderate bounce. Over-anxiety? Tubs's revival has hardly aided his cause, of course. Indeed, all the signs are that his second tour is destined to be as dispiriting as his first was rapturous.

Awaiting a taxi to ferry me to the tourists' hotel, I strike up a regrettable conversation with a burly, unkempt chap who warns me that, should Tubs have the gall to repeat his Edgbaston staunchness, he'll hit his girlfriend. Much as my bones have already supplied the answer, I can't help but ask why. 'Because,' he reasons with impeccable logic, 'she's there.' Before I can make my excuses, he insists on telling me how unreasonable she is: 'When we were watching the game on the box on Sunday I asked her to say Blewett was a wanker. She told me to fuck off. Why would she do that?' Wary that the wrong words might result in extreme bodily discomfort, I delicately suggest he shouldn't take his frustrations out on her. 'All right then,' he snaps, 'I won't pay my rent to the council. Not that I do anyway.'

15 June 'Fire bomber stalks "fat cat bosses" '
(Sunday Telegraph)

Can't remember the last time I felt so marooned. The old man is celebrating Father's Day cruising the Med, water-bound holidays being his only option now that diabetes has forced his legs to swell, rendering walking quite agonizing (or so he assures me). Anne and the kids are in Devon with my mother and stepfather but there's no phone at their cottage, so I can't contact them if I get in a jam, such as screwing up the washing-machine cycle. Even Stinger has deserted me, schlapping out to Windsor to play for the Australian Taverners against their Lord's counterparts. I had planned to tag along, but the batteries are running low.

Terrific to see Stinger again. For all the frequency of our phone conversations, our paths hadn't crossed since '89. During the winter, Peter Roebuck had accused him of being anti-English, which comes as news to me. 'I'm not anti-

English,' he insists, 'just anti-English incompetence.' As ever, the difference between our respective native customs is a prime source of debate. 'You lot pass on the left,' he exclaimed querulously as we descended the escalator at Bounds Green Tube yesterday en route to Cardiff. 'On our escalators, anyone wanting to overtake has to go on the right. Just like on a motorway.' Love–fifteen. 'How many points do you get for a first-innings lead?' he wondered while Middlesex were inching along in a morning session at Sophia Gardens that produced 66 runs in 32 overs and approximately three minutes of enterprise. I explained, somewhat sheepishly, that the visitors were pursuing an extra batting point. Stinger's eyebrows leaped heavenwards. Love–thirty.

The ennui finally ended when Tufnell was bowled swishing at Darren Thomas, as if fed up with all this apparently purposeless mundanity. With Croftie listed to bat at six, I proposed a chat over coffee. No chance. The Lions are in action on the dressing-room TV. Could I wait until the transmission was over? Sixteen overs and barely an hour later, Glamorgan, trailing by 38, were all out for 31, dismantled by the die-straight seamers of Fraser and his richly promising young apprentice, Jamie Hewitt. Croftie was one of the unluckier victims, dismissed by a grubber that would have done Barry John proud. 'Don't rub it in,' chuckled one Glamorgan member as I dictated the words 'lowest-ever score at Sophia Gardens' to the *Sunday Times* copytaker from the phone in the main bar. By the time I'd expanded my original 410 words into a hastily reordered 1,010, Croftie was on his way home, a night with the lads in store. Non-Test Sundays mean a lie-in; the hangover promised to be sizeable. And was. 'Never seen anything like it,' he assured me an hour ago. 'The pitch didn't help but they caught every edge and everything we missed was straight. Crazy.'

'Have England broken the deadly spell of Warne?' posits the headline over an article in the *Sunday Telegraph*.

Underneath, Kerry O'Keeffe, the last Australian wrist-spin-ner before Warney to take fifty Test wickets, offers a prog-nosis of his successor's ailments. Warney is dropping his left shoulder at the point of release, he observes, and hence bowling with only one half of his body. 'He is slinging the ball out, so he's not generating the loop and bounce he wants . . . Early in every spell Shane wants to rip a leg-break and see Healy take it up by his hip, and then his confidence soars. But if there is no bounce, as at Edgbaston, and he sees Mike Atherton waiting on the back foot, then his psyche changes and he feels he has to push the ball through and frustrate the batsman out . . . He was bowling three or four of these front-of-the-hand nothing balls and either getting cut or picked off through the leg side by the right-handers. Previously, anybody who did that did so at their peril. When Hussain and Thorpe were about to reach their hundreds, in both cases he gave them the flipper – he always does when a batsman is about to reach a landmark – and in both cases the ball was too short and the trajectory too low because the left side of his body had fallen away.' All of which suggests that the promised presence at Lord's of Terry Jenner, Warney's trusty technical guru, cannot come a moment too soon.

O'Keeffe, who took 53 wickets at 38.07 in his twenty-four Tests for Australia in the seventies, also felt that Warney ('a far better bowler than me') was missing his spin twin of 1993, Tim May, as friend and in-house humourist as well as foil. 'When Bevan comes on, Shane will never know whether he is going to take 5 for 40 or bowl 5 overs for 40. In 1993 they had Merv as well to relieve the intensity and provide some slapstick. Nothing against this party, but there are a lot of pretty intense cricketers in it who don't smile much.'

On a neighbouring page, Atherton stresses the impor-tance of continuity after the New Zealand tour: 'People felt at ease in each other's company [at Edgbaston] and the old mickey-taking, puerile jokes about Croftie's weight, Nasser's hair, Creepy's lack of, and Thorpie's height

returned. It's part of what David Lloyd calls Team England.'
No shortage of smiles there, then.

Stinger returns with tales of Windsor. Of particular interest was an amusing tête-à-tête between Jenner and John
Snow as the former readied himself to face his erstwhile
adversary. 'Just thought I'd remind you,' said the maverick
leg-spinner whom Snow had felled with a bouncer at
Sydney in 1971, provoking one member of the affronted
crowd to grab the Sussex poet by the shirt and so prod
Illingworth to lead his team off the field. 'It's been twenty-
odd years since you did what you did to me. Times have
changed.' And with that he tugged on a helmet. Snow
laughed heartily.

The other noteworthy exchange in the castle grounds
followed the dismissal of one of Snow's teammates. A cue
for mild rejoicing? Not on your nelly. Turning to Paul
Sheahan, the man who preceded him as his country's finest
fielder, Ross Edwards articulates the general disenchantment: 'Why can't we play a *proper* game?'

17 June 'Clinton may give blacks an apology over slavery'
(Daily Telegraph)

To Lord's, now shorn of scaffolding and getting in trim.
Fresh from beating Leicestershire and reaping £2,500 for
their first meaningful win of the tour, the Cobbers are
stretched out on the grass in front of the Grandstand. Hooter
conducts the exercise routines, as he has done ever since the
Caribbean tour of 1983–84. Originally a rugby league
physio, his only hiccups occurred in the late eighties, when
Mike Whitney and Geoff Lawson, convinced he was an ACB
stooge, put it around that he was feeding rumours back to
the board. Then it's the turn of Steve Smith, the diminutive
fitness instructor with a springbok tattooed on one of his
buttocks (the other is being kept vacant for a lion). He whips
the ranks through a frantic slalom run round a series of
yellow cones followed by five push-ups. Warney, keeping

one eye on Smith, declines the last part. Then comes the fielding drill. Warney is sparing with his right shoulder.

Stinger and I are a mite apprehensive as we spot Tugga and Matthew together and looking our way. According to Swan Richards, Tugga had approached Matthew in South Africa and asked him if he would support any industrial action, to which Matthew allegedly replied that he was only interested in playing for his country. Although Stinger referred to this in his story without recourse to names or pack drills, fingers quickly pointed to Matthew, who denies all. Denis Rogers has warned Stinger that the players are gunning for him. Not knowing which way to turn, Stinger tackles Tubs. 'Are you talking to me?' he asks. 'Not really,' comes the atypically curt reply. 'You're keeping us on the wrong side of the ACB.' Tubs explains that there had been discussions about the players' workload in South Africa but insisted there had been no talk of pulling out of the tour. Which clarifies matters to a degree but does little to address the reports of internal ructions, let alone dispel the possibility of action in the longer term.

Matthew, naturally, is obliged to err on the side of discretion. 'For me, the Players Association is a very positive move forward because we're becoming more professional and businesslike and want to be seen as such. The formation of a union reflects that. It's too simplistic to see any disputes as being solely about money. It's also about respect. We're being asked to train more and play more, so the best players could be absolutely knackered by their early thirties. Do we really want to go back to the bad old days when our country's finest cricketers were forced to retire early for financial reasons?'

Over by the nets at the Nursery End, Baum curses his workload. 'There's been Taylor, Warne, selection issues. We never had any in '93 because we were winning all the time.' Mick Hunt, the groundsman, walks by looking imploringly at the skies, eyebrows stiff with panic. Concerned about the legacy of the storms, he shows us a core of soil he has drilled from the pitch: 'See – damp.' Not a happy bunny.

Stinger stands behind Warney's net. 'Are you talking to me?' he calls out to the man whose autobiography he has just finished ghosting. 'Yeah,' replies Warney. 'Well,' says Stinger, 'that makes one.'

Adjourn to the ECB boardroom where the future of the game is taking its latest turn for the better. Hotfoot from an ICC meeting described by one delegate as 'harmonious and boring', Jagmohan Dalmiya, the poker-faced new chairman, sits at a table next to a perma-smiling David Richards, his chief executive. He eyes the assembled media warily, as well he might. An Indian as the leading light in world cricket? Imperialist feathers are bound to be ruffled.

The good news is that Kenya and Bangladesh have been been granted first-class and one-day international status, a measure taken at the recommendation of the new development committee headed by Dr Ali Bacher. A world Test championship, moreover, will be examined at the next ICC confab. Best of all, in the event of bad light, Test grounds will henceforth be permitted, if so equipped, to switch on their floodlights. The *Sun* and the *Mirror*, predictably, are more concerned about plans to stage a triangular one-day tourney at Disney World. 'The development committee has a mission to make a Commonwealth sport into a global sport,' states Richards, who reminds us that the game's oldest international fixture is that between Canada and the USA. 'Other sports are going past us at a great rate of knots. I don't want to name them because I don't want to give them publicity.'

Aside from stressing the need for 'collective responsibility, unity of purpose, quicker decision-making', Dalmiya says precious little, no doubt recalling an interview with the BBC last summer, wherein he ill-advisedly advocated that first innings in Test matches be restricted to 100 overs and the draw outlawed. Sensing he could do with a bit of moral support, I approach him at the end of the conference and wish him the best of luck, adding that it was high time the game lifted its head above the parapet and confronted changing leisure habits, that globalization was indeed the way forward. He seemed to appreciate it.

At the Nursery End, Lillee and Thomson kindle visions of John Belushi and Dan Akroyd's *Blues Brothers*: matching shades, matching jeans, matching 'Raw Power' T-shirts. 'Is my run-up long enough?' one aspiring southern quick asks Lillee. The answer is characteristically succinct: 'Too bloody long.' Thommo reveals – make that boasts – that they had been 'kicked out' of Tramps the other night, albeit only because they wanted to stay at the nightclub past closing time. So far as he could recall, they'd hadn't been to bed before 7 a.m. since their arrival. Nice to see the boys haven't lost their contempt for the straight and narrow.

18 June 'Shane can't grip his balls'

(Sun)

The other day, a vicar wrote to *The Times* complaining about 'the baying masses' at Edgbaston. Roger Knight, the MCC secretary, appears to have taken this very much to heart. He has warned spectators coming through the Grace Gates that they will be ejected for hissing, booing or chanting mindlessly, and asked them to applaud both teams with equal zest. He needn't have bothered. Over the years, the crowds at HQ have been about as helpful to the home team as an outbreak of the pox.

Warney had been remarkably buoyant on the second evening at Edgbaston. The pitch was easing, he asserted to the reporter ghosting his column for the *Sunday Age*, the footmarks widening. Who knows? If the batsmen did their bit, he might even have something to bowl at in the fourth innings. Besides, even if the least the Cobbers achieved was a draw, there was always Lord's. Brazen braggadocio? More like impeccable logic. Lord's is to the Cobbers what the world used to be to Britain: a place to conquer at will. Sixty-three years have passed since they last lost a Test behind the Grace Gates, and that was the only time this century. Vienna had just staged a pow-wow between Mussolini and Hitler; Bonnie and Clyde had just retired, extremely hurt; Londoners were adjusting to a new-fangled contraption known as the pedestrian crossing; Richie was 3. Talk about a lifetime.

'Australians will always fight for those twenty-two yards. Lord's and its traditions belong to Australia as much as England.' John Curtin, the Australian Premier, uttered those heartfelt sentiments in 1945; his descendants have yet to let him down. Since 'Verity's Match' in 1934, there have been 14 clashes for the Ashes at headquarters, 7 won by the visitors. But for the stubbornness of Willie Watson and Trevor Bailey in 1953, it would have been 8. Where did the Cobbers amass their highest total against the Poms? Lord's. Where did Bradman play his finest hand? Lord's. Where did Bob Massie enjoy his fifteen minutes' worth? Need we go on?

Even in the otherwise bountiful summer of 1985, the jinx never wavered. Border's men may have been trounced in the first Test, and then shunted out for 76 by Hampshire, but they still prevailed with more than two sessions to spare. Only once, in fact, have the hosts gained so much as a technical knockout. In 1968 Bill Lawry and his comrades followed on after David Brown and Barry Knight had harried them out for 78, only for rain, inevitably, to have the final titter. Even the weather gods have taken sides.

Wembley and Twickenham may be virtually impregnable, but cricket is as much about patience as passion. Besides, how can any crowd sustain a roar for five days, let alone one so unfailingly polite? The Cobbers, lest we forget, are not the only regular visitors to NW8 with an unnerving knack of making monkeys of their hosts. Think of Ramadhin and Valentine, of Mudassar and Mohsin, of Wessels and DeVilliers. Since beating New Zealand and Pakistan in 1978, England have played 27 Tests here, winning 5, losing 9. Is it stretching things to suggest that to succeed there, even now, is to storm the citadel, to thumb noses at Empire? Maybe the Dutch would be more compliant.

Matthew, who had an uneasy introduction to the slope in last month's one-day international – 'I kept feeling as if I

118

was falling over' – is not about to break with tradition. 'The place definitely gives you a lift. You look up there on the dressing-room wall and there's this honours board listing all the visiting players who've made a Test hundred there. How can you not be inspired by that?'

The home team, conversely, tends to be cowed by the size of the stage, by all that unremitting tradition. Familiarity, Crawley concedes, has bred, if not contempt, then certainly a degree of flatness. Even the locals struggle. As he made his way through the Long Room on his first day as captain of his country, Mike Brearley recalled being watched 'as through the cage of a zoo'. Wearing his psychologist's hat, Brearley might well conclude that some Poms underperform because, subconsciously, they are either embarrassed or repelled by all the -isms Lord's stands for: elitism, imperialism, sexism, ageism. In many cases, this may be precisely what inspires the opposition. Even if the ICC does move its HQ to Calcutta, nothing will change.

All the more reason, then, to reel in the years. Trapped on a drying wicket after a sodden Sunday, Bill Woodfull's 1934 tourists failed by 9 runs to avoid the follow-on and surrendered their last 14 wickets in a day. A leggy purveyor of briskish left-arm spin fated to die in his prime, in an Italian POW camp (albeit not as a prisoner), Yorkshire's Hedley Verity claimed 7 for 61 and 8 for 43: still the best haul in 120 years of Anglo-Antipodean warfare by an Englishman not named Laker. 'All lovers of the game,' rejoiced Neville Cardus, 'were unanimous that Test cricket was itself again, chivalrous and magnificent.' Cardus never was over-fond of Australians.

Two survivors endure: Bradman, and Bill Brown, the dairy farmer's son from Toowoomba. The first Queensland native to captain Australia, Brown, now a spry 84, will be in attendance tomorrow, just as he was at Edgbaston. A graceful opener with a penchant for felicitous glances, he averaged nearly 47 in 22 Tests, angling his shots with such precision, wrote Ray Robinson, it was as if his bat 'had an inbuilt protractor'. The generosity of spirit remains, the self-effacement, too. Speaking from his lodgings in Newbury last week, he rhapsodized over Wally Hammond's 240 in 1938 ('without being disloyal, you wanted to see him get a few'). Naturally, he omitted one minor detail: his own double-century saved the day.

Brown, who is adamant that Warney imparts more turn than either Bill O'Reilly or Clarrie Grimmett, was also the only Australian to derive anything remotely resembling pleasure from Verity's Match. Opening in a Test for the first time, he made 105; no compatriot reached 50 in either innings. 'I got my runs when the wicket was good. But when it got wet, it turned quite a bit. Verity speeded up and bowled magnificently. His length was immaculate. Whenever a ball lifted you had to play at it. There was quite a festive air afterwards, quite a bit of champagne flowing around, but not in our dressing room.'

Verity had disposed of Bradman in both innings amid mounting concern for the whereabouts of the immortal's marbles. When The Don came to the crease, his side, facing 440, were 68 for 1. The situation, surely, called for a careful recce. But The Don was not himself. Even Brown, with whom he added 73, was taken unawares. 'I was a bit surprised,' he recalled with diplomatic understatement. 'He was normally fairly selective but he almost threw caution to the wind. He took to Verity like I have never seen anyone taken to before, went right down the wicket, struck some magnificent cover drives. Woodfull sent out a message, urging him to simmer down.' Before long, The Don advanced to drive, remembered his skipper's plea in mid-dart (or so it is said), checked his shot and donated Verity the simplest of return catches. He always blamed Woodfull.

Ever eager to detect a chink, the critics were less convinced. On the Monday, indeed, The Don fell for the sucker punch, tempted by a vacant outfield and top-edging a catch to Les Ames behind the stumps. As he wended his way back to the pavilion, the tuts were loud, the headshakes vigorous. 'I was not well,' The Don insisted in a radio

Apocalypse postponed. Mark Taylor nearly became the first Australian captain to be dropped during an Ashes tour, then rebounded with a century few Englishmen begrudged. At Southampton a week later, the sense of renewal was inescapable. *(Mark Ray)*

The Godfather Mike Brearley, another captain whose brain demanded retention even when his bat did not, is reminded by a press box colleague at Old Trafford that his highest Test score was inferior to Eddie Hemmings's. *(Mark Ray)*

The Good Life. Croft, an avid fisherman, bemoans the one that got away at the team hotel prior to the Lords Test. There were times when the suddenness of fame intimidated him. 'I'm still pinching myself' was a constant refrain. *(Mark Ray)*

Uneasy rider. Elliott adjourns after a net at Lord's. Beset by knee problems all winter at one juncture he was laid up for two months he contemplated pulling out of the tour two days before departure and was seldom free of discomfort thereafter. *(Mark Ray)*

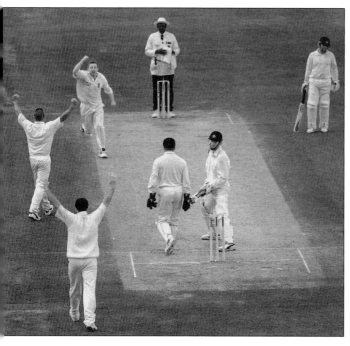

Look back in rancour. Betrayed by an angled bat, Elliott is bowled by a gleeful Croft for 66 in the second innings at Edgbaston. The pair would tussle keenly all summer, but never again did the Welshman have the last word.
(Graham Morris)

Paper fortress. Elliott drives Gough through the covers en route to his maiden Test century at Lord's. A draw meant that Pom had still not beaten Cobber at HQ since the invention of the pedestrian crossing.
(Graham Morris)

Global warning. Jagmohan Dalmiya (left), the newly elected chairman of the International Cricket Council, and David Richards, his chief executive, face the press at Lord's after announcing plans for a major tournament at Disney World. *(Mark Ray)*

Life's a pitch. Before the Test began, Mick Hunt, the Lord's groundsman, was anxious about the dampness of the wicket. 'Our boys gave their wickets away too easily,' he declaimed after England's dismissal for 77.

Smiley smile. David Lloyd, England's affable coach, finds no end of reasons to be cheerful after his batsmen's stirring defiance on the final day at Lord's. That disarming smile would seldom be glimpsed by the press thereafter. (Mark Ray)

Drinking it in. Glenn McGrath tries to disguise his delight from the media after his record-breaking 8-38 at Lord's, and succeeds admirably. A stranglehold had been imposed. (Mark Ray)

Mark his words. Mark Butcher, whose mature batting in his second Test helped England save the day at Lord's, avails the author of his panacea for English cricket: 'Something absolutely drastic'. (Mark Ray)

Roll up, roll up. Mostly homeless and unemployed, the cleaners await the call of duty outside the Nursery End car park at Lord's. Pay amounted to £14 for an evening's labour, £15 if wet. Cheques only. *(Mark Ray)*

Age shall not wither them. The Bruise Brothers, Dennis Lillee and Jeff Thomson put some aspiring fast bowlers through their paces at Lord's. *(Mark Ray)*

Keith Miller, prince of Australian all-rounders, tells the Crusaders touring team one of his favourite footie yarns. *(Mark Ray)*

Dedicated followers of passion.
Colin Ingleby-Mackenzie is an unusual, if
not unique, MCC president: he does not
seem too averse to women members.
(Mark Ray)

John-Paul Getty at Wormsley, his
enchanting, purpose-built ground. Has any
American ever been so hopelessly
smitten? (Mark Ray)

Parental support. (Above) Bev Waugh, squash-champion mother of the Waugh twins, and No 1 son are united on the eve of the Old Trafford Test. *(Mark Ray)*

Ditto Shane Warne and father Keith. That Australian's finest promptly found their form and dominated the game may or may not have been mere coincidence. *(Mark Ray)*

Pearls for Dean. Accompanied by his captain, David Graveney, the chairman of selectors, informs Dean Headley he will make his Test bow at Old Trafford. After numerous false starts, he emerged as England's bowling find of the summer. *(Mark Ray)*

At a distance. Michael Slater, so ebullient on his Test debut at Old Trafford in 1993, contemplates fortune's slings on his return. Superceded by Elliott, he remained a sad, peripheral figure all tour, barely scraping 100 first-class runs. *(Mark Ray)*

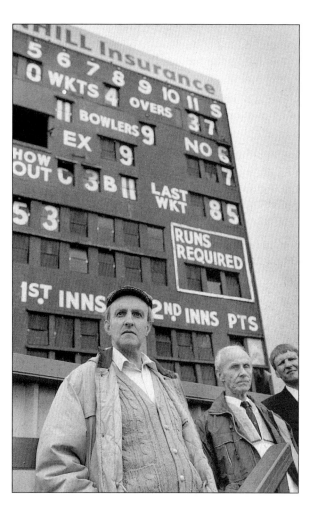

Foreboding. Old Trafford, day one, Steve Waugh just in. *(Mark Ray)*

Fruition. Old Trafford, day four, Ian Healy and McGrath acclaim the elder Waugh's second hundred. (Mark Ray)

The engine room. Atherton (above), Darren Gough (below left) and Nasser Hussain (below right). Atherton became McGrath's rabbit, yet ended the summer as secure as ever. Gough and Hussain began superbly, but injury and fatigue told. Or did that escape the counties' attention? *(Mark Ray)*

The scribes. (Above left) Scyld Berry of the *Sunday Telegraph* stares ruefully at the action from the Old Trafford press box.
(Above right) John Woodcock, Sage of Lóngparish, partakes of retirement.
(Below) Chris Lander (left) of the *Mirror* and John Etheridge of the *Sun. (Mark Ray)*

All quiet on the Western Terrace. Threatened with closure after racial incidents in 1996, Headingley's hotbed of ill-will to most men was on its best behaviour for the fourth Test's rainswept opening day. It couldn't last, and didn't. (Mark Ray)

Hmmm. Alan Crompton, the Australian manager, listens sceptically as Graveney explains why the wicket for the Headingley Test was switched. The pitch doctors did their utmost all summer, to scant avail. Until it was too late. *(Mark Ray)*

The last cut is the deepest. Elliott sheepishly accepts the acclaim after his 199 at Headingley, disappointment acute: 'I didn't look up enough'. *(Mark Ray)*

What if ... Elliott faces the pens and tape recorders after his match-winning knock. What if Thorpe *had* caught that sitter when he'd made 29? *(Mark Ray)*

Definitely No Poofters. Ashes retained, inhibitions shelved, the Cobbers celebrate as Devon Malcolm is last out at Trent Bridge. It was their fifth victorious quest in succession; never has the gap yawned wider. *(Graham Morris)*

interview a few years ago. 'I didn't feel I had the stamina to play a big innings: my mental outlook was wrong.' It is exceedingly difficult to envisage his descendants being guilty of a similar felony tomorrow.

19 June 'Lord's buffers ban the National Anthem'
(*Daily Mirror*)

Awake at 6.30 to the swish of tyres over damp tarmac. Talk about déjà vu all over again. In my youth, just about every trip to Lord's for a Test brought grisly skies and a Pacific's worth of covers and tarpaulins. In 1974 I spent two-thirds of the day waiting for the rains to cease, only to tune in to Peter West and chums on my return home and discover that Derek Underwood was mowing through the Pakistani order. Was I being punished for my impatience? There is one consolation for Josef and his generation. The impressive blueprint for Yorkshire's proposed new purpose-built home at Wakefield incorporates a retractable roof. The sooner the vicissitudes of our less than beloved climate are removed from the equation the better.

Stinger and I head for St John's Wood nonetheless. Even if there is no play, I'll still have to file something for the *FT*. As we walk down Wellington Road, the effervescent strains of Booker T and the MGs' 'Soul Limbo' ring out courtesy of a couple of young musicians in the Tetley Bitter concession stand. 'Gerry Adams has a lot to answer for,' moans one egg-and-bacon tie to another as their bags are checked at the Grace Gates, conveniently forgetting that the stewards are after booze, not bombs.

No play before lunch, and scant chance of any beyond that. Atherton might reasonably have wished for a more fitting start to his record forty-second Test as captain of his country, but then repulsing slings and arrows are his stock-in-trade. Rummaging in the bookshop, I scanned the new postscript to *One-man Committee*, the tome originally published last year by his purported nemesis, Ray

Illingworth. 'He's tough,' warrants the author. 'Tougher than I thought at first . . . He's stubborn, but that's no crime – so am I. I think we have more in common than perhaps either of us realized at the beginning. We've had a few laughs and there are many more pluses than minuses in our time together. I can only repeat something I wrote earlier: I just cannot imagine how I would have coped with leading England at his age. He is improving as a captain, but only slowly because of the number of times he has had to juggle a moderate attack. That is why he has to learn to be more flexible; he needs to try and make things happen more, rather than sit back and wait.'

Atherton, lest we forget, was 25 when he succeeded Gooch, whereas Illy was 37 when he ascended what was then an immeasurably more forgiving throne. To see the present incumbent interviewed on *The Pavilion End* last night was to observe a man at one with self and job. Working with Graveney, whom he finds 'very approachable and more open to cricket chat', has evidently been beneficial. He had come close to resigning his commission after the last World Cup, he said, so infuriated had he been by both itinerary and administrators. He recalled asking Illingworth whether he thought bringing back National Service would be worthwhile, and receiving an affirmative response. Having originally bought his portrayal by the media hook line and sinker, conceded Lord Tesco, 'my opinions have changed on their head – I found him very intelligent, very gutsy, a good leader, nice sense of humour'. Hansie Cronje, the South African captain, felt he was 'ready to die for his country'.

Image, Atherton professed, 'was never that important to me', recalling his comments in the latest *Wisden Cricket Monthly*. 'I don't do myself justice,' he confessed, 'in that I just try and be as I am. And often that means being uncomfortable . . . Certainly I'm very reserved in a written press conference, because I've found from experience that the more you say, the more rope you give yourself to be hung by . . . I basically don't trust that I'm going to be quoted correctly. There was a classic example at the end of the New Zealand tour. Colin Bateman of the *Daily Express* – we lost the game at Auckland, chasing 150, and he asked me about the defeat. I said very simply, "if you play as we did today, obviously you give the opposition a chance". That was just an obvious comment and it was taken the piss out of in the *Daily Express* – "this is what the England captain thinks, aren't we glad he's a wise old bird" la-di-dah. Complete pisstake. You don't need that.' But then nor, it could be argued, does the public deserve to be patronized. Happily, a change in tack has been apparent of late, purportedly urged by Lord Tesco and facilitated by success. The knives have been sheathed, for now.

Stinger introduces me to the statuesque Tom Brooks, the former Test umpire. He is in town with the Kingsgrove Sports Club Supporters Tour, led by that inimitable rapscallion Doug Walters. Brooks had the misfortune to be involved in some of the least pleasant Tests in history, notably at Sydney in 1971, when Illingworth marched his team off the field only to be advised that he would have to concede the match if they didn't get back out there sharpish. 'I was a bit lucky,' the ruddy-faced ex-copper acknowledges. 'Most of the problems in that series were at Lou Rowan's end. He was the one who warned Snowy for persistent bumpers. He and Lou didn't get on. To be honest, I never really enjoyed umpiring, or at least not until it was all over. Robin Baillache and I did all six Tests in '74–75, and it was very draining. I told Ian Chappell there were to be no bouncers at Underwood or Willis: he was not pleased. When Lillee or Thomson came on I told them after two bouncers – no more, and not every over. I remember Fletcher turning to me at Adelaide, having made a few runs after Thommo had been injured playing tennis, and saying, "It's not so bad facing one of the fuckers". By the time Baillache and I walked into the hotel in Sydney at the end of the series, I found myself turning to him and saying, "Thank God – I can't wait to finish." '

While waiting for play to be called off, I spend a couple of stimulating hours getting drizzled on with my friend Mike Marqusee, the native New Yorker who describes himself as 'an indigent bohemian' and whose seminal book, *Anyone but England*, stands as one of the most perceptive dissections of the foibles of English cricket. We note how those we have seen milling around the ground are overwhelmingly male Caucasians between the ages of 30 and 60. 'When I came to my first Tests in '76 and '77,' Mike recalls wistfully, 'we'd sit on the grass verge and there was a more spontaneous atmosphere, probably because there were more children. There were also more women, whereas the ratio now is, what, 20 or 30 to 1? Whenever Pakistan or India played here, the Asian families would come, but not now.' The advent of advance booking (with priority for club members) has much to do with all this, of course, which begs the question: why not increase capacities? Not one cricketing stage in this country holds 30,000, a figure exceeded by every major venue Down Under. As an investment, both in financial and social terms, what could possibly make more sense?

Not until 4.55 is word leaked to the press: play abandoned for the day. At 5.02 the punters are informed. The recent decision to award refunds under such circumstances (a grand total of £650,000 in this instance) would appear to have decelerated the decision-making process. One estimate has it that 1,800 bottles of champers have been quaffed by the 3,100 occupants of the hospitality boxes. As the ground-staff sweep the pools off the covers, Malcolm puts in a few laps at the Nursery End while Matthew and Warney loosen up in front of the pavilion, punting around an Aussie Rules football. The egg-and-bacon ties look on, still quaffing.

When the Victorians have finished their fun, a pack of autograph hounds pursue Warney to the gate. 'Sorry guys, not today,' he tells them. 'You've ruined it for everyone,' he adds, indicating one of their number who had shouted something wholly untoward about his sexual preferences. I cast back to some xenophobic drivel I'd spotted in this morning's *Sun*. Readers had been invited to send limericks to a section entitled 'Clobber the Cobbers', and one of the £30 prizewinning entries ran thus: 'Once the world's best spinner/His bowling is now a dog's dinner/So poor whingeing Warne/Is now just a pawn/As England become Ashes winners'.

One cannot discount the tensions of impending fatherhood, but a man can only take so much abuse, however thick his hide may be. If Warney isn't at the end of his tether, he must be pretty damn close. Still, if he needs any lessons in resilience, he could always have a chat with David Morris and Helen Steel, who, eleven years after the fact, have finally been found guilty in the so-called McLibel trial, at 313 days the longest in British history. Their crime? Producing leaflets accusing McDonald's, among other sins, of destroying rainforests, exploiting children, treating animals inhumanely and causing Third World starvation. The judge agreed with some of this, and awarded a cursory £60,000 in damages (costs were £10 million). Warney's crime? Destroying the rule of brute force, exploiting his own genius, treating the game as something to be enjoyed and causing no end of Poms to look utterly stupid. The very least the man deserves is the Nobel Prize for Chemistry.

20 June 'Kick 'em in the Cobbers'

(*Daily Star*)

Encouraged by Michael Parkinson, Keith Miller returned my call last night, consenting to an interview at Wormsley next week. If I could rent the TARDIS and witness a legend in his or her pomp, he would assuredly get the nod, just ahead of Grace Kelly, Mozart and Stanley Matthews. Much to my surprise, he expressed a keen desire to see the Poms reclaim the urn. 'It's about time. Besides, I'm not so sure I like what's happening to these Australians.'

Still, I am quite certain that Pigeon's form when play finally gets underway would have met with his unstinting approval. Noting the oppressive cloud cover and muggy atmosphere, Tubs calls correctly again and inserts, whereupon Butcher, Atherton and Stewart all fall inside eleven overs as Pigeon reaps the benefits of a fuller length and a moist pitch. Being a Friday, I view all this from the Wapping bunker. Like everybody else in the office, I revise my hitherto sceptical opinion of Heals's notions of sportsmanship when he claims a catch off Thorpe then trots over to David Shepherd like some conscience-stricken fourth-former and admits he wasn't entirely sure whether he got his gloves under the ball before it bounced. To think this was the man who was supposed to be scruple-free.

At 12.32, as Warney is about to deliver his first ball, the rains return, preventing further play. He and his colleagues settle for an afternoon of cards, newspapers and goggle-boxing. In the presence of the man himself, Colin Ingleby-Mackenzie unveils *Bradman's Walk to Glory*, a painting of The Don being ogled by a bank of female admirers behind the boundary at Melbourne in 1936–37. Composed by an Englishman, Colin Dudley, it will be displayed in Bombay before being taken back to Adelaide; bids in the region of £500,000 have already been received, with limited-edition prints fetching £9,000. All proceeds are destined for the Bradman Museum Trust and the Wheelchair Sports Foundation, fine causes both. Atherton and his sternest critic Graham Otway declare a truce and arrange a round of golf.

Return home to find a fax from John Paul Getty's personal assistant: Miller has changed his mind. Drat and double-drat, as Dick Dastardly would doubtless have put it. Stinger is feeling low. He had proposed a conciliatory beer with Tugga and Heals when the tourists reach Southampton, but Warney said this would be unwise. Tugga is reputed to have little time for our profession, hence, presumably, his insistence on writing his diaries without the aid of a ghost. At least you can't accuse him of hypocrisy.

Daily Accumulator: Poms 0 Cobbers 5

21 June 'MOD spends £73.50 buying 98p padlocks'
(Daily Telegraph)

Midsummer's Day and the square at Derby resembles a scaled-down model of the Great Lakes. Sit in front of the TV in the member's bar and cobble together a piece about the Dean Jones fracas while Pigeon craps all over the Poms. By lunch, the execution is complete: 77 all out, the hosts' lowest low at HQ since 1888; Pigeon 8 for 38, the most destructive analysis by a Cobber under Father Time's gaze. To describe the batting as meek would be putting it mildly, but blame must run a distant second to admiration. When Pigeon and his mother first left the western New South Wales bush for the bustle of Sydney, they lost their way in the outskirts of the city, just as Pigeon would mislay his bearings at Edgbaston. In both cases recovery was swift. What was that about a hoodoo?

Read Rory Bremner's column in the *Telegraph* on the train home. He recalls the time a friend visited that eccentric showman Derek 'Arkle' Randall, to be greeted at the door by a chap in jeans and pads. 'Oh, don't worry,' Arkle assured him, 'they're a new pair. I'm just breaking them in.' Ushered into the lounge, the friend beheld the sight of Mrs Randall 'wearing a smile, her everyday clothes – and a brand new pair of pads'. They can't possibly make them like that any more, can they?

'It's all over,' smirks Stinger upon his return from Lord's, depression gone. Matthew, who has survived three presentable chances to fine-leg, slip and bat-pad, the last off Croftie, not to mention a missed run-out, is unbeaten on 55 out of 131 for 2. In all, five catches had gone a-begging, including one offered by Junior to Hussain at slip off Croftie before he had opened his account. Was Edgbaston a mirage? 'You shoulda seen McGrath,' adds Stinger, rubbing it in. 'Off-cutter, leg-cutter, then – pfing!' The local press apparently spent much of the afternoon averting their eyes from the unfolding tableau and watching the Lions beat South

Africa. We'll take our consolations any way we can.

That said, it's a toss-up as to who had the worse day: the Poms or Bob Massie. Back at the scene of his one and only crime, Massie turned up with the wrong pass, missed most of the morning's dramas dashing back to his hotel for the correct one, then suffered the indignity of having to put a tie on over his T-shirt before being permitted to shake hands with his country's prime minister. Protocol: the code that separates the dignitaries from the dignified.

Daily Accumulator: Poms 0 Cobbers 10

22 June 'Commons recognises gay MP's boyfriend as "wife" '

(Sunday Telegraph)

Whoever said God isn't an Englishman? A thunderstorm half an hour before play prevents any resumption before lunch. Spend most of the day ambling around Camden Town and Primrose Hill with Stinger and the family, waiting for the clouds to start behaving seasonally. Stinger maintains contact with Malcolm Conn via his mobile phone but by mid-afternoon we decide to head home, whereupon another deluge descends. Given that the distance from Alexandra Palace to Lord's is around five miles, the chances of Matthew making his hundred today seem roughly on a par with Jonathan Aitken's prospects of finding gainful employment in Tony Blair's Cabinet.

Warney, we learn to our undisguised delight, had been spotted exhaling smoke in the Long Room yesterday. Attaboy! Stinger's day is well and truly made when we switch on the TV to find Hawthorn and Geelong locked in combat, prompting him to do his level best to convert me to the untold alleged delights of Aussie Rules. He points out that Kevin Sheedy, a promising leg-spinner in his youth and now a highly vaunted Australian Football League coach, gave a motivational talk to the cricketers prior to the Adelaide Test against West Indies earlier this year. The trouble with this game, I bemoan, is that there are too many points, too many players (eighteen-a-side) and none of the flow of rugby. The athleticism, on the other hand, has to be seen to be believed.

Much to our disbelief and dismay, play resumes at Lord's at 5.40. We contemplate driving back to cheer on Matthew but the absence of parking at the ground means stumps could be drawn by the time we make it. John Logie Baird: where would we be without you? The orders are clear: quick runs are para- mount, individual concerns go hang. Junior soon slices Caddick to third man, where Malcolm accepts the chance on his knees. Enter Warney, the pinch-hitter, but he doesn't tarry either, carving Gough high to backward point where Hussain hangs on, puffing out his cheeks and tapping his heart. Tugga comes out and Stinger boos. 'Get a duck!' he urges, jest and earnestness fighting tooth-and-nail. Lo and behold, Tugga obliges: leg-before to Gough first ball. 'You beauty,' exclaims Stinger, slapping me on the back. We hug. (I realize, of course, that this is purely his instinctive reaction to the events of the past few days, not evidence of some deep-seated dislike for the man. Nor, I assure you, is my own response predicated by any personal antipathy. I just don't care for the way he saves his best for those who least deserve it.)

Matthew remains unmoved, stroking Gough through the covers to bring up the 150, then allowing a short one to strike him on the elbow before collecting another boundary with a textbook on-drive. Bev bottom-edges a pull off Caddick to Stewart but the rains return as he trudges off. Only briefly, mind, and Matthew is swiftly into his stride when hostilities recommence, hooking then square-cutting Gough to the perimeter hoardings. *Star Trek* has been held over to accommodate the extra hour, announces Richie, 'and I'm a *Star Trek* fan'.

One light on the scoreboard as Matthew survives a close call for leg-before against Caddick, then plunders three consecutive boundaries off Gough to reach 99. Umpire Shepherd purses his lips as he consults his light meter and eyes the morose skies: now two bulbs are glinting. Cue more drizzle, a third bulb and an earnest discussion between the white jackets. The light is offered but Heals and Matthew decline. Atherton shrewdly brings on Croftie: slip, silly point, everyone else saving the single. Three dot balls go by before Matthew, using his feet, pushes to mid-off and beats the throw with ease. The fielders applaud warmly as he removes his helmet and smiles bashfully. Nor is he finished. Advancing to Croftie, he on-drives majestically: the shot of the match so far. No sign of poorly knees there. In the following over he departs, hooking Caddick to backward square. The congregation rise as one. A star is well and truly born.

Convey my felicitations to Matthew's answering service at the Westbury. I probably deserve to have my head hoisted on Traitor's Gate for admitting as much, but I'm ruddy well proud of him. I can only compare it to the days when I championed Steely Dan and waited for the rest of the British record-buying public to catch up. Even if his knees gave out tomorrow, the skill and selflessness he displayed today would assuredly not be forgotten in a hurry.

A hundred years ago today, Queen Victoria taught the band to play. To mark the occasion of the old goat's Diamond Jubilee, Sydney Harbour was illuminated, 3,000 children assembled at the SCG to sing songs of patriotic fervour, and the city's paupers were each given a square meal. 'The people of Australia', declared the South Australian Premier on a visit to England that year, 'might be depended upon as being capable of strong and faithful adherence and support in all that concerned the integrity and defence of the Empire.' Only 'might', please note.

Daily Accumulator: Poms 4 Cobbers 6

23 June 'Police hunt Ku Klux Klan recruiters in Scotland'
(*Guardian*)

Sam Chisholm, the fearsome Australian boss of BSkyB, has relinquished his position owing to ill-health. During his days at Channel 9, his desk carried a slogan that encapsulated man and myth: 'To err is human. To forgive is not my policy.' Should the Poms contrive to lose a match that has already been deprived of all but three-quarters of its timespan, the national mood may be just as malevolent.

Those who saw Pakistan brush aside the last seven home wickets for 18 here last year are not alone in their foreboding. Tubs declares first thing with a lead of 136 and the Met Office vouching for a day of interrupted fare. The clouds are gloomy, the fears darker still. Stinger pops off to snap some snaps and I find a pew in the Grandstand, scarcely a tall order with the premises three-quarters empty. The contrast in ambience from the opening day is stark. No executive boxholders, no Hooray Henrys for whom munching and imbibing take precedence over runs and wickets, just connoisseurs and devotees, immersed in every twist and turn. If only every day of a Test could be the fifth.

'Get a bat,' yells a chap in his mid-twenties to mild amusement as Butcher presents the full face of the blade to Pigeon and misses. Matthew, the only Cobber bar Heals to disdain a sweater, plays cheerleader from his station at mid-off: 'C'mon lads . . . c'mon Pidgie . . . c'mon Pistol.' Pigeon's line to the left-hander is frequently awry, allowing Butcher to shoulder arms without compunction. Pistol is more of a handful, and in his third over draws a seemingly routine edge from Butcher to first slip; Tubs fluffs it. 'Get one and we'll get two,' the skipper cajoles his crew, clapping his hands briskly.

The sun begins to beat down as Butcher reaches double figures with a half-intended shot that skews through midwicket. So vibrant during the first hour with their chants of 'Aussie, Aussie, Aussie – Oi, Oi, Oi', the Cobbers in the Mound Stand appear muted, all the more so when Butcher leans back and cracks Pistol square. Warney finally enters the fray at 12.37, the body language listless. Did Tubs's drop mark the end of hope? Surely not. Atherton bides his time before indicating his readiness, taking a leaf out of the West

131

Indians' book. He knows how much it annoys his would-be tormentor. Chances are that he will see a fair bit of Warney next season. Four counties are said to have made substantial offers, with Notts the early favourites. Matthew believes captaincy will have to be part of the package.

The batsmen strive to impose themselves. Atherton drives Warney's first ball to cover and scampers a single. Butcher thick-edges the next past slip then collects 2 with a sweep. 'Turn it up boys,' urges Tubs, but apart from the obligatory 'catch it' as Butcher is struck on the pad, twirling leather seldom beats broad willow. Kasper's inswing is more troublesome, and in the last over before lunch he clangs Atherton amidships. 'C'mon Atherton,' exhorts a prim lady in a green skirt, hair fastened in an equally fastidious bun, folding a serviette neatly around the remnants of her sandwiches. Butcher leaves the final ball of the session with a flourish. Seventy without loss, a third of the job done.

Bump into a peeved Mick Hunt during the interval. He has been stung by criticism of some odd-looking cracks in the pitch, the legacy, one assumes, of his efforts to keep it dry. 'Isn't it funny how the press go on about it being a bad pitch rather than good bowling?' he grumbles. 'Our boys gave their wickets away too easily.' Outside the Nursery End gates, the cleaners are sitting in a line against the wall. Most, if not all, are homeless. The rates? Fourteen quid a day, £15 if it's a wet day. The cheques invariably arrive a week later. One bloke says he gets them to send the payments to his sister. Stinger and I empty our pockets.

Warney and Pigeon are in harness upon the resumption, the Grandstand fuller, the mood lighter, panic subsiding. Progress is leisurely, painfully so at times, but mishaps kept at bay. Atherton, on 41, survives a vehement appeal for caught behind off Pigeon: one replay only on the giant video screen, from a distance at that – such tact! The bloke behind me consults his portable TV and assures all and sundry that it came off the forearm. Mired on 24 for 37 minutes, Butcher plays Warney to leg for a single. 'MCC stands for Male

Chauvinist Citadel,' proclaims a buxom woman in a purple T-shirt. Tubs, she argues, should have declared on Sunday: 'He couldn't lose, could he?' The man sitting beside her recalls his first Test here in '38: no advance booking, ninepence admission, ha'penny for a cuppa.

The sun peeks out as Butcher, gaining in assurance, unfurls a crisp cover drive off Pigeon, then freezes in the follow-through as if posing for David Bailey. All around him, shoulders are beginning to droop; all is quiet around the bat. Warney's grunt is almost apologetic as Butcher cuts him for four to bring up the 100, whereupon Bev comes on and contributes four legside byes. Atherton tucks Warney off his legs to reach 50 off 114 balls then stands aside as the wizard bowls a wide. Never shy of experimenting, Bev pings down a bouncer: Atherton swats it fine for four. Pistol returns and Warney retires to point, plainly disgruntled. Atherton cuts Bev's long-hop for four and I head off to meet the family at the Grace Gates, a contented bunny. Anne is interviewing somebody important at the Royal Free Hospital and we had agreed that I should look after the kids until she is done. As we drive off to Primrose Hill, Laura asks me why I seem so much happier than at breakfast. 'We're going to save the match,' I tell her. I can't quite decide whether her expression denotes bemusement or pity.

'Swing Low Sweet Chariot' booms out from the Mound Stand on my return, the score a robust 250 for 4. The openers had raised 162 before Atherton (77) retreated too far against Kasper and stepped on his own wicket. Three wickets then fell in the space of eighteen balls, Pigeon making short work of Stewart and Warney offing Butcher (87) and Hussain (0), but now liberation is in the air as Thorpe and Crawley see the vessel serenely into port with barely a mark on the hull. When the end comes ten minutes later, Warney extends a matey arm around Thorpe's shoulders then walks off with Matthew, who looks a little broody. An invader makes off with a brace of stumps. A steward runs him down and retrieves them. As Pigeon receives his undisputed award as Man of the Match, Warney, dragging heavily on a cigarette, is a picture of ruefulness.

Thus ends one of the more noteworthy sequences in Test history: after eighteen conclusive results, the Cobbers have remembered how to draw. Tubs, who admits he had considered declaring on Sunday afternoon, acknowledges that his gaffe at slip 'didn't help too much' but insists that the ball swung away in mid-flight. 'I was lucky to get a finger to it. It might have made a difference but we only created four or five chances, which suggests the wicket played pretty well.' Had Mick Hunt been in the vicinity, he might well have been prompted to kiss his feet. Captain Sensible pronounced himself 'very encouraged' by the way his side had responded to adversity, noting that Matthew 'hit the ball as crisply as I've seen in a Test for a long time'.

As Atherton takes his turn to address the press he is handed a note, presumably of the 'well done, old boy' variety. He blushes as he reads it, then grins. Contrary to widespread supposition, he had not been apprehensive at the start of play. 'I can't ever remember treading on my wicket,' he says of his dismissal, cheeks reddening from the effects of whatever potion is in his plastic tumbler. 'It doesn't surprise me. I've never made a Test hundred here.' Today, he stresses, 'has done no harm to our confidence'.

Spotting Butcher on the stairs after the conference adjourns, I go over and shake his hand. Relief, naturally, is writ large. He had found it difficult to motivate himself in the first innings ('the adrenalin was pumping so hard on Thursday I was exhausted by the evening, even though I hadn't done anything'). Father Alan, a one-cap wonder in 1979, had been in attendance on Friday, but he wasn't sure about today. 'That was the hardest net I've ever had. I got a bit of chat from the fielders as the innings wore on, but I was concentrating too hard really to notice.' A phone call before play from Dave Gilbert, the astute Surrey coach, had helped appreciably. 'He told me he had a day off and fancied sitting in front of his TV and watching me bat all day. It was a fantastic gesture.'

Graveney insists he would have been retained regardless. Fair trials, it would seem, are now in vogue.

The final bell finds the Poms on the upswing, but a vexing thought occurs. The Three Ws – as Stevie Wonder once sang with Richard Nixon in mind – haven't done nothing. Warney's highest score, moreover, exceeds that of either Tugga or Junior. Can't last, can it? Can it?

Daily Accumulator: Poms 8 Cobbers 2
Match total: Poms 12 Cobbers 23

MATTHEW ELLIOTT

Of course I was relieved at making my maiden Test hundred. To do so at Lord's obviously lent the achievement added lustre. But the glow was diminished by the result. Isn't that the way it should be in a team game? Had we had three clear days we would have won. The disappointment was especially acute for guys like Tubs and Heals and Tugga: the weather ruined what could well be their last Lord's Test.

There were variations in bounce but I didn't think it was a bad wicket. Pigeon bowled superbly. His line was so relentless the batsmen must have been wondering how on earth they were ever going to score. Pistol gave him great support, and might easily have had five wickets himself. On the last day there was always a sniff of victory if we could get an early wicket but I can't attach any blame to Tubs for dropping Butcher. The ball really did swing a great deal once it left the edge; it may even have come to him slower than he'd envisaged.

It was a strange way to make a century. With all those interruptions I felt as if I'd opened the innings seven or eight times. On the first two days I played cards for hours on end – 500, which is quite similar to bridge – but when it was our turn to bat we were mostly toing and froing between the showers; there was no opportunity to take off your pads and relax. 'Come on,' I'd keep saying to myself, 'come on,' just trying to stay tuned. It wasn't easy. I was pretty lucky with those catches going down on the Saturday. At that stage I was playing all right, no more. I was hooking really badly, not getting over the ball. I was using a heavier bat than usual and it was coming down a bit slowly. Then I remembered that Venkat had also been umpiring when I made that 85 in Johannesburg, which I took as an omen.

The aim when we finally resumed on Sunday was to get 100 runs in 20 overs. There wasn't even time for a warm-up. I was about to have a shower when we heard that play would start. When we lost a wicket quickly I decided it wouldn't make sense to go at it right from the off, just try and bat for five, maybe ten overs and then give it a shot. But we kept losing wickets, and when Warney came in I told him I wasn't sure whether it was the right approach. They had two men back for the hook throughout the innings so I didn't want to chance anything, but then I had a good over against Gough, cutting one four, top-edging another, which took me to 95 – one good shot away. 'If he bowls a bouncer,' I told myself, 'I'm just going to try and get it up and over for six.' But he pitched it up; I was moving on to the back foot and hit him down the ground for four. Three in a row. After that, everything seemed to fall into place. Just about everything I tried came off.

When Croftie came on with one run needed I thought, 'Oh no, that's all I need,' but I decided to be positive. The abiding feeling was relief. I thought back to the collision with Junior in Sydney, retiring hurt for 78, the knee operation, those eight idle weeks, the depression, then mishooking in Johannesburg on 85: all those bad memories. I wanted to get rid of all those feelings. After being given those lives, I'm not sure how easy I would have found it to forgive myself if I hadn't made it, but the needs of the side came first, which meant I couldn't just plod along, playing it safe. When I got there, I looked up and saw Megan in the stands, cheering me on. She says she can tell when I'm going to do well. If I look comfortable, as if I'm happy going about my work, as if I ought to be there. That's the way she said I looked.

For me, batting is all about the search for perfection. No chances, no playing and missing. I got close when I made 187 against New South Wales last season, but not quite. Tugga says he's done it a couple of times, and I saw Deano make 320 in a Shield game, so it is possible. Getting that hundred was a big step, but I know I still haven't done myself justice at this level.

ROBERT CROFT

The atmosphere was totally different to Edgbaston. Quieter, not as patriotic, less inspiring. At Edgbaston the Aussies probably felt as if they were playing away from home, but it wasn't like that here. I was amazed when I heard that Tannoy announcement about cheering both sides equally. What sense does that make? It's a lovely idea, and it probably happens more at Lord's than anywhere else, but that's not what a team needs. Playing the national anthem is a good idea. I can't think of another team sport where it isn't played. You're playing for your country, representing Britain. Why shouldn't we have it? Mind you, the Welsh anthem would be even nicer.

Keeping occupied during all the delays may have been easier for me than some of the others. Some of the guys played cards but my family were there, and a few other people from Wales, so I spent quite a lot of time going round the ground, catching up with people. Staring at those four walls can get to you after a while. I watched the Lions on the Saturday morning: they kicked off as I went out and by the time I got back they were catching it. I messed around in the dressing room: playing football, indoor cricket with a tennis ball, taking the mickey out of people. I was calling Ealham 'Fat Man' so he christened me 'Mr Blobby'. The next thing I knew he had put a sheet over a chair on the balcony complete with cap, glasses and a ball under the shirt. Richie Benaud spotted it while he was commentating and said: 'They tell me that's Croftie, but to me, I think not.' I'm glad he can tell the difference.

I don't think we had any difficulty staying focused through the interruptions and delays. Having played so much three-day cricket during the early part of my career, and consistently seen results manufactured in that space of time, I always felt there might be one here, so we had to be on our guard. That said, getting out for 77 is unacceptable. Batting first on a wicket that looked very cracked didn't help, of course, and the bounce was variable, but McGrath exploited the conditions amazingly well. Unlike our seamers, who tend to skid the ball through, he hits the deck hard. He also bowls extremely straight.

Beating Peter May's record definitely meant a lot to Athers. He's a very proud man, the sort of man who doesn't show his hand that readily, but you could tell he was pleased. What a pity the weather put such a damper on it. Matthew Engel made a comment in the *Guardian* about the MCC members chuntering away when Athers made his way back to the pavilion at the end of his innings, suggesting that this may be an indication that he has yet to win over the public. If that really is the case, then the British public need to grow up. He's been tremendous for British cricket. I think he knows how I think now, so he lets me set my own field. He knows I'm an attacking bowler, knows I like people up in front of the bat, not necessarily to take wickets but to let them know they're in for a battle. And I reckon he likes that approach. We've been to a few river-banks together. He doesn't catch much, mind. To be honest, he's absolutely hopeless.

I don't think they played that much better than us. Had we caught our catches they might have been 100 for 5 on the Saturday. I don't think those errors were indicative of a lack of concentration. It was quite murky out there, so it was difficult picking the ball up against the stands. Goughie and Caddick bowled well again, and I was happy with my

138

performance with the ball. Matthew excepted, we kept their batsmen out of nick, getting them out when they were chasing quick runs. Matthew played very well. We gave him three knocks but he grasped his chances. I thought I'd got him at silly point: that's twice he's got the breaks against me. Perhaps we'll have a chat at some point.

We showed true British spirit in that second innings and we finished holding the upper hand. The heavens were on our side. And we've left Lord's one up, for the first time this century.

24 June 'Boss sorry for being beastly'

(*Daily Telegraph*)

Elton John was wrong. Sorry, it would appear, is not the hardest word after all. In the wake of Bill Clinton's apology for slavery and Tony Blair's acknowledgement of the British government's culpability for the Irish potato famine, Peter Birse, the chairman of Birse Construction, has expressed profound regrets to his staff for his unreasonable demands and general beastliness. All we need now is for Pol Pot to go cap in hand to the Cambodians and Frau Thatcher to own up to depriving this country's workers of their theoretically inalienable rights and the world will have been well and truly turned on its head.

Arrive at Sophia Gardens for Glamorgan's NatWest tie against Bedfordshire to discover that Croftie, due to receive his award as Swansea's Sportsman of the Year on Thursday, has been invited to join the Bardic Circle at August's Royal Eisteddfod, in recognition of services to his homeland. Will he be invested as Rob the Dyddiadur (Rob the Spinner)? Rob of Hendy seems likelier. This is an honour confined to Welsh speakers, and he will be only the second greenswardsman, after that splendidly cussed opener Alan Jones, to be so regaled. To describe him as chuffed would be something of an understatement. 'As far as I see it, it's for putting Wales on the map. It's a great honour to be accepted by your own people. It'll be a rushed job, mind. We're playing at Colwyn Bay that day, so they're sending a helicopter to pick me up at the ground at eight in the morning and have promised to drop me back in time for warm-ups. Thankfully, I won't have to sing.'

For the life of him, Matthew, who is enjoying a day off, cannot fathom how the Poms can be expected to go straight from a Test to an important county match, however modest the opposition. Croftie readily admits it's easier for a spinner, and takes 1 for 14 off his alotted 12 overs to underscore the point. After play concludes, nevertheless, he plans to head for the riverbank with a friend and fish well into the wee small hours. At the end of the Bedfordshire innings, scores of small boys swarm on to the middle, patting fielders on the back and politely demanding signatures. The elders tut, but the players actively encourage such enthusiasm. They relish the attention. These are heady days indeed for cricket in the Principality. In Croftie's absence Glamorgan had rebounded from the debacle against Middlesex by routing Lancashire for 51 in 14 overs, moving up to joint third in the championship. Steve James heads the national batting averages, Waqar Younis is beginning to justify his handsome salary, confidence is boundless. With devolution in the offing and the nation's footballers and rugger buggers enduring a protracted lean patch, the renaissance could hardly be more timely. 'I tell you what,' says Eddie Bevan, 'I'd prefer us to win the championship than England to win the Ashes.'

Does Croftie share those sentiments? Even if he did, he couldn't possibly admit it publicly, but even a denial can be instructive. 'No,' he replies, firmly, unhesitatingly, calmly. 'I can see why you might believe that, but no.' Had he treated the question with scorn or outrage my suspicions might have been alerted. Those references to 'Britain' and 'British', nonetheless, seem more than a little pointed. He has seen Union Jacks fluttering in stands from Bulawayo to Birmingham: how could he not believe the name of the team

140

to be something of a misnomer? He would not have been alone.

25 June 'Man survives 12,000 ft fall'

(Guardian)

Tugga is sitting reading *The Times* in the foyer of the Oxford Moat House hotel, surrounded by besuited businessmen and looking for all the world like an undercover cop. Heals and Junior are watching rugby in the pool room. Mrs Heals and Mrs Slats stumble towards reception with heaving shopping bags. Matthew and Megan have gone to town for some sightseeing. The first day of the Cobbers' match against the Combined Universities has been called off: of their last 72 scheduled hours of play, the tourists have seen action for barely 30; Gilly has had 14 minutes' batting in a month, Punter two innings in 40 days. The wettest June since records began may be doing wonders for home hopes, but embarrassment is beginning to border on outright guilt.

26 June 'Bidding frenzy over Princess's cast-off dresses'
(Daily Telegraph)

Hamish Mansbridge had ordered thirty-two rounds of sandwiches and enough bottles of Mâcon to get him and his chums through the night. Mr Clapham's party contented themselves with turkey and cranberry pie plus twenty-four rounds of sandwiches. Fully twenty years after Packer had set the ball rolling Down Under, Surrey had shelled out £100,000 to stage English cricket's inaugural competitive nocturnal contest (Surrey Lions *v* Nottinghamshire Outlaws, if you will), but the elements, inevitably, nip their hubris in the bud, preventing so much as a ball being bowled. The Luddites snigger.

Martin Crowe emerges from the commentary box. The former New Zealand captain is in town to promote his new brainchild, Cricket Max, whose relationship to Test cricket is

141

roughly akin to that between Boyzone and Bach. 'The aim is to promote the one-day game rather than provide a means of easing kids into Test cricket,' he elucidates. 'According to a recent poll back home, 60 per cent of respondents prefer the one-dayers, while Tests run neck-and-neck with Cricket Max.' Be afraid. Be very afraid.

30 June 'Doctors to decide if mercy killing should be legalised'

(Daily Telegraph)

A solemn day for some, for others a belated confirmation of Britain's true place in the modern world. At midnight, Hong Kong will be handed over to China, ringing the curtain down on the Empire. John Casey, a Fellow of Gonville and Caius College, Cambridge, declares it to be 'a noble thing, sustained by generations of noble men'. What, like those Scottish businessmen who instigated the acquisition of Hong Kong solely in order to secure trade advantages over the Chinese, particularly in the opium market?

Ominous rumblings from Southampton, where centuries from Tubs and Junior, augmented by a hatful of wickets for Warney and a fit-again Dizzy, help the Cobbers thrash Hampshire by an innings. The Met Office does its patriotic best to deflate them by forecasting another fortnight of the soggy stuff.

Nothing, though, can dampen my spirits. While driving to visit an old friend near Kilburn, I espy a bunch of assorted youths – black and white, boys and girls – playing cricket at the junction of Summerfield Avenue and Brondesbury Road, the wicket a dustbin. The lump in my throat bears a passing resemblance to Gibraltar.

ACT 3

2 July 'TV dating show accused of being "pimping service"'
(*Daily Telegraph*)

'Sorry, that's all I could get.' Junior apologizes to his mother for not being able to sneak any more sandwiches out of the Old Trafford dressing room. Slight of frame and tightly curled of hair, Bev Waugh reminds me of Carla, the formidable cocktail waitress from that classic American sitcom, *Cheers*; as the Australian Masters squash champion for her age group, she is by no means less indomitable. As the woman responsible for the most illustrious twins in the annals of athletic endeavour tucks into her lunch outside the pavilion, she chews the cud with Warney and his father, Keith, a slim, trim financial consultant whose pride in his offspring knows few bounds. Might the presence of their parents be just the inspiration the Cobbers' leading lights need?

With practice impossible on the puddled outfield, the players would have expected to transfer to the indoor nets. Unfortunately, these have been converted to hospitality suites. Priorities, priorities. Not that this stops Warney from having a productive session with Jenner, nor Slats from doing press-ups on his own near the square while the groundsman, Peter Marron, whirrs by on his mower. A bevy of autograph hunters encircle the out-of-favour opener as he wends his way back to the dressing room on the ground where he kick-started his international career in such vivid fashion four years ago. He seems grateful for the attention.

Warney returns from an inspection of the middle. 'What's it like?' asks Keith. Cue puffed cheeks and bulging eyes: 'Green!' Interviewed in the *Manchester Evening News*, Crawley pleads for his home crowd to give Warney a break: 'We want all the support we can get but I wouldn't like it to go too far. Warne was booed in the one-dayers and at Edgbaston and there is no need for that. He is a great player and should be respected for it.'

Tufnell completes an unenviable hat-trick, sent back to Middlesex for the third match in succession, which would appear to affirm Warney's pitch prognosis. In 1993 Warney and Peter Such took eight wickets apiece here but the spinners can hardly expect anything like the same assistance. While Dizzy has already been informed that he will return in place of the unlucky Kasper, Malcolm's place is under threat from Dean Headley, who would almost certainly have played earlier but for injury. The day's two casualties are The Hacienda, Manchester's most renowned music venue, which closed its doors last night when the owners went into liquidation, and Gilly, who tore medial ligaments in his left leg when a colleague fell over him during training. Further involvement in the tour seems highly unlikely, but he'll be back. There are some, indeed, who believe he could well captain his country before the millennium is out, Matthew, a close companion, among them.

As the Poms run through their training routines, Croftie and Stewart stage an impromptu rerun of last weekend's shameful Tyson–Holyfield farce: Stewart, playing Tyson, pretends to sink his molars into Croftie's right ear, whereupon the latter leaps about like a dervish. While the opposition conduct their preparations with a grim intensity, the mood here verges on the carefree. The sign of a unified collective? No bout a doubt it. Nor can the feelgood factor be discounted, fuelled as it is by the presence of two Brits in the Wimbledon quarter-finals for the first time since 1961 (or rather, one true Brit, Henman, and one converted Canadian,

Greg Rusedski). Mind you, when Atherton returns from a golf match in aid of his benefit fund, he remarks that the ruckers and cross-court volleyers were stealing his team's thunder. It may or may not comfort him to know that no team has lost at Old Trafford this century and won the Ashes.

MATTHEW ELLIOTT

You can almost taste the atmosphere in the dressing room. It's virtually at fever pitch. Everyone is starting to gear up, to lift themselves that extra notch. You can see Warney and the Waughs starting to prickle. Even Junior. We were watching TV the other day and they were going on and on: 'one-nil, one-nil'. He really got stuck in. 'What about the last ten years?' he yelled. You can see the guys trying to generate that bit of fire. Everywhere we go, people are digging at us: 'one-nil, one-nil'. Everywhere. That can only help. An Aussie Rules coach once said that to win at professional sport consistently you had to be carnivorous. I agree. If you're not strong, you get walked over. We have to be carnivorous.

Warney's wife gave birth last week and he's been pretty quiet since. It's bound to be hard on him not being at home, not being able to hold Brooke. Talking on the phone can never be a substitute. I know how difficult I would find it if Megs gave birth when I wasn't there, and that may happen because she's due during the Melbourne Test, but at least I'll be within reach. Judging by some of the insulting behaviour towards him, people must forget what Warney's going through. It was the same in South Africa, and I don't believe he's as thick-skinned as the public imagine. Deep down, it probably gets to him a lot of the time, no matter what he says. He does have the occasional blow-up, after all, but who can blame him? He's such a genuine guy, so down-to-earth. He's been an enormous help to me down the years. He gets a lot of satisfaction from giving players advice and then seeing them progress. He loves talking about the game.

At Hampshire he was reading this book full of statistics and firing questions at me. How many people had taken a hundred wickets in Ashes Tests, who'd scored this century or that. As much as he sometimes makes out that he doesn't enjoy playing, I don't know what else he could do.

ROBERT CROFT

I don't really regard us as being one up in the series. To me, if you're in this position, you have to make yourself imagine that the series is level, so you're always thinking, 'we must win one more game'. Sometimes when you're one-up you can relax a bit. The key is to regard each game as a single entity. What happened at Lord's might be just what we needed. It may turn out to be a valuable kick up the backside. We expected them to come back at us, and now they have, but we got away with it.

Up to now Warne and the Waughs have not been able to get going. We intend to keep it that way. Even though his figures might belie it, and the lads played him well, Warne bowled any number of wicket-taking balls on that Monday at Lord's. He's a world-class bowler: you don't become a poor one overnight. I don't think he's on the down-slope at all. He's still a threat.

3 July 'Doctors back cannabis treatment for the seriously ill'
(*The Times*)

'A rainy Manchester day seems greyer than any other,' Richie once opined. 'The roofs seen from the hotel windows look wetter, the houses more sombre.' Even when the heavens are merely hinting that they might be about to deposit their load, it still feels devoid of colour. Stinger reckons Old Trafford (the ground) is rather grotty, which it is, yet there is something endearingly innocent about the place. A tram ferries you to the gates, there are no electronic scoreboards and any number of stands remain unnamed. A Dixieland band tootles away as Tubs calls correctly yet again. Rosencrantz and Guildenstern would probably accuse him of witchcraft.

All the signs point to an insertion: grassy pitch, melancholy clouds, clammy atmosphere, showers afoot. Yet Tubs opts to bat. Peter Marron, whose preparations have been hampered by the weather, feels the surface will iron out, thus aiding Warney as the match wears on (the bare, mottled patches around either crease will surely have him licking his fingers with relish). Maybe that was what persuaded Tubs. Or maybe he's been mugging up on his trivia. No side has inserted the opposition in a Test here and won.

Having displaced Malcolm as anticipated, Headley is presented with his cap by Atherton before the off – a worthy innovation – thus making his clan the first to sire three generations of Test cricketers. When we spoke last season, he availed me of his stock answer to those who query his capacity to cope with living in the shadow of his forebears, notably Grandad George, the 'Black Bradman': 'I just say I'm a darn sight better bowler than either of them.' With the government on the verge of curbing the powers of hereditary peerage, the irony is striking: Headley is one of four members of the home XI whose fathers played first-class cricket (Butcher, Stewart and Ealham being the others). So much for nature v nurture.

Headley, whose jerky, elbow-led action contrives to make him look appreciably shorter than his 6 feet 5 inches, is known to fancy his chances against the left-handers and soon demonstrates why. Squared up by the last ball of his third over, Tubs can only fend as it cuts across him and Thorpe completes the hanging at first slip, stooping low to his right. The conditions are well-nigh perfect for the seamers: ample bounce at the Warwick Road End, lateral movement at the Radcliffe Road. Matthew is leaving the ball well but Headley beats him with unnerving regularity. Blewie collects the first authentic boundary with a cover drive off Gough then aims something inordinately lavish outside off in the Yorkshireman's next over whereupon the ball clips the leg bail via an inside edge. Troubled endlessly by Headley, Junior takes twelve balls to break his duck then snicks an Ealham leg-cutter to a horizontal Stewart. Croftie comes on just before lunch and Matthew immediately clips him for four through midwicket. Tugga flips Headley to the square-leg boundary to end a session that the Poms may suspect could have gone even better than it did.

Rain delays the resumption by twenty minutes and Matthew soon falls prey to a decision long on dubiousness, adjudged caught behind off a Headley lifter that brushes his left arm. He rubs it as he departs but doesn't linger. Six overs later, Bev's uncertainty against the short ball surfaces once more as Headley squares him up; going down at first, Stewart rebounds to intercept the edge: 113 for 5. A sea of brightly coloured umbrellas signifies another unscheduled intermission – this time of forty minutes, ensuring the extra hour – by which time Tugga, unusually capricious outside off amid the early going, has recovered his poise to reach 42. After Caddick had polished him off first ball at Lord's he declared his intention to remedy the situation. Defending meticulously, cutting with withering force, he appears to be in the mood to do precisely that.

Heals hangs around without ever looking comfortable before gloving Caddick down the leg side: the appeal is strangled but valid. Relatively quiescent to this juncture, the crowd perk up as Warney enters, booing lustily. Their wishes are quickly rewarded when Venkat errs again, upholding Ealham's appeal for a catch at the wicket. The *FT*'s deadlines oblige me to file rather earlier than I would have liked, but when bad light brings another hiatus at 173 for 7 the prospects of further play seem remote.

Stinger and I mosey on down to the E2 Stand, the source of most of the jeers when Warney came out. We get chatting to a lass from New South Wales who has painted one side of her head yellow and the other green. Her name is Rachel and she is spending the summer working at a hotel in

Morecambe Bay. 'I wouldn't normally do this at home,' she assures us, 'but there's so little support for our boys here.' We are joined by Glen, a breezy sort from Melbourne who has daubed his face with the Southern Cross. He is spending his last day in the country before popping off to Pamplona for the running of the bulls. Like Rachel, he is dismayed at what he perceives as a lack of atmosphere. 'In Melbourne a Test match is a social function. We have a laugh and a sing. Here it's just about cricket.' Billy, who normally works alongside Glen at Channel 9, says he enjoys the social inter-action and the mutual baiting. 'You're not singing any-more,' taunt a few Barmy Army types, spurring Glen to lead a clutch of compatriots through a strident riposte of 'Aussie, Aussie, Aussie – Oi, Oi, Oi', followed by a stirring rendition of 'Advance Australia Fair'. The Poms respond with 'God Save The Queen'. The banter seems amiable enough. Rachel is not so sure: 'When they booed Warne, I said, "I don't like him either but I wouldn't boo one of your blokes." '

Five bulbs gleam on the scoreboard as a folically chal-lenged streaker, the first of the day, is engulfed by half-a-dozen stewards. Judging by the size of their necks and the brusqueness of their tackles, the rumours about them having been requisitioned from a local rugby club are prob-ably spot on. As the offender is escorted away with inordi-nate roughness, he raises a fist in triumph. 'He'll get a £1,000 fine for that,' reveals Billy. 'We sussed that out. He probably had a whip-round first.' Ten minutes later, a pair of invaders try their luck without success. One is felled by a high tackle that comes perilously close to beheading him. Granted, Matthew's experience at Edgbaston has made me see such transgressions in a rather more sinister light, but these particular trespassers surely warrant more gracious treat-ment. Who, pray, are they threatening?

The video screen serves up flashes of Henman in action but the news for those who care about such things is grave: the housewives' choice has lost his quarter-final in straight sets. Back up in the press box, the visiting journos rub it in.

'Did Woodbridge get through?' asks Jim Tucker. 'Yeah,' smirks Ian Jessup. 'Four sets.' And with that, to general amazement, play gets underway again. Needing one catch to match the Ashes innings record of six shared by Russell and Rod Marsh, the hitherto flawless Stewart fluffs a sitter as Pistol prods at Headley. The significance of this becomes increasingly apparent. Tugga ploughs on with impenitent intent, shot selection beyond reproach, placement unerring, respecting the good balls, contemptuous of the bad. Utterly free of aesthetic appeal, but then that's little brother's job. Twice he and Pistol are offered the light; twice they decline. With four lights penetrating the murk, Atherton recalls Croftie, more out of necessity than desire. The first ball of his second over is short and wide: rocking back, Tugga lashes it in front of square for four and punches the air in celebration of his fourth century against the Poms; it feels more like the fortieth. The emoting stops there. Extraordinary to relate, all of those tons have been made in this country: what has he got against us? Stinger's instinctive reaction to that golden duck at Lord's is but a hazy memory as he and I stare at each other with a blend of awe and stupefaction. What is this guy on? Four Shredded Wheats a morning? Robert Mitchum, the tough guy's tough guy, died yesterday; his spirit endures.

A bagpiper drones a plaintive 'Auld Lang Syne' as the crowd shuffles away, smiles erased. In the space of 14 overs and 51 runs, superiority has been reduced to parity. A thought for Pistol, a straight man in every sense. Ron Reiffel, once an Aussie Rules notable, certainly ensured his son grew up in the right environment. The run of *Wisdens* in Ron's Melbourne study extends back to 1879; among the most cherished items is C B Fry's *The Book of Cricket*, published in 1899, a gift from the treasurer of East Lancashire CC, where Pistol did stout service from 1989 to 1991. Accompanied by his own peacock-proud father, another Ron, Headley informs a BBC interviewer that the erstwhile Worcestershire and West Indies opener never coached him, just as George had never coached Ron: 'Dad doesn't believe in coaching; he believes in guidance.' When Dean took his first wicket, Dad was stuck in a traffic jam.

Tugga receives the media in the library. To his left is the Duncan Mutch Collection, an elegant bookcase boasting assorted gems such as *W G Grace – Cricketer*. What will he call his autobiography: *Steve Waugh – Australian*? He is certainly not about to short-change himself now. How did he rate his innings? 'Up there with the 200 I scored in Jamaica,' he declaimed matter-of-factly, referring to the seemingly incomparable innings that terminated notions of Caribbean invincibility two years ago. 'The wicket was a lot tougher. Hopefully, the stand between me and Reiffel could be the difference between winning and losing. We won the day.' What did he make of the pitch? 'Pretty good pace, a bit hard underneath. It would have been a good pitch given more time to prepare it. As it is, it's a bit underdone. Moist, balls are taking divots out. I would think there'll be turn.' Warney will sleep soundly tonight.

Over in the Cornhill tent I ask the third umpire, John Hampshire, about the principles underpinning the benefit of doubt. His eyes twinkle: 'There's *never* any doubt.'

Daily Accumulator: Poms 5 Cobbers 5

4 July 'Sex at 11, Mum at 12'

(*Sun*)

A pigeon lies slumped at the entrance to our hotel, one wing short of the full complement. A metaphor for the tour? Twenty-four hours ago perhaps, but not now. No way, José.

The wind is up, the restart deceptive. Gough and Headley require barely half an hour to polish off the last three wickets, the former's summary ejection of Tugga's middle pole via a compliant inside edge sending E2 Stand into raptures. As Atherton gloves a hook off Pigeon in the ninth over of the reply, a grim cloud drifts over from behind the MacLaren Stand and that sinking sensation descends.

151

Mild boos as Warney is summoned for the fourteenth over. For one surreal moment, as the back of his shirt bulges in the semi-gale, we could be watching Robert Redford playing the Hunchback of Notre Dame. His first offering spins sharply and scurries low but Butcher, cool and watchful, has time to turn it off his pads for a single. 'He's back,' trumpets Alasdair Ross, Warney's loyal ghost for his *Sunday Mirror* column. Stewart thumps the next straight for four to hearty acclaim. 'He'll never bowl another dot ball,' pronounces the *Sunday Telegraph*'s Scyld Berry, deadpan as ever. During lunch, Chappelli observes that, on a pitch as sluggish as this, patience will be Warney's greatest virtue; at Lord's, Jenner said he thought he'd lost it. Indeed, little in his initial spell beats the bat, and the Surrey twosome middle most everything else, but then comes '93 Revisited. Essaying a flick behind square to one pitching a good foot outside leg stump, Stewart can only get an outside edge as the ball breaks across him. You'd swear it was giggling. So acute is the deviation, Tubs has to fling himself to his right to take the catch. Stewart's successors must be swallowing hard.

Butcher drills a rare full-toss through the covers, then reaches his 50 off Bev. The bat rises shyly, helmet doffed without conviction. Two balls later he goes to glide a rapid full-pitcher to fine-leg and misses. The back leg is airborne for a tenth of an instant, but that's ample for Heals, who whips off the bails with a stealth worthy of Knott to notch a century of Ashes victims (only the Kentish imp and Marsh now stand ahead of him). Butcher waits for the replay, less in hope than confusion, but there is no reprieve. Bev's lips come desperately close to parting. Thorpe, the one Pom down the years consistently to have given as good as he gets against Warney, rolls his wrists and sweeps smoothly but Victoria's wiliest has his measure this time. The ball dips, nudges the pads and arcs to slip. Tea is served at 110 for 4 off 48 overs. On this evidence, the meek have no earthly hope of inheriting anything.

Having received the benefit of no doubt whatsoever when

Warney bellows for leg-before, Crawley misses a squatter in his next over and experiences the obverse side of the coin when Venkat raises his right index finger as if directing traffic. 'Bollocks,' fumes Scyld Berry, doubling his career total of oaths. 'Will we ever regain the Ashes in our lifetime?'

The Mexican Wave is suitably half-hearted as Croftie gets off the mark with a Chinese cut off Pigeon. I've never seen him look so jumpy. In Pigeon's next over he guides a four throug the cordon then finds his ears buzzing as the following missile cracks him on the head. Thank heavens for little girls and helmets. Croftie staggers back but quickly unscrambles his senses to scamper a single as the ball balloons over Heals. In Pigeon's next over he spoons gingerly to extra cover where Tugga swoops full-length to put him out of his misery. Over in E2 Stand half a dozen cardboard Merv Hugheses do a jig.

So subservient is the mood, Gough resists his customary urge to send every ball into a neighbouring galaxy. Warney's top-spinner brings a close call for leg-before; two balls later, an identical shout brings an affirmative response. Warney's spell has yielded 5 for 19, his first nap hand for 16 Tests and more than 18 months. Better yet, his 248th five-day scalp has drawn him level with Richie. 'This Test is over,' announces Stinger.

'I wouldn't know the last time I took a five-fer,' Warney advises the fourth estate; you almost believe him. What about the booing? 'The home crowd should always support the home team. They all pay money to get in – they can do what they like.' Do you have aspirations to lead your country? Pause to inflate cheeks. 'Don't know about that. I'm happy captaining Victoria. Steve Waugh and Ian Healy and Mark Taylor are the senior players.' Then the warning: 'You'll be seeing the best of us from now on.' The throng disperses. Heads are shaken, pessimism rife. Warney beckons over Alasdair Ross. 'Who's this Mike Walters?' he demands to know, clearly furious. Walters, one of Shameful Street's most industrious and talented reporters, had interviewed him for the *Mirror* a couple of days ago, the focus *that* ball to Gatting. It isn't quite clear what he finds offensive: the 'exclusive' tagline or the headline – 'One Giant Fluke'. As Stinger and I walk through the car park on our way out, one crewcut teenager is tossing leg-breaks to another. At their age, the words 'fame' and 'fortune' never occupy the same sentence as 'get', 'on', 'my' or 'tits'.

Daily Accumulator: Poms 2 Cobbers 8

5 July 'Shane on the lot of you'

(Sun)

Seldom one to miss a trick, Tubs calls on Warney to recommence proceedings. Caddick turns the fourth offering to leg; darting out of the rough, the ball bounces off the back of his bat and spirals towards silly point for Junior to cling on at the third time of asking. Warney thus eclipses Richie as the most proficient wrist-spinner in Test history and moves to third in the Twirlers' Hall of Fame behind Bishen Bedi (266) and Lance Gibbs (309). For the record, the King of St Kilda's jewels have come at a rate of one every 63 balls; Richie struck once every 77, Bedi 80, Gibbs 88. Three overs later, Pigeon flattens Headley's off stump with an inswinging yorker. The Cobbers part to let their joker through the gate first. At first he breaks into a jog, then turns back, clapping his sunhat, glancing at Heals, his trustiest accomplice. Wristman and Bobbin, anyone?

The Poms rebound immediately. Headley's second ball, the eighth of the Cobbers' second dig, lifts and nips Taylor's outside edge for Butcher to grasp a chest-high catch at second slip. Matthew seems tentative. On as early as the ninth over, Croftie lures Blewie, who advances to drive and miscues. Hussain, at first slip, propels himself forward, stretches fingertips and emerges with ball, roaring. Croftie joins in, but did it carry? The doubt is immense. Blewie, who should by rights have incurred the benefit, stands his ground, gazing up at the video screen, which cannot, of course, be used in evidence. Venkat consults George Sharp, his comrade at square-leg. Up in the commentary box, the jury is split: Lewis and Chappelli say aye, Gower and Boycott nay. At length, Blewie is sent on his way. As he walks back, the cameras capture his fury. With himself? With the umpires? With Hussain? Warney rushes on to the dressing-room balcony, fag in hand, plainly agitated. The press are also on their feet. 'Contrary,' I declaim, referring to the refusal to use technology and thinking about John Hampshire's comment on Thursday evening. 'Any more of those you can come up with I'll take,' grins Mike Brearley, looking for all the world like a Bordeaux viticulturist in his silvery mane and red-and-white neckerchief. I oblige with two: 'Stubborn. Luddites.' Only the slo-mo camera from the Stretford End manages to capture the moment in close-up, and this suggests the ball did bounce first. I don't believe Hussain would knowingly cheat, but the point lies elsewhere. Why, in these days of ever-soaring stakes, must we rely on the word of those with the most to gain and lose? Or deprive the officials of every aid possible, for *all* eventualities? In the interests of keeping ex-players employed?

The Cobbers are little more than 100 to the good when Matthew is caught at second slip off Headley but Junior is soon pulling out shots from another solar system and the advantage at lunch is 151. He then picks up from where he left off, pulling Caddick imperiously to reach his first half-hundred of the rubber with a six then coming within inches of another as he sallies forth to Croftie. Alas and alack, he regales us for another ten minutes before allowing Ealham to bowl him through the gate. The sense of deprivation is acute. As the replay zooms in towards the exultant bowler, Tugga's face, pale and taciturn as ever, is a picture of ambiguity: part professional empathy, part incredulity that somebody from the same womb could have committed such heresy. Making light of the bruised and swollen webbing between his right thumb and forefinger, a legacy of the first day's constant jarring, he upholds the family's honour for the remains of the day. By then the lead is 335 and he requires a further 18 to become the first man to register a century in each innings of an Ashes debate since Arthur Morris and Denis Compton at Adelaide fifty years ago. How fitting that he and a cock-a-hoop Warney should be conjoined for the final hour. The effect is numbing. It feels so inevitable, so preordained.

Crommo makes a rare appearance at the press conference. For diplomatic reasons, one assumes. Warney is alleged to have yelled 'fucking cheats' after Blewie's dismissal; as Heals took guard, his ha'apworth is said to have included a sizeable flea in the ear for Stewart. 'The captain and coach,' explains the manager, 'have excused the players their media responsibilities.' For his own part, Crommo has 'no comment to make at all in relation to umpiring decisions' but speaks his piece anyway, albeit with a lawyer's penchant for superfluous adjectives. 'My personal view is that if a third umpire can be used to make correct factual decisions he should be used.' Besides, where was the sense in half-opening Pandora's box?

An hour or so later Stinger and I get into the lift at the Palace Hotel with Warney and father, who are on their way to spend the evening with a tour party from St Kilda. Warney tells Stinger he's pissed off with the *Mirror*. Still. I recall a conversation I overheard between Jenner and Warney Sr at Lord's, something about their boy not being as self-assured as the world imagines. Must have been the headline.

Daily Accumulator: Poms 3 Cobbers 7

6 July 'Why is sex fun?'

(*Observer*)

'Don't you dare cross the track!' booms the Tannoy as we disembark from the tram. Cue guffaws all round as a couple of red-faced chaps hurry sheepishly from track to platform. Get up to the press box and dive into the *Sunday Telegraph* to see how well Scyld Berry has recovered from his outburst of emotion. Superbly. Above his pearls, however, lurks unabashed parochialism. Instead of Warney's record-breaking wicket, or one of Tugga's boundaries, or even Hussain's 'catch', the main image of yesterday's play is Bevan leaping, eyes shut, just before Headley's short-pitcher loops to gully off an involuntary edge. The headline is a good deal more justified: 'Australia slam the door shut'.

Tugga turns the key and casts it into the Ship Canal. Croftie misfields horribly at short cover then comes on to stem the early flurry (32 in 4 overs); respect is earned and given but everyone else Atherton turns to is dispatched at will. A chorus of 'Delilah' strikes up from E2 Stand as Caddick stands at mid-on, arms folded, resignation in every step. Warney boogies on to 53 then fends Caddick to Stewart with his partner on 97; the sustained ovation from the pavilion sounds a lot like an apology for the rudeness of the oiks. 'Yesss!' cries Pigeon as Tugga takes half a pace forward and shovels Caddick through midwicket to complete his century. Hoisting his bat with apparent reluctance, he turns full circle, saluting all four corners. Stinger and I are propped up against the wall below the Cobbers' dressing room as Heals almost topples out of the window in his zeal to hail the conquering hero; that toothy smile could dazzle Greater Manchester. A banner in the MacLaren Stand, the handiwork of some vacationing loyalists from Moore Park, near the SCG, mirrors his enthusiasm to a T: 'S WAUGH = GOD = ASHES'.

A browse round the museum yields several fascinating curios. A tinted photo of W G and a grinning Ranji (at Lord's?). A 1926 letter to a newspaper wherein Cecil Parkin, that hard-bowling, hard-living Lancastrian, conveys his gratitude for a cheque then chips in the immortal p.s.: 'I am just going to partake of a little "tonsil varnish".' And then, there it was, in a cabinet beside an array of antiquarian bats:

a baggy green cap. After Matthew's stormy battle to preserve his, I'd assumed this was something that never left its owner's side. A call to the curator, Keith Ayres, reveals it to have been a donation from the unfortunate Ron Archer, the Man Who Would Have Been Keith Miller The Second. A king-size all-rounder from Brisbane, Archer was 24 when, in the 1956 Ashes series, he finished second to Sir Robert Menzies's favourite flannelled fool in the bowling lists (average and aggregate); in Pakistan two months later, he trapped his spikes in the matting, twisted a knee and never represented his country again. Life thereafter was prosperous, but was this something he wanted to distance himself from? I'd far rather believe it was proof of the ties that bind.

Tubs allows Pistol and Dizzy to make merry then waves them in twenty minutes into a sun-soaked afternoon, the target a nominal 469. 'Three an over,' reveals the *Daily Mail*'s Brian Scovell, helpfully. The Cobber journos are pissed off with Ross. The *Sunday Mirror* had carried a 'world exclusive' with the alluring headline 'Shane quits tour', a reference to nothing more sensational than the fact that the new father was being allowed to take advantage of the fortnight's break between Tests and return home to meet his daughter. 'What was I supposed to do?' bemoans Ross, who had kept the tale to himself. 'Issue a press release?'

As Atherton and Butcher set off, there is one factoid they probably don't need to be apprised of: the highest winning total in the fourth innings of a Test on this ground is 145 for 7. For an hour, all is hunky dory. Warney comes on at the Warwick Road End and the boos are subsumed by a defiant burst of 'Rule Britannia'. Hell, when Dizzy returns for a second spell in the fifteenth over – Tubs is shuffling his pack with the dexterity of the Cincinnati Kid – Atherton hooks him for six. Unheard of. He pays for his temerity in Dizzy's next over as the South Australian whippet persuades one to dive-bomb and elicits a leg-before decision that grows increasingly dodgy with each BBC replay (the punters only get the one). The score moves from 44 for 1 to 45 for 2 as

158

Stewart lunges forward to Warney's top-spinner, bat and pad estranged: timbers are shivered. Hussain goes leg-before in the first over after tea, pinned on the back foot by Dizzy and beaten for pace. E2 Stand takes it out on Warney, who at some point yesterday is supposed to have given them the finger: 'He's blond, he's bent, his arse is up for rent'. Then the plea for forgiveness: 'Warney, Warney, give us a wave'. Turning around at third slip, the target of the abuse does their bidding with a winning grin, then strokes an imaginary pot belly. Nothing, one suspects, can spoil his humour today.

Impressively stoical up to now, Butcher top-edges a hook off Dizzy; Pigeon hares in from fine-leg like some knock-kneed stag and intercepts on his knees. Four prime bats have gone for 11 in the space of 37 balls. A barrel-chested bloke with a pink tan and maroon underpants runs on to the square in the 25th over, a prelude to the first bona fide streak of the match in the 33rd. In the 34th, Thorpe slashes at a wide one from Warney and Heals does the business. If the first innings was shot through with timidity, here, or so it appears, is self-assertion gone mad. The despairing gestures of spirits broken by an irresistible force? Or merely confirmation of Junior's pre-tour jibes about fibre deficiency?

Classical, upright and composed – and fighting to retain his place for Leeds – Crawley evokes what little footage I have seen of P B H May (so why isn't he batting at first drop?). Ealham helps him restore order, ekeing out 5 in the final hour. The spotlight, though, is now squarely on the bare of behind. One invader rumbles on in a Viking helmet brandishing a plastic billy club, and hurdles the stumps at the bowler's end. At which point I decide that I miss my family. An hour after stumps I'm on a standing-room-only 125, steaming back to Euston, a rat shamelessly deserting a sunken vessel.

John Woodcock's top twenty 'Greatest Cricketers Of All Time', as unveiled in yesterday's *Times* magazine, is such a riveting read I almost forget I won't be able to sit down for the best part of three hours. W G at one, The Don at two and Sobers at three brook no argument, but Woolley ahead of Warney? Granted, I am completely, irredeemably and irretrievably biased towards the titans of my own lifetime, but even so. If the Sage of Longparish was in this carriage I would have no option but to say to him, 'Oi, Johnny. No! How can you prefer the Pride of Kent and his five Test hundreds to the beach boy who singlehandedly saved his profession from death by a thousand shattered visors?'

En route to the loo I find a couple of blokes smoking in the corridor. I cadge a fag from Keith Roberts, an extractor-fan manufacturer from Uxbridge who has just sampled his first taste of Test cricket alfresco. A long-time regular at Lord's for county fixtures, this is the first time he has been able to obtain tickets. 'I went with an Aussie mate. He prodded me into it. Really enjoyed the camaraderie. Some of our lot were helping the Aussies smuggle in their beer, in exchange for the odd can. A bloke in a Marge Simpson wig started a conga and everyone joined in. Mind you, they didn't half give Warne some stick. How did that one go?' The question is directed at Richard Huntley, who is studying for a degree in economics and politics at Cardiff University and is whiling away his vacation in the City, working for a merchant bank. He duly obliges: 'Three men went to mow, went to mow a meadow, three men, two men, one man, and his sheep – baaah – went to bed with Shane Warne. It doesn't even rhyme.'

Richard's biggest bugaboo, however, is the over-exuberance of the security guards. 'Some guy started chucking orange peel at one and got dragged away by four of them. They were really rough on him, as they were with the streakers. So unnecessary.' Keith prefers to reflect on an incident that saw snooks cocked with the utmost ingenuity. 'You know that woman who streaked yesterday? Apparently, she collected five grand on the spot before doing it.' The ECB marketing department should sign her up pronto.

Daily Accumulator: Poms 0 Cobbers 10

7 July 'Parade sparks Ulster riots'

(Daily Telegraph)

Standing tall on the burning deck, Crawley goes expertly back to something short and spiteful from Pigeon, neutralizing the threat as if he were Pete Sampras executing a stop-volley. As he does so, however, he retreats a pace too far and a heel dislodges a bail. As a metaphor for this game – indeed, for the state of the series – what could possibly be more apt?

Manchester had steadfastly refused to pull its finger out, letting the side down with another concerted blast of sunshine. The most languorous of slow deaths finally draws its last breath half an hour before lunch, Crawley and Ealham extending their liaison to 74, the most protracted home resistance of the contest, before Pigeon surges through with 4 wickets in 6 overs. One of these is Croftie, who gleans his 100th Test run but otherwise has another torrid time of it. Jogging on the spot between deliveries, geeing himself up, he was under no illusions. He knew from the outset that there would be fewer offerings in his half of the pitch than there are druids in Dubai. Moving into line, deflecting well off his legs, he proceeds gamely then fends a chin-high bouncer to backward short-leg. Hammering the turf with his bat, he departs in a funk. Grunting like a famished warthog, Warney applies the *coup de grâce* as Caddick swipes him for successive boundaries then chips to mid-on, where Dizzy accepts the dolly, pauses to consider the magnitude of it all, then does his level best to puncture the ozone layer. For some reason, Warney seems quite disgusted. Does waiting the best part of three hours between scalps gnaw that much at his self-esteem?

At Lord's, the Poms were halted in their tracks; the last five days have seen them shoved backwards, by inches then feet. It would be ludicrous to suggest that dusk has settled on the new dawn, just as it would be insulting to their opponents to dwell on the home team's shortcomings. Admitted free for the last rites, the diehards are certainly nowhere near the dumps. Up goes the chant: 'Enger-land, Enger-land'. The way they probably view it, had Warney and Tugga, the Man of the Match, been reared in Bury, the result would have been reversed, and who could blame them? What they may not have noticed is the way Dizzy and Pistol have imposed themselves, or that the bottom half of the order outscored the top in both innings, by 2–1 in the second, a sure indication of unified purpose. A scan of the victors during the prizegiving proves most revealing. Pistol fondles Warney's shoulders and does his best Cheshire cat impression. Pigeon giggles. Tugga, however, looks positively scornful of such levity. The job, after all, is only half-done.

Ring Croftie during the evening for his assessment. 'One-all at half-time,' he asserts, puckish as ever, albeit sounding eminently ready for his impending ten-day break. He has been told he can miss Glamorgan's game against the tourists at the weekend. 'Why take the risk that they might go after me and damage my confidence?' he reasons, worryingly.

Daily Accumulator: Poms 1 Cobbers 9
Match total: Poms 11, Cobbers 39

ROBERT CROFT
It was a difficult wicket on that first day and they probably scored 20 or 30 runs more than they should, but we bowled well. Let's be fair, bowling them out hasn't been the problem. We seem to have an attack capable of taking 20 wickets. Where we let ourselves down was in not getting enough runs in the first innings. As a consequence, they went out with a lead when the wicket was at its flattest.

Warne had some nice rough to bowl into – very rarely do off-spinners have that sort of advantage – but the point is that he put enough balls into the right area. There hasn't been any talk of getting down the wicket, getting to the pitch, but we did try to play him positively. Personally, I would look to kick away as much as possible, make him bowl over the wicket, use the flatter part of the wicket, but each batsman is different.

Steve Waugh played superbly well. That innings on the opening day was one of the best I've seen anywhere. I don't think he was very happy when Taylor chose to bat – probably not many of the batsmen were – and it was almost as if he felt he had to bale his captain out. What he is so good at, apart from getting stuck in, is not missing the bad balls. He is so engrossed in what he does, in one of the innings he all but punched the ball to Stewart and just stood there. He'd scored a hundred but you still had to prise him away.

When I went out to bat, the only thing I was scared of was failure. Of letting the side down. I didn't see the ball that hit me on the helmet. Again, I don't want to make excuses, but the sightscreen is small there and there are red buildings behind it. I don't want to take anything away from McGrath because he bowled well. Nor do I want people to make too much of my struggles against him because in ten years of county cricket I've never had a problem with short-pitched bowling. The crucial thing for me is not to make too much of it. Yes, I probably did let myself down, but I'm there as a bowler first and foremost. If I made 50 and bowled like a drain, I would lose my place. You can't lose sight of that.

As far as my bowling is concerned, I still feel I'm in the form of my life. I feel more experienced, more confident. It would be nice to have Tuffers at the other end but the conditions haven't allowed that. I bowled nearly 40 overs in the second innings, went for less than 3 an over and could have picked up a few more wickets. Unfortunately, I was aiming for the hard part of the surface so there wasn't much spin, however much of a rip I gave it. Some people have suggested I'm being used as a stock bowler, but I've never bowled in that way. I want a wicket every ball.

My first reaction to the Blewett dismissal was 'great catch'. Because I was following through I obviously didn't get the best view, but that was my immediate response: I honestly thought Naz flicked it up. He was convinced, and

163

in circumstances like that you have to take the fielder's word. Had the third umpire been consulted, a couple of other decisions might have gone the other way. There was a good shout in the first innings against Steve Waugh before he'd scored; Reiffel was given not out when he was caught behind; I thought I had Warne caught at short-leg. I couldn't believe they didn't give that one, but it's swings and round-abouts. I don't agree with using cameras to make these decisions. What need would there be for umpires?

MATTHEW ELLIOTT

Whenever I've played for Australia and we've had even a sniff of a strong position, half an opening, everybody seems to make the most of it, really going in for the kill. This was no exception.

When Tubs saw the wicket he assured us it would be OK. With his experience, I took it on trust, so I was quite happy batting first. In the event it seamed as much on that first day as any Test wicket I've ever played on, but although some of the guys were surprised, nobody grumbled. The key was the footmarks, which were quite deep. Tubs obviously knew what he was doing. Most of our victories have come when we've been able to be the front-runners. He read it beautifully in the end.

That's not to say I thought it was a good wicket. It certainly wasn't the best that could have been prepared. Which is why the stand between Pistol and Tugga was so critical. It was one of those swings in momentum, just when it looked as if we might be steamrollered. And when we lost those three early wickets on the Saturday Tugga came in and did it again. Fantastic is the only word for it. I've been watching him carefully. He is always looking to bring the odds back into his favour, letting a lot of balls go by outside off, playing the percentages. He's superb off his legs, and off the back foot through the off side, but once he's in he won't give an inch. He's become more ruthless. As a bloke he's hard to get to know. He's generally very quiet during a game, sitting in the corner of the dressing room, watching everything but not communicating a great deal. He likes his own time, being with his family.

I'm not sure how I would play Warney. It would be hard to hit the ball on the on side or sweep without getting a leading edge but I would probably aim to bring the odds back in my favour by batting outside leg stump. I'd give him a good look at it, and hope he aims at it, because then you have a chance to score through the off side. My priority would be to keep scoring.

Having said all that, I thought Dizzy turned the game our way in the end. Although the wicket had died a little, the bounce was a bit uneven and he bowled with a lot of pace. Getting Butcher, Atherton and Hussain in quick succession either side of tea effectively ripped the heart out of their second innings.

Gough is beginning to bowl world class, good pace and swing, always trying to get you out, and Headley really impressed me. He gave us left-handers no end of bother, bowling middle-and-leg, forcing you to play, then darting the ball away. The ball came off the back of my arm in the first innings but I've no qualms about being given out. I knew I wasn't out. I was going to appeal and then thought better of it, but if every decision required a replay it would detract a great deal from the game.

The umpires we've had in this series are the best in the world – Bucknor, Venkat, Shepherd – but they're not going to get it right all the time. Having said that, I don't think they used their common sense over the Blewett catch. I was at the non-striker's end and I thought the ball bounced, but I couldn't see the sense in asking the square-leg umpire because he has to worry about the line decisions. He's not going to be watching the ball as keenly. Which is why I believe we have to look at using the third umpire to help out in those situations.

Some of our players did get a bit hot under the collar. Warney was furious.The impression I got from the guys was that if the shoe had been on the other foot a lot more would have been made of it. There is a perception in the side that we always tend to be the bad guys, the guys who don't have the game's best interests at heart. When Heals stuck his neck out at Lord's it was as if that was expected, but nobody suggested that was expected of Hussain.

8 July 'Coalmine may sink Byron's home'

(Guardian)

Almost a fortnight ahead of schedule, in an unprecedented and admirable show of faith, the G-men nominate the same eleven Poms for Headingley plus Tufnell. Notwithstanding my suspicion that Ealham is out of his depth and at least one Hollioake should have been in from the start – the Surrey captain, to be fair, has hardly made a run since the Texacos – I hereby salute all concerned.

Ian McGeechan, who coached the British Lions to their wholly unexpected triumphs in South Africa, has been asked to address the squad at Upper Heythrop on the Sunday before the fourth Test, the subject 'motivation'. Lloyd has organized it in conjunction with Insights, the company run by Will Carling and Frank Dick, the former national athletics coach, to help the players 'improve levels of mutual support and communication'. Digging up an Irish grandmother for Tugga or Warney would be even more useful.

21 July 'Essex man bows out before career goes on too long'
(Daily Telegraph)

I now have a fair idea of what it must feel like to spend a week inside a Turkish wrestler's jockstrap. Mayor Guiliani may have given the streets a decent wash and brush-up but my first taste of a New York summer since 1981 sent the sweat glands into hyperdrive. Four showers a day minimum. At least the cultural stimulation compensated: *Face/Off*, a terrific slab of bloody cinematic psychodrama starring the endlessly watchable Nicolas Cage and John Travolta; Earl Klugh and his soothing six-string at the Blue Note; Christopher Plummer imperious as John Barrymore. I cannot think of anywhere else on the planet where I would choose to be alone.

Not that I was entirely without company. Over dinner at Old Trafford I had told Matthew Engel I was going over for a friend's wedding, which prompted him to persuade his wife that he, too, was in need of the Gross Pomme's unique injection of oxygen. The barman at the Blue Note will probably never forget the night he kept a pair of Limeys going with Jack Daniels and Absolut while they came close to blows over something called a county championship. We also attended a couple of baseball games, losing ourselves in a world of pinstripes, pinch-runners and pretzels. A world where sport and nationalism are divisible. They don't know the glorious angst they're missing.

Inspired by public acclaim for experimental mid-season inter-league matches and the prospect of all those dollar-spinning derbies, the owners of the Major League franchises are proposing to kill off a century's worth of tradition by scrapping the National and American leagues. At a time when Lord Tesco is said to be modelling his championship blueprint on baseball's conference system, how ironic that the guardians of the diamond should be on the verge of revamping it.

Shea Stadium, home to my cherished New York Mets, furnished further evidence of this divergence in attitudes. The bevvies of Benetton-clad kids shrieking holes in our eardrums were all admitted gratis, a stark reminder of how far our own supposed national summer pastime trails behind in its efforts to foster passions. Baseball is to Americans what cricket is to us Limeys: a reminder of what we like best about ourselves. The main difference between the two is that baseball attaches as much importance to tomorrow and today as yesterday. When I got home this morning, Mike Marqusee rang to tell me about a trip to Lord's with his 11-year-old American nephew. 'You should have seen him,' he exulted. 'First game ever, watched intently for half an hour and got it!' Notwithstanding the fact that the tourists were the attraction, the proud uncle was somewhat less taken with the pricing policy. Understandably so. Admission to the upper tier of the Compton and Edrich stands – £8 admission plus supplement – came to £10 a head, adults and children alike. If that's marketing, Mae West was the apogee of subtlety.

In my absence, Blighty appears to have waived the rules (in my determination to cut off from everyday concerns when on holiday, I make a point of avoiding news of home come what may). Piqued that the BBC's man, Malcolm Ashton, has secured his third winter tour on the trot, strike action is being threatened by the Association of County Cricket Scorers, a breed about as prone to militant tendencies as laboratory rats. Radley School (Ted Dexter's alma mater) have cancelled their annual fixture with Marlborough (nursery to A G Steel and Reggie Spooner) in the wake of a wholly unsporting declaration and a hail of 'unpleasant and abusive comments'. And Goochie has hung up his box. Mired in the worst slump of his career, he has evidently decided to get out before embarrassment gives way to pity. He always was adept at extricating himself from tight corners.

In Cardiff, meanwhile, Punter has been doing himself no end of favours. In his third first-class innings since docking in west Middlesex, the shrimp from the Launceston back-streets made what was by all acounts a sparkling hundred, albeit against a Glamorgan attack shorn of Waqar and Watkin as well as Croftie. Until then, his most impressive score had been the 75 he shot round the Old Course at St Andrews. When he was dropped for last winter's third Test against the Windies, having made 88 in the first, it was hard to avoid the conclusion that he must have upset somebody.

With Bev out of sorts with bat as well as ball, the wrist-slapping may be over.

Though Steve James took the opportunity to elbow the selectors with a brace of half-centuries, winning the race to 1,000 runs, Tubs has expressed disenchantment with the reluctance of the counties to field full-strength XIs, no doubt recalling that he, Slats, Junior and Bev all turned out for New South Wales against the Poms in '94–95. Nor is Captain Sensible overly chuffed with the decision to use a different strip to that originally designated for the Headingley Test. Then again, where would we be without a bit of argy-bargy over a Yorkshire stage? Those demonic surfaces served up in 1961 and 1972 certainly had the Cobbers foaming (fuserium my bottom). 'There's a bastard in my family,' Keith Boyce, the square's recently retired minder, once pronounced on the eve of a Test, 'and it's sitting out there.'

Before re-acquainting myself with the pleasures of occupying the same mattress as Anne, I catch a few frames of Mick Jagger mugging his way through the title role in Tony Richardson's biopic of Ned Kelly. Short of Michael Hutchence playing Dick Turpin, I cannot imagine how the Cobbers will ever wreak any commensurate revenge.

23 July 'Why shouldn't the Home Counties have Home Rule?'

(*Daily Mail*)

Arrive at Headingley to spot Crommo and Graveney sitting in an otherwise deserted stand, ankle-deep in huggermugger. The Cobbers are mightily pissed off, not so much that the pitch had been switched, but at Graveney's purported part in the move. The chairman of selectors, who is said to have been asked to curtail his Spanish vacation when the issue came to a head, is all smiles and bonhomie, presumably making the point that the shift was made on the instructions of Harry Brind, who felt the designated surface might not last the distance. Crommo seems sceptical, as if he's back in court, listening to a loquacious but unreliable witness. Not even Graveney's mother would believe him were he to suggest that Brind acted alone. The board's policy all season has been to influence pitch preparation; with the series all-square, why would they desist now?

The host club, it scarce needs adding, is having its own barneys. Needled by the proposed relocation to Wakefield, Paul Caddick has unveiled his own ambitious blueprint for the redevelopment of Headingley, where cricketers and rugby leaguers have cohabited uneasily for a century. On Monday night the ground's owner appeared live on TV with his long-time adversaries, Sir Lawrence Byford, the Yorkshire president, and Chris Hassell, its far-thinking chief executive. Predictably, tempers rose, Caddick accusing the club of not giving members an opportunity to assess the merits of staying put. Now he has offered to renegotiate the remaining eighty-four years on the lease. Given the pressing need to distance itself from the racist rabble who triggered those ugly scenes on the Western Terrace during last summer's Test against Pakistan, the members would be doing the game a favour if they were to tell Caddick where to put his extension.

Bespectacled and self-effacing, Mike Smith handles his interrogation by the press with aplomb. A son of Dewsbury whose academic leanings found him at odds with his fellow aspirants during a brief sojourn at Yorkshire in his teens, he paused to collect a degree in languages then found his *métier* at Bristol. Now heading the country's wicket-takers by a street, he appears likely to make his debut in place of either Gough (knee) or Headley (side strain).

According to the *Yorkshire Evening Post*, Ian Botham's website offers a sneak preview of the Barmy Army's single, 'We Are England', scheduled to hit the high streets next month. The chorus includes the lines: 'We are England, we are mighty/In our hearts we know that this will be the year'. A month ago, maybe.

To Edgbaston, for Warwickshire's floodlit bash against

Somerset. Dennis Amiss, for once, is finding words elusive. Or at least the right ones. Peering searchingly at his feet, he delves deep for the most diplomatic means of expression, then opts for the immaculate forward defensive that once reduced bowlers the world over to servitude. How did the Warwickshire chief executive feel about the idea of a chunk of those juicy Ashes receipts being used to install floodlights at every county HQ? At £4.5 million all told, after all, it would hardly be that crippling an investment. Didn't the Indian board have the foresight to employ its share of last year's World Cup proceeds to illuminate its major venues? 'It's a big question,' Amiss acknowledges. Pause. 'The counties need that money.' Another pause. Another dead bat. 'The Board do have to look seriously at the future of floodlit cricket.'

Of all the pronouncements on the Poms' belated entry into the twilight zone this week (the Roses rivals dipped their toes at Old Trafford on Monday), none, assuredly, has been more apposite, nor more blindingly obvious. As one of Kerry Packer's pirates, Amiss had himself been part of the first such foray nearly twenty years ago. Ask him to name World Series Cricket's foremost contribution to mankind and the answer is unhesitating: night games. Which is why Amiss's feet had barely touched the ground all evening. The northern hemisphere's first competitive floodlit match was going spiffingly. More than 15,000 had turned up for this rescheduled Sunday League affair, three times the ground's Sabbath average. The cost of hiring that quartet of humongous monuments to the genius of Thomas Edison had been amply offset by estimated receipts of £120,000, yielding profits of £70,000, nearly twice the county's total gate income from last season's championship programme.

True, the attendance has put a strain on parking, so much so that, in exchange for modest considerations of up to £10, residents hired out their driveways. Little else had been left to chance. Board approval had been obtained to drag a rope through the square between innings, and hence minimize

171

the effects of the dew (as it transpired, a balmy evening had rendered such concerns needless). Edgbaston's new MP had done her bit, assuaging local fears of drunks running amok in their tidy suburban streets, generating goodwill. Public transport had been extended, a crèche supplied. Yet something niggles. In strict cricketing terms, granted, gimmicks have been kept to a minimum, even if there were doubtless those for whom the banana-coloured stumps bordered on heresy (Lord's, mercifully, had drawn the line at pink). But it wasn't that. Nor the basketball net behind the R E S Wyatt Stand, for all that its presence is somewhat at odds with the point of the exercise. The packaging, in almost every respect, is impeccable. Shame about the content.

The blame, of course, lies with the shortcomings, not only of the forty-over game, but the limited-overs format *per se*. When the first five Somerset wickets clatter for next to nothing, seats vacate at an unseemly rate of knots. The contest was in a coma, but takes two hours to expire. There is no referee to step in, let alone any means of prolonging the drama. Even though the hosts are heading for the top of the league, boredom sets in, polite yet palpable. The first streaker sets sail at 10.20, the first Mexican Wave two minutes later. Occasion is everything, the stage a sideshow. For the moonlight-and-Roses challenge match, on the other hand, the book seems to have been vastly more satisfying than the cover. A fifty-over affair divided into quarters, it ensured fairness, each side batting half an innings in the unfamiliar conditions, a formula that attracted no end of scoffing when Atherton's men encountered it in Perth at the outset of the last Ashes tour. The upshot, better still, was a contest that swung this way and that, gripping to the final frame. After twenty-five overs apiece, the scores were level, whereupon Yorkshire, having looked certain to outstrip Lancashire's eventual total at a canter, abruptly lost their last 4 wickets in 5 balls. The crowd may have been barely a third of that at Edgbaston, but at least they remained riveted to their pews.

Combine Edgbaston's multicultural theme park with Old Trafford's onfield dramatics and we might have something. What cannot be disputed, in the increasingly fraught tussle for both public and sponsorship pound, is that cricket's future in the forefront of the national psyche lies with fixtures at sociable hours. Tonight's toe-dunking exercise has shown beyond doubt that the demand is there. It has also furnished evidence that the counties, given the tools, might even learn to fend for themselves.

MATTHEW ELLIOTT

The guys are not happy about the wicket. It doesn't look as if it has been prepared. People pay good money to watch these games and they should get the best wickets possible; if they don't, they're not getting value for money. Do they really want another wicket like the one we had at Old Trafford, where only one batsman was able to conquer it? Do they want to see results or good cricket?

As a professional, I think I'm entitled to expect a certain standard, too, but of late, here and in South Africa, the wickets certainly haven't been of Test standard. The weather obviously hasn't been friendly to the curators who tend the wickets but I can't understand the point of preparing a wicket that's soft at the start, just to take Warney out of the contest. This is probably the key match of the series and the ECB is trying to give England an advantage by nullifying Warney, but to do all this just to take one player out of the game? The same happened at Port Elizabeth. It's absolute bullshit.

The selectors have dropped Bev, and I feel for him. He seems to be caught in two minds against the short-pitchers, whether to play at them or not. You have to be so clear in those circumstances. But Punter plays pace well and he is ready to take his opportunity. He seems to have coped better than most with being one of the reserve batsmen. The biggest difficulty is not so much the boredom as having to go out and prove points in county games when some of your colleagues aren't approaching the game quite so seriously. The key is not to take yourself too seriously, which Punter doesn't. As well as being a giving person and a good team man, he is also worldly for his age, a strong character. You had the feeling he knew he just had to bide his time. You never heard him say, 'I've got to get runs today.' He took his chance at Cardiff but you never had the sense of him putting himself under pressure.

I've decided I'm going to hook in this match. Tubs always tells me to go for it, but I've never executed it as badly as this season. When the bounce is uneven, as it has been on the surfaces we've encountered, you can be a bit hesitant to play it, and I've been top-edging a lot. But you have to back yourself, don't you?

Did you know the Queen was a fan of *The Gladiators*? We found that out when we went to Buckingham Palace. Somebody asked her about this TV challenge match they'd had on TV between the Gladiators and her guardsmen, whether it was her idea. 'Oh no, oh no,' she said, but then she started doing all the moves. It was funny. She seemed pretty with it on most things. I stood back and let the other guys talk to her. I was a bit on edge; the hands were definitely clammy. In some ways the monarchy is a good thing, although I don't think too many countries look at the Queen as the Queen of the Commonwealth. What intrigues me is how they accumulated all that wealth.

ROBERT CROFT

Surely, as the home team, we are entitled to select the pitch we want. If you go to India they don't produce wickets that seam, do they? You play on turning pitches, dust bowls. Same in Sri Lanka. The West Indies have been producing wickets to help their pacemen for twenty years. It's the same everywhere. I wouldn't have any complaints. You accept what you're given. At the end of the day it's twenty-two yards with stumps stuck at either end. Now let's go and play.

174

We were given a fitness programme by Dean Riddell so those ten days off weren't completely idle, which was good. You don't want to switch off too much. I popped in to see the lads at Cardiff when they were playing the Australians, played a bit of golf and did a lot of fishing on the River Tywi in west Wales. Caught a nice six-pounder. I've also been working on my batting.

Announcing the same twelve straight away was great for the fellows. Maybe those days of bringing in five new faces at the first sign of defeat are gone. It made us feel as if we have everybody's backing. The selectors seem to have identified a group of seventeen to twenty players whom they feel have the potential to create a top-quality side, if not now, then in two or three years' time. That has to be the right approach.

The weekend at Upper Heythrop was superb. We were divided into teams of four or five and went off on various exercises – laser clay-pigeon shooting, golf, team-building activities, getting everybody working together again, recreating the buzz. Seb Coe addressed us instead of Ian McGeechan, chatting about his experiences, particularly the way he came back to win the Olympic 1,500 metres in 1980 after losing the 800. Not only did he have to pick himself up after losing a race he should never have lost, he had to beat Steve Ovett, who'd won the 800 and hadn't been beaten over 1,500 for two years. What struck me most was the inner belief, the conviction that he could never run as badly again as he had in the 800. We played badly at Old Trafford; we have to have that same inner belief that we can't play as badly again. This is now a three-Test series, so it's important to grab the initiative. I still think we have the edge.

24 July 'TV viewing is linked to mental illness'
(Daily Telegraph)

'I've paid a hundred and fifty quid to come here from Paris,' bemoans Michael Caine (no relation). A typographer originally from hereabouts, he is wearing an East Leeds CC sweater and a pained expression. Hard to blame him really. Headley and Gough have both reported fit, Smith has come in for Caddick, Tubs has underlined his credentials to toss for Earth against Mars but drizzle has delayed the start. Michael and I, it transpires, were contemporaries at the London College of Printing. I ask him why two old boys of such an upstanding institution should care so avidly about the antics of eleven chaps in jockstraps. 'Sport brings out the chauvinism in me,' he admits. 'The buzz you get when Goughie sends someone's stump cartwheeling!' I should be so honest.

Two spells of action are possible before lunch, one of four overs, one of five balls. Atherton and Butcher emerge unscathed. By early afternoon a torrential downpour reduces outfield and square to a mass of pools. Brian Murgatroyd, Sky stats supremo turned smartly blazered ECB press officer, informs us that Tubs has formally complained to the Right-on Tim about Graveney's alleged hand in the decision to swap pitches. The Board, inevitably, claims that Brind acted alone.

Stinger and I venture on to the Western Terrace and find Sikhs, Jamaicans, Poms and Cobbers in various states of sombre wetness. A few of them exchange good-humoured banter with Cyril Mitchley, Venkat's replacement as 'independent' umpire. A plane circles the ground trailing the message, 'Bog off Fat Boy – The Sport'. This is a reference to the headline in the country's scuzziest newspaper after Warney availed Old Trafford of his Harvey Smith impression. 'Bog Off Fat Boy' T-shirts are apparently doing brisk business.

We also meet the Spice Girls. Or, rather, a quintet of hirsute students dressed up as the newly anointed Fab Five. The instigator was Andrew Archer (leopardskin top), who has just left Ripon Grammar and is currently working on a farm. 'They wanted a lift so I told them they had to dress up. I hatched the idea with Gary when we were on holiday in

Benidorm. A few Newcastle fans took the piss.' Gary is Gary Oliver (pink top, tracksuit bottoms), fresh from A levels and shortly to go up to Northumbria University to study business administration. 'It's a shame about Bevan,' he sympathizes. 'He played great for us last summer.' Andrew is excited about the mooted move to Wakefield, especially all the talk about a retractable roof. 'I'll be able to watch games after work,' he enthuses, eyes widening.

As we continue on our way, Stinger espies Geoff Lawson in the commentary box and beckons him down. The two are firm friends – Stinger ghosted his fellow New South Walian's 1989 Ashes diary – but 'Henry' seems distracted. By way of keeping the customers entertained, the video screen is transmitting extended highlights of *1981 And All That*; Lawson, who was on the receiving end, watches Botham's Herculean slogging with rather greater intent than one might imagine. 'Look at all those slips,' he exclaims after one outrageous slice whizzes to an untenanted third-man boundary. 'We were giving him runs. Great knock, though.'

Working with the likes of Willis and Paul Allott, he says, 'has been like meeting long-lost buddies'. During the early eighties, he assures us, the rival camps mixed freely at the end of a day's hard-nosed labour, 'chewing the cud, empathizing with each other's plight'. He is convinced the ECB's pitch manoeuvring was indicative of Pommy panic. 'Anyway, it's no big deal. I remember a Test we played in Pakistan when there were two strips side-by-side, one bare, one green. Imran passed a fitness test on the morning of the game so they plumped for the greentop.' Did he agree with my theory about memories of Empire and imposed inferiority being a factor, however subconscious, in his successors' determination to hold on to the Ashes? Not in the slightest. 'We'll be a republic in five years. These kids know nothing about the Empire, nothing about history. You've just told me that Matthew Elliott wants to find out about the history of the Ashes. I was eight when George Davis ruined the Test here in '75: I cried.'

Cue hoots of derision as the PA announcer informs us that dispersing the loose water has been sheer hell. Play, nevertheless, will resume at 4.45. Five minutes later comes another cloudburst, persuading me to give up the ghost. The *FT* have decided they don't have space for a report and I have to be back in London for my Wapping shift. O ye of little faith! Upon my arrival home I learn that hostilities recommenced ten minutes after my exit. The Poms finish on 103 for 3, balance tilted by Hussain's dismissal two overs from stumps via a pearler from Pigeon and a nifty catch from Tubs. Oh, and Butcher has clipped a Reiffel half-volley into Blewie's armpit.

I'm too preoccupied to get depressed. While driving me from Edgbaston to Leeds this morning, Matthew Engel told me that he has been apprised of Lord Tesco's plans for the championship. No promotion or relegation, or even two parallel regional conferences, but three non-regionalized conferences! Preposterous. 'Take it from me,' he insisted when I expressed the view that his mole might be winding him up. Of course I know he is the editor of *Wisden* and must therefore have impeccable sources, but I still can't credit it. Of course compromise is necessary, if only up to a point, but whatever happened to common sense?

Daily Accumulator: Poms 4 Cobbers 6

25 July 'Wickets galore in the Test (but sorry we're now switching you off)'

(Standard)

What on earth my father was doing listening to *Test Match Special* I really couldn't tell you. His fondness for cricket, after all, is roughly on a par with his affinity for good health (we are talking about the world's most shameless hypochondriac here). But he was. Hence his call to the office a few minutes ago. Had I heard? Come the end of the series, the last garden party in town, currently celebrating forty years of cheers and chides and choccie cakes, will cease to be a ball-by-ball operation. A similar threat was made nine years ago but the public outcry obliged Auntie to rethink. Given the prevailing philosophy at Broadcasting House, it may be too much to hope for another stay of execution.

Admittedly, I haven't tuned in to *TMS* for more than five minutes at a stretch since the Berlin Wall fell – the very thought of having to hear Freddie Trueman witter on about how much better things were in his day is merely the first repellent to spring to mind – but that doesn't mean I fail to recognize its value to the nation. Its passing would signal intolerance, both for minority interests and, more specifically, for a form of cultural sustenance that refuses to conform to the wham or the bam, let alone the thank-you ma'am. 'There is no place for a sport that takes up hours and hours of the schedule during the summer months,' the *Standard* quotes a BBC mole as saying. Particularly one so hopelessly inept at boosting morale. Would it have made any difference had the Old Trafford result been reversed?

Oddly enough, the announcement came just as the Poms appear to be on the cusp of a decent day. The pre-lunch session, it must be said, had been inauspicious in the extreme. Atherton, a model of temperance for the best part of four hours, hooked Pigeon to long-leg and the walls did not so much tumble as melt. Thorpe came out blasting from the hip, twice clattering Dizzy to the boards with have-at-thee hooks, only to be bowled off the bottom edge attempting another. Dizzy was too hasty for the rest, too, taking 6 for 23 in his second spell as the total puttered from 154 for 4 to 172 all out inside 10 overs. Crawley, caught off a rebound from short-leg's instep, once again found the fates giving him a wide berth. But then, lo and behold, Gough and Headley snarled back. Thorpe dropped Matthew in Smith's third over (gentle, two-handed and maybe six inches above the forehead; on a 1–10 scale of complexity, we're talking a 3) but Tugga went next ball, leaving the Cobbers on 50 for 4. In they flocked from every nook and cranny: designers, arts

179

editors, news reporters, chief subs, production editors, cran-
ing necks to catch a glimpse of the sports desk TV,
colleagues united in pursuit of boyhood.

Matthew, though, is sticking to his word, hooking and
pulling with elan and precision whenever the gauntlet is
flung down, which is not infrequently. To date, pitching the
ball up, letting soil and clouds do their worst, has proved
much the most profitable avenue; after Matthew's first few
clean connections, might it not have made more sense to
revert to the tried and trusted? Still, I'm sure Atherton
knows what he's doing. My own sentiments are not so much
mixed as fried, scrambled and poached. I dearly want
Croftie and his confrères to get shot of this pesky Victorian
yet find myself willing him on with ever-increasing vigour
as the afternoon progresses. 'That's my boy' is my stock
riposte whenever anybody shouts over the score. But this is
about more than reflected glory. I have grown extremely
fond of him. Hell, there are times when my instincts are
paternal. Unlike Croftie, for whom I share an equal affection, Matthew has felt able to let his guard down. Would the
situation be reversed were he the one with the attendant
pressures of representing the home nation? Quite possibly.
And yet I wonder. Where Matthew has been strengthened
by disappointment, Croftie, I am beginning to fear, may
have been unnerved by the suddenness of his ascent.

Come early evening, turmoil. Dropped shortly before
stumps at long-leg by the luckless Smith, Matthew has
galloped on to 138, matching the sun ray for blessed ray. In
a stand already worth 208 at better than a run a minute,
Punter, whose footwork and driving through the V have
been an absolute revelation, has aided and abetted with
cocky impishness. Large and little, leftie and rightie, upper-
cut and jab. Bulls have been taken by horns, initiatives
grabbed and locked away. They haven't even allowed
Croftie a maiden. At Tower Hill Station, Matt Loup, who
helps design the sports pages, is in skittish mood: 'Who's
going to play Botham?' Even my extensive reserves of self-

180

delusion don't stretch that far.

Slump in front of the highlights and wallow. And kvetch. On a day when Tugga and Warney fail to muster a wicket or a boundary between them, the apprentices have stood up and demanded to be counted. Matthew, it goes without saying, reaches three figures dispatching something short and silly from Headley. At one juncture he even manages to draw Richie to the brink of inelegance. 'I tell you, that's a hell of a shot,' the Ice Man acclaimeth as another pluperfect pull off Headley lasers its way over the hoardings. 'Absolutely brilliant.' Then it's Gough's turn: an off drive as smooth and creamy as anything authored by Messrs Gower or Lindt. The square pull with which he puts the Cobbers ahead seems nothing if not symbolic. As the ball thwacks off the boards, Croftie casts around frantically at fine-leg, dazzled by the sun, foggiest-free.

Drive Anne crackers in bed with my incessant ramblings. Torn as I am, the abiding feeling is one of gloom. There are other factors. I've been a miseryguts ever since I returned from New York, but until now I have attributed this to a combination of jet lag, general fatigue and over-exposure to that moving yet faintly depressing new tape by Radiohead. Maybe it all began at Old Trafford, with Tugga the unbend-able? Seeing my team beaten by a genius like Warney is probably the closest I will ever get to outright masochism, but where, pray, is the compensation in being beaten by superior will? But today wasn't like that. Today was about skill, inspiration, courage, daring and optimism, everything I look for in sport, and just about all of it oozing from the wrong pores.

The unedifying truth is dawning. However many times I remind myself none of this matters, however hard I tug on my New South Wales cap and strive to maintain a veneer of neutrality, however much I convince myself that defeat is an acceptable price to pay for progress (I still can't believe that guff about three conferences), it bloody well hurts. Anne, who is no more knowingly patriotic than I, can recall only two occasions when she has experienced the frisson of caring about the result of a sporting contest: the 1990 World Cup semi-final between our boys and Germany, and the night Frank Bruno beat Oliver McCall. Which makes her parting comment somewhat alarming. '*I'm* beginning to feel depressed about this team of yours. Can't you do something?' Stuart Law, I tell her, has submitted one plausible solution. 'The only way England can win,' he recommended the other day, 'is to get the Aussies down the pub the evening before each day's play and keep them there.'

Daily Accumulator: Poms 1 Cobbers 9

26 July 'Junk food's thin link to waistlines'
(Daily Telegraph)

Euston, 09.42: British Rail is awfully sorry about this, but the 9.54 to Birmingham New St via Northampton will be running a little late – 'We're waiting for the driver.' 10.03: Another polite cough over the intercom. 'Ladies and gentlemen. Sorry for the delay, but we've been waiting for the driver. And the driver has just arrived.'

Read Matthew Engel's report on yesterday's proceedings en route to covering Northants–Surrey. The warnings of Old Trafford had come to fruition. 'This was the day the fun and laughter went out of the Ashes series, in more ways than one. As England's cricketers walked dejectedly off the field, believing the Ashes had now finally slipped from their grasp, a man was injured when he was bashed against the advertising hoardings by stewards trying to get him off the field. The injured man was apparently playing the back legs of a pantomime cow.' The back legs, I subsequently discover, belonged to one Branco Resik, who was knocked senseless and remained so for nearly two hours. A confused message was sent to the hospital before his arrival, prompting staff to prepare an operating theatre in readiness for a casualty who had been crushed by a cow. Thankfully, no permanent damage was diagnosed and Branco was soon released. The chills persist nonetheless.

Even though there is precious little action to report, actual or meaningful, the TV in the Wantage Road press box spends most of the morning in Coventry. The overriding concern is for Doug Ibbotson, long one of the wittiest and most perceptive sportswriters in the land, whose final assignment for the *Telegraph* this is. Besides, whenever I turn around, a Pom is dropping short or overpitching and Matthew and Punter are still raising hell. The latter's maiden Test century means that the top seven in the Cobbers' order have all got off the mark against the Poms. Coincidence or fact of life? Discuss.

Play is suspended for good after lunch, by which time the Cobbers lead by 201 with 5 wickets intact and Matthew on 168. Gough and co. can count their blessings they don't play football for Iraq. FIFA have dispatched investigators there in the wake of allegations that members of the national team have been beaten and tortured on the orders of Saddam Hussein after failing to reach the World Cup finals. Seldom was that ancient Latin saying more apt: *Ludus non nisi sanguineus* – it's only a bloody game.

Daily Accumulator: Poms 0 Cobbers 10

27 July 'Thieves in wheelchairs pose as disabled shoppers to rob stores'

(Sunday Telegraph)

Notes from a small man on a small island. Lousy cold, book in for day on sofa. Nod approvingly at Tony Lewis's *Sunday Telegraph* column when he urges 'the dignity of death for Headingley as a Test match ground' and compares the stand between Matthew and Punter to 'Menhuin and Oistrakh performing the Bach Double Violin Concerto in Steptoe's yard'. Warney is booed in and laughed back, a blob against his name. Cheers as Reiffel drills Smith to cover where Croftie saves at the cost of a nasty bang on the left wrist; jeers as Croftie dives at another educated biff by Reiffel, realizes he can't make it and pulls out at the death. Did he think better of risking further damage? Matthew reaches 199, cracking Gough in front of square as Croftie scampers off in vain pursuit, then falls two balls later to a snorter of a yorker and departs head down, chin adrooping. 'Wonderful innings,' enthuses Gower, 'beautiful strokes.' Tubs declares after a morning of one-sided barbarics, 128 runs and nearly as many fielding goofs; more than half the 447 scored off the bat in the innings came in boundaries. Staggering. Chappelli asks Richie how 'thrilled' he would be if his attack had conceded 500 runs on this pitch. 'Only moderately.'

Stinger calls, though not to gloat. Not his style at all. I should have seen Matthew's performance at yesterday's press conference. Cooler than an air-conditioned igloo. The key for the Poms, Gooch advises Sue Barker in the *Grandstand* studio, 'is to be positive'. Gower concurs. But how to be positive when the bowling is this straight, this disciplined, this mean? Butcher cover-drives Pigeon's second ball, cuffs a couple of stray leg-siders then succumbs to an unanswerable leg-cutter. Pop out to save Josef from decapitation by a falling chair and miss Atherton fending Pigeon to third slip; that's five times in eight innings the latter has bested him. At least Atherton can console himself in the knowledge that he shares a hutch with Lara. Hussain does his damnedest to commit hara-kiri, chancing a single off a no-ball, to the speedy Punter, but the latter's throw from cover, which would have run him out by feet, yields four overthrows. An omen? More like a tease. First Stewart jams down on Reiffel's yorker and the ball dribbles back into his stumps. Then Thorpe pokes at a screamer from Dizzy, Heals spills and Junior scoops up the rebound as if it were a rehearsed routine. The fates are beginning to snigger.

184

Then relief. Hussain hangs on with Crawley, whose place, in Gower's carefully worded estimation, is 'almost' on the line. Hussain scales three figures and puffs hard – one mile down, a marathon to go. A tache-less Gooch leads the applause from the balcony. 'Just a window open for England if these two can be there overnight,' vouchsafes Boycott as eleven balls remain. Crawley keeps Pigeon's yorkers at bay, giving the more grievously afflicted among us another night of fond imaginings. Hope is so much more fun than certainty.

Daily Accumulator: Poms 2 Cobbers 8

28 July 'Many pupils "steal to gamble" '

(Guardian)

J E Fletcher writes to the *Telegraph* to take issue with E W Swanton's contention that a two-divisional championship would 'lower the moral tone'. 'To carry Mr Swanton's point to its logical conclusion,' he reasons, 'we should play only friendly championship matches with no financial bonuses in order to ensure that players will not be tempted to be too competitive.' Well put, that man.

Those nocturnal visions – whether of monsoons, typhoons or Hussain and Crawley apeing Bailey and Watson – dissolve with the usual abruptness. Warney does for the twitchy Hussain after 35 minutes of strokeless toil, coaxing dip from his top-spinner to induce a mistimed drive, then steps aside for Pistol to dip his wick with 4 wickets in 22 balls. The agony ends with the first offering of the afternoon, Croftie wafting and caught behind. In the final over of the morning, gobs had been widely smacked by his decision to turn down a blatant single and hence keep Smith exposed to Dizzy. The less-than-delirious debutant promptly clumped a boundary, which at least gives him something tangible to take back to Bristol, but the questions linger.

In a telephone post-mortem for *Sportstalk* – a cable TV show commanding an audience of four men and a mangy moggy – I was asked the question which is apparently on every pair of lips from Land's End to John o' Groats: why are we so crap? On the contrary, I asserted, the opposition are rather useful. Last night, a sports editor of a national paper is said to have had a snipe at his cricket correspondent shortly after the latter had filed his copy. 'How many "England Days of Shame" is that now this season?' In fairness, not as many as expected. Mind you, there are still two Tests to go.

Up on the Cobbers' balcony, Warney sprayed the bubbly as Slats conducted a resounding chorus of 'Aussie, Aussie, Aussie'. Stinger and I calculated that more than half the victorious XI would be around for the next Ashes tour to these shores. Now there's a sobering thought. Manners made a sharp exit when Tubs was greeted with a smattering of boos while accepting the winners' cheque. 'Not the flattest wicket I've ever seen,' he conceded, and left it at that. 'How can you leave him out?' Gower asked him, referring to Punter. 'We just keep 'em hungry,' smirked Tubs.

Botham, in his less than infinite wisdom, plumped for Dizzy as Man of the Match ahead of a Foster's-slurping Matthew. 'Sorry guys,' the habitually reticent nominee had apologized after his maiden press conference last year, 'I'm not very good at this yet.' He must be getting the hang of it. Asked how he planned to celebrate, he paused at length then stated his intention 'to drink a few drinks in a very short space of time'.

Atherton's relationship with the popular prints has shown a sharp upturn this summer, but knives are emerging in the quest for scapegoats. This morning's tabloids had been full of a purported 'clash' yesterday lunchtime between the captain and an MCC member. Hearing the bacon-and-egg tie accuse his side of being 'garbage', Atherton is reported to have suggested, not unreasonably, that he say so to his face. What was that about not caring?

This afternoon he elaborated, insisting he had merely been 'politely enquiring about the gentleman's health'. He also denied that his team's failings stemmed from mental deficiencies yet bemoaned a match of 'missed opportunities'. Are the two not interwoven?

If any one moment can be said to have defined the force of the pendulum's swing, it was Junior's awesome effort at slip to send back Ealham. Whizzing to his right as if propelled from a .45, the edge had actually passed him before he pocketed it one-handed, the Artful Dodger filching silk hankies for Fagin. Chappelli was quick to draw needless comparisons: 'Someone was saying to me that Thorpe was as good a slip fielder as Mark Waugh. I said codswallop at the time.' Though hindsight isolated it as a turning-point – Tugga's immediate exit, it bears reiterating, seemed vastly more critical at the time – to heap all the blame for defeat on Matthew's let-off by Thorpe is tantamount to fingering the snake as the only villain in the Garden of Eden. The fact nevertheless remains that, since Edgbaston, the Poms' fingers have been as buttery as their opponents' have been coated with Araldite. Confidence and uncertainty have not so much swapped chairs as planets.

Shortly before the *Nine O'Clock News*, a journalist friend rang for some advice on a delicate matter. He said had been approached by an ex-employee of a certain cricket board who claimed to have had a bun deposited in her oven by a prominent colleague. Her story went as follows. As soon as the bounder found out about his impending responsibilities, she was left in the lurch and offered a loan of £400 by two senior officials to have an abortion and not be a silly girl. Declining, she went ahead with the abortion but suffered severe complications. Told to take her time returning to work, she recently received a letter informing her that her contract had been terminated, here was five grand and don't be a silly girl. What was my friend to do? The law, after all, offers no redress: it's her word against theirs. The only option, he has concluded, is to rope in Max Clifford and stoke up the tabloids. I wish him the best of British luck, whatever that means.

Daily Accumulator: Poms 0 Cobbers 10
Match total: Poms 7 Cobbers 43

MATTHEW ELLIOTT

That was a big night last night. Ordinarily I'm not much of a drinker but by the time I left the ground I was talking gibberish.

A win is a win, but to recover from 50 for 4 was an enormous achievement. That was probably as well as we've played all tour. The bowlers built up so much pressure, bowling so straight. Heals said some of Dizzy's deliveries in the first innings were as quick as any he'd seen. Losing Hussain just before the close on the first day may have affected their confidence, because he was in full flow, but it was a brilliant ball. Luck played its part, mind. It probably helped to bowl first because the wicket was at its worst then, and then the overcast conditions helped our bowlers swing it around on the Sunday.

One stand changed the match. If Thorpe or Atherton had caught me, who knows? I can't tell you why a game that lasts for five days can be decided by one moment but that was one, and we seem to have the habit of making them count. Look at Warney. He only took one wicket in the match, but it was one we really needed. He knew he had to break through before the second new ball. I was standing at 45 degrees to the wicket and I could see him rising to the challenge, really giving it everything, like a pace bowler. You can't buy that.

Fortunately for Punter and me, the sun came out during our stand and the wicket seemed to flatten out. 'Let's go for it,' said Punter, and so we did. Although I slowed down after giving that chance to Thorpe, I was pretty pumped when I went out. They kept bowling short, and that got me going. I felt as if I was scoring freely, in control, playing to a plan. The time hurtled by.

Building an innings is like driving a car. You move through the gears and then you head off into the country, brain in neutral, almost on auto-pilot. There are no thoughts at all. All you see is the bowling. When you get to this level you have be in neutral because your body is programmed. In between balls I get away from the wicket, remember a snatch of music, look at the crowd, distract myself. It's all about switching on and switching off. And that way you don't get involved with any of the chit-chat among the fielders. You block out everything, build a cocoon.

I was a bit nervy on 199. I'd padded up to Tim May's arm ball within 1 of my maiden Shield hundred, been run out for 98 off the bowler's hand on another occasion, and made 99 against New South Wales. Gough bowled me a pretty good ball, although I could have played it straighter. I was looking to turn it to leg; one moment I saw it full, the next thing it had knocked my off stump past Stewart. The crowd gave me a great reception but I didn't look up enough when I walked off. Even though it was a more satisfying innings than the one at Lord's, I was disappointed with myself. Mind you, I was pretty chuffed when I sat back at the end of the game. I felt as if I'd put a lot in and got a lot out.

I like Punter and I really enjoyed batting with him. It was great to see him hitting the ball so well, making amends for his own disappointment. He felt he got a bad decision in Perth when he made 96 on his Test debut and although he's not an animated guy you saw the emotion when he reached his century. I found myself standing there and admiring his shots. There were a couple of beautiful on drives that whizzed just past me. It may not be as flashy a shot as the cover drive but it's the sign of a very fine player.

Their bowlers looked a bit worn, didn't have quite the same zip. Croftie's struggles with the bat must impact on his bowling, although I can't help but feel he's paying the price for Warney's success in '93. The wickets have been designed to blunt him but they've probably done more to blunt Croftie. I felt a little bit for him when he came in to bat. The boys were coming in for the kill and they'd spotted a weakness. Test cricket could hardly be more aptly named.

ROBERT CROFT

As you might imagine, it was pretty quiet in the dressing room when the game was over, quieter than at Old Trafford. After losing two matches on the trot, it's only human, for all the selectors' assurances about us as having been recognized as the best players, to worry whether you're going to be around for the next game. I felt low because I might lose my place because of my batting. I have no worries about the bowling.

You sometimes get the impression that the public expect us to lose, but to lose the way we did was disappointing. There were two key moments: when Nasser went at the end of the first day and when Thorpie dropped Matthew. Australia seem to have come up trumps whenever those crunch moments have come but I don't put that down to any more than their being accustomed to winning. It becomes a habit, and in a 50–50 situation you've been there before so you know how to tackle it. I'd compare it to Glamorgan never having won a one-day final, although I hope we'll put that right this year: you're just not sure how to win. Nobody in this dressing room knows what it feels like to win the Ashes.

Some people suggested I left Smith to face Gillespie at the end of the second innings because I was scared. The fact was, I couldn't see the ball because Gillespie had followed through and Ponting had moved. He normally fields on the line at point because he backs himself to attack the ball quickly, so I thought the shot had gone straight to him. The press and the media are bound to have a go. I'm convinced they build you up to knock you down. Yes, they say and write good things, but I honestly feel they may enjoy writing the bad.

I'm disappointed with the way I batted and all I want to

do is prove everybody wrong. It has dented my confidence, especially when people say I'm not playing with the same smile on my face. But I can divorce the two: I'm still a bowler first, and I didn't think I bowled too badly. Perhaps I am paying for Warne's success in '93. I struggled to get into a rhythm, which may have had something to do with that ten-day break. Spinners don't need time off to the same extent as fast bowlers.

Matty played brilliantly but I actually enjoyed bowling to him; I like bowling to left-handers and I like the challenge of trying to outwit a superb batsman. Unfortunately, after getting the better of him at Edgbaston, I didn't bowl much to him at Lord's or Old Trafford, and even in this match I only had short darts at him: two overs here, two overs there. What I did notice was that their batsmen approach spinners differently to ours. If you make the slightest error – bang – they're after you. Ponting especially. That hundred of his was one of the best innings I've seen.

No, I didn't take a wicket, but if I had I would have finished with the same figures as Warne. You have to find a sense of perspective.

29 July 'Mike Batt scores for Germany'

(*Daily Telegraph*)

Quite what Uncle Bulgaria would say, I shudder to think. Mike Batt, the songwriter behind The Wombles, those cuddly be-snouted citizens of Wimbledon Common conceived during the seventies to declare war on the litterbugs, has been commissioned to write a World Cup anthem for Germany's national football team. It's not as if they need any help. 'The idea felt uncomfortable for about five minutes,' he admitted, 'but goals win matches, not anthems.'

This is Stinger's last day before returning to New South Wales via Bombay. I'm going to miss him hugely. It's been like having an older brother around the place. I know he regards me as a philistine for preferring Bowie and Coppola to Mahler and Joyce; I've had a go at him for being a cultural snob. Yet above and beyond all our differences, inevitably exacerbated as they have been by virtually six weeks of constant companionship, lies a commonality of outlook and an undying passion for the five-day theatre, more than enough to sustain any friendship.

Anne, he and the kids visit Karl Marx's grave – I'm barred for being in possession of a cigarette and a cocker spaniel – after which we repair to a café to discuss what Stinger loves and loathes about this green if not always pleasant land. The soft spots: the sense of history, of humour and irony; London; the culture (literature especially); the pubs; the stone houses around Wetherby; the Hampshire countryside. The peeves (discounting the weather, naturally): pessimism, privilege, elitism, lethargy, the weight of the past and – his biggest bugbear – the sullen waiters. Their counterparts Down Under seldom receive tips, he reasons, but their wages are higher; being employed in the service industries is not deemed a passport to second-class citizenry. When he gets home he intends to join the Republican Party, whose founder members, he points out, include one I M Chappell.

There again, our nations still have some things in common besides a mutual adoration of cricket and horses. The Royal Commission investigating corruption in Sydney has provoked several suicides among top-ranking officers. In Yorkshire, meanwhile, officers attempting to nail a black suspect are reported to have assembled an identity parade by bootpolishing a few of the faces in the line-up. Trouble was, they omitted to do likewise to the owners' hands. Ah, the universality of improbity and incompetence.

31 July 'Boy drowns unnoticed in crowded swimming pool'
(*Daily Telegraph*)

Today I became a Teletubbie. 'Jojo's Po, Mummy's Dipsy, I'm La La coz she's yellow, and you're Tinky Winky,' announced Laura, who for some unfathomable reason espies a likeness between her sleek and svelte father and the tubbiest Tubbie. Ludicrous as it may seem, these cheery television creatures, cult heroes to everyone from environmentalists to England cricketers, have provoked no end of impassioned outcries. Some decry the dearth of educational content; others that these alien beings converse in interstellar gobbledegook rather than the Queen's English ('Aha', Laura advises me, means goodbye); others that the actor who plays Tinky Winky has just been sacked, allegedly for carnal indiscretions. How can they be so curmudgeonly about a children's show whose stars 'love to love each other very much'?

Matthew Engel really must have an exceedingly good mole. On Monday, the *Guardian* ran a story claiming that Lord Tesco's plans do indeed encompass a three-conference championship. Its intricacies, apparently, will see even more flabbers gasted. Each division will comprise six counties, who will play each member of the other divisions twice, but not their direct rivals. Final places, moreover, will be decided by a series of round-robin playoffs between the first-placed teams, the second, and so on, down to sixth. In order to finish sixteenth, say, the bottom side in Conference A would have to beat both its table-propping counterparts. With me so far? The two-tiered concept, meanwhile, will be confined to a national one-day league, which would have the decided advantage of creating more space for night games, thus enabling the counties to be more self-reliant. The drawback, however, is that this would mean an increase in limited-overs fixtures when what is required is precisely the opposite. Compromise gone mad, or what? Even now, I cannot accept that the intellectual might of the ECB management board could devise such arrant nonsense. Or is it a Machiavellian ruse?

With official publication of the blueprint nearly a week away, the *Sunday Times* ask me to solicit some views. Discretion and conjecture reign:

Paul Sheldon (chief executive, Surrey): 'The principle of fusing the one-day competitions would be sensible and appropriate but where it all has to start is in bringing the best cricketers through at the top level, which therefore means concentrating on the championship and making it as competitive as possible. Without two divisions, without promotion or relegation, it is very difficult to see how we are going to give it that edge.'

Matthew Fleming (chairman, Professional Cricketers' Association): 'Seventy-five per cent of respondents to a PCA poll voted for two divisions with promotion and relegation: it was a reaction born out of frustration. We're fed up of being considered second rate, of being tagged as underachievers, and, more important, of not being given the best chance to prove how good we are.'

Steve Coverdale (chief executive, Northants): 'Personally, I would do very little with the structure at the top level. At our supporters' club's AGM, the overriding feeling was: please, please preserve our game. They weren't bothered about the England team. One bloke said: "Them lot at Lord's are ruining our game." Yes, we are probably too hidebound by tradition but I honestly don't think winning or losing makes that much difference when it comes to selling Test matches. The quality and attractiveness of the opposition does that.'

Sheldon's reaction throws up the possibility of a Premier League-type breakaway but must it come to that? Unfortunately, judging by Coverdale's comments, it will probably have to. Short-termism and self-interest, the twin cankers of English cricket, are alive and kicking hard. To spit or to weep, that is the question.

2 August 'Australian landslide survivor found trapped after 54 hours'

(*Guardian*)

Earwig-o, earwig-o, earwig-o. 'Football is our everything' exults the giant billboard round the corner from Taunton station, plugging Sky's coverage of the people's opiate. Another new season is already upon us. Granted, the advent of so many of the world's finest foot-fetishists to these shores has prompted a rise in skill, recharging my own waning interest, but I still feel as if my cheeks are turning chartreuse. The fact that the blessed thing will be hogging the nation's sporting consciousness until after next summer's World Cup is only part of it. Can you envisage any advertising agency worth its salt trying to persuade us that cricket was our everything?

Pick up a copy of Warney's autobiography at the Taunton bookshop and notice he has nominated Matthew – given a richly deserved match off here – as one of the openers in his World XI. Victorian bias? More like uncommonly fine judgment. Bristling after his questionable exclusion at Leeds, Caddick wrings lift and movement from a comatose pitch to whisk out the first five in the tourists' order, but the stroke-play on both sides thereafter is nourishing and satisfying, particularly that of the strident young Somerset pair, Rob Turner and Simon Ecclestone. The day, though, is blighted by another baiting for Warney. So incessant is the abuse, Tugga, captain in place of the resting Tubs, complains to the umpires and the law is summoned.

On Radio 5 Live's *6-0-6 Show*, hosted by Sir Geoffrey of Boycottshire, the verdict of the telephone participants was unanimous: Atherton Must Go. Earwig-o, earwig-o, earwig-o.

3 July 'Catholic priests seek return of priests who wed'

(*Sunday Times*)

The headline in the *Sunday Times* was nothing if not eye-catching: 'Caught out: W G Grace "bribed" Aussie player'.

Describing his subject as 'a bit of a rogue', Robert Low, the dodgy doctor's latest biographer, claims that when W G burst into the Cobbers' dressing room at Lord's in 1878 and spirited Billy Midwinter off to The Oval to play for Gloucestershire, he 'appealed more to Midwinter's wallet than his better nature'. E M Grace's great-grandson, Dr Richard Bernard, who played for Gloucestershire in the fifties, concurs with the theory: 'Grace regarded Midwinter as a fully paid professional and couldn't understand what he was doing. Midwinter was trying to get it both ways.' Jonathan Agnew urges the selectors to try a similar tactic with Junior.

The cultural exchange continues. Boddington's, Bass, Stones, Newcastle Brown and McEwan's are 'spearheading a small but growing British beer invasion Down Under', according to the *Sunday Telegraph*. Scottish & Newcastle have signed up 180 pubs across the land to serve the likes of Theakston's Old Peculier and Beamish; thanks in the main to the popularity of their eponymous ale, promoted as 'Pommy holy water', Newcastle Brown claim sales have grown 40 per cent over the past three years, even though their pints cost twice as much as a draught Tooheys or Foster's. Mind you, given that such products still account for less than 1 per cent of the market Down Under, the word 'invasion' seems a mite excessive. 'I got used to the dishwater jokes,' recalls Scottish & Newcastle's regional MD, Andrew Theakston. 'One guy said: "Sorry, I can't serve that mate. We don't have a microwave behind the bar." '

'He is a born captain,' Scyld Berry observes of Atherton, his fellow *Sunday Telegraph* columnist, adamant that he should remain in charge, 'but he is a leader of such a defensive cast that he has to have a vibrant vice-captain.' At present, with Stewart's concentration presumably diffused, at least to an extent, by concern for his ailing wife, he doesn't even appear to have that. Not that it would have made the slightest difference to the outcome at either Old Trafford or Leeds. When the Cobbers are strutting, as they assuredly are now, even a leader with the combined perspicacity of Moses, Gandhi and Attila the Hun would be hard pushed to make a difference.

On the same page, Chappelli, for once, hedges his bets. He has never been able to decide whether the spirit of his countrymen on the field is 'a by-product of isolation or maybe even our convict heritage, or a combination of those and other factors'. What he is certain of is that the ritual singing of 'Under the Southern Cross' after a Test victory symbolizes that spirit. He suspects the words were the handiwork of either one of those two fine writers, Henry Lawson or Banjo Patterson, but for him, the origins lay in an Indian restaurant in Manchester called the Khazi. It was there in the early sixties, while Chappelli was honing his craft in the local leagues, that he first heard a recitation by Raymond Patrick Hogan, a former New South Wales player, 'and he heard it, I reckon, from the South Australian John McMahon (ex-Surrey and Cambridge), who recited it to Lawson and Patterson when homesick'. Its inception as a ritual came after the first Test of the 1974–75 Ashes series. Chappelli and his confrères were in the Wally Grout lounge at the Queensland Cricketers' Club when the secretary, Lew Cooper, the man who had invited them in, offered them a case of beer if they would return to the dressing room. Grabbing the grog, the players duly adjourned and, during the ensuing frolics, Rod Marsh cleared his throat and led the chant. From then until his retirement, Marsh did the honours, and the baton has since been handed down to Border, then Boon, and now Heals. Only those with an indecent ration of balls need apply.

With victory at Trent Bridge imperative, *les très* Gs have gone for broke. Out go Ealham, Smith and Butcher (what!); in come the Hollioakes, albeit four matches late, plus Malcolm as cover for Gough, whose knee injury is a source of mounting concern. Atherton will reactivate his opening partnership with Stewart, who might well have been dropped but for the fact that his glovemanship will enable both Hollioakes to be accommodated. In which case they will become the first brothers to make their England Test debuts simultaneously since Alec and George Hearne in 1892. The only trouble is their form since the one-dayers. Or, rather, lack of it. While Major has yet to make a championship hundred, Minor's sole performance of substance has been the exhilarating 98 that won the B&H final. As with Gower, only the most dazzling spotlights seem worthy of his all. Over the coming days he will be lionized and canonized: Messiah, Big Ben, Mighty Oak, New Botham XXII, the greatest breakthrough in the history of organized entertainment since the advent of the laugh. Don't expect miracles just yet, but do believe at least a smidgin of the hype.

5 August 'Poverty is "cause of ethnic ill-health" '

(Daily Telegraph)

'Let's face it, it's bollocks!' Dominik Diamond, the no-piss-left-untaken presenter of Channel 5's late-night sports show, *Live and Dangerous,* is in one of his more equivocal moods. The first viewer to ring up with so much as a remote understanding of Lord Tesco's new-fangled, hopelessly mangled county championship, he promises, will win one of Brian Clough's gardening gloves.

To be fair, for all that the word hotchpotch is being bandied around with gay abandon, most of the other recommendations in the good lord's blueprint, *Raising the Standard,* unveiled amid much pomp and ceremony at Lord's today, seem spot-on. As a balancing act it works wonders. No stone, it would appear, has been left unturned, no nook unscoured. A two-divisional limited-overs league to replace the B&H Cup and the Sunday League; a sixty-team NatWest Trophy; leaner county staffs; a feeder competition linking clubs and counties to replace the 2nd XI championship; a national network of 'Premier' club leagues; a new variant of the game to spread the gospel in secondary schools. '[It is] the best possible plan we could put to the counties,' Lord Tesco exclaimed, alluding to the degree of compromise. 'Life is a progression and this is not the limit of our plans.' In which case, can we take it that the issue of board contracts, which are understood not to have been considered germane in this particular instance, will be saved for another, less sensitive day?

News at Ten's announcement of the proposals was accompanied by film of a pensioner nodding off at a deserted ground, typifying the view of county cricket held by the vast majority of the population: boring, anachronistic, pointless. 'Football has captured the middle classes, people are watching rugby league and basketball in the summer,' acknowledged the Right-On Tim. 'If we don't watch it we'll become a minor sport.' Some would say that status has already been achieved.

Anorak heaven in Colombo, where the end of the fourth day of an uncommonly purposeless Test against India finds one and a bit innings complete and the poor misbegotten bowlers having paid an average of 102 runs per wicket. Sayanath Jayasuriya, the belligerent balding bantamweight whose mighty smiting provided the most vivid and enduring memories of the last World Cup, adjourns with 326 to his name, having thus far added 548 with Roshan Mahanama, a new all-wicket record in Tests and 29 shy of the first-class mark. The pair have now been entrenched for two entire days. What was all that guff about pyjama parties denuding the concentration? The best master both.

Big trouble in Littlehampton. A Rolf Harris impersonator has been moved on by police after repeating the same three tunes on his didgeridoo for more than three hours. Now that really is pushing the special relationship a tad far.

6 August 'County egos get in way of progress'
(Daily Telegraph)

A gaggle of boys of assorted hues gather at the foot of the stairs leading to the Trent Bridge changing rooms, pens primed. Watched by a throng of 32,000, including their president, Sri Lanka have swept on to 952 for 6 (Jayasuriya 340), but indifference rules. As the players descend, none is safe, save Caddick. Twice he lollops past, twice he is ignored. As a cucumber-cool Hollioake Minor obliges them with an elegant flourish, I ask a couple of Asian lads why the lack of attention for Caddick. Shoulders are shrugged in unison. 'Do me a favour,' I say, 'ask him to sign when he comes down again. He'd like it, trust me.' I'm bullshitting, of course. Never met the man. For all I know, he couldn't give a stuff, but I doubt it. He still comes across as someone in urgent need of a hug. Half an hour later he returns and those nice boys do me that favour. Caddick's face lights up dimly, almost shyly. Their mothers should be proud.

'We should bloody give 'em the Ashes,' exclaims my cabbie. 'They haven't really battled, have they?' I beg to disagree but my efforts to stress the quality of the opposition prove futile. In the foyer of the Poms' hotel, Caddick is engaged in conversation with a middle-aged couple whom I take to be his parents. Rather than being relaxed, he seems overtly self-aware. The receptionist informs me that Atherton brought in a freshly snaffled trout yesterday evening and requested it be cooked for his supper. What was that about absolutely useless, Croftie? Hussain natters in the bar with Gooch. He looks drawn and weary, and admits as much.

ROBERT CROFT
People keep calling for more time off but that doesn't really work for me. I had no bowling rhythm at all for a couple of days when we were in the nets at Headingley but I've just bowled fifty-odd overs at Colwyn Bay and taken six wickets: I feel a million dollars again. What will be, will be, but I'm going into this match feeling really confident with the ball.

I've been working on my batting with Goochie but we've kept that out of the press. The way they cut you to pieces can stir the public up. That's why you get the odd letter from people, saying you're crap or whatever. Mind you, I've also had a lot of nice letters. 'We know you play with spirit, Croftie, keep your head up,' that sort of thing, which is very gratifying. Last week, however, I read an article that had a go at me for having my feet under the table, for lacking enthusiasm. That's what I take exception to. What made it worse was that it was written by a fellow Welshman, Tony Lewis. I rang him up and conveyed my feelings. He didn't apologize. He said he wanted me to do well. I suggested this was a funny way of showing it and that he should know I never give anything less than everything I can.

I won't deny it. I have been a bit down lately. I've been on the back foot for the last two Tests and it does get to you. You get home and it hurts for a few days. You're bound to be a bit snappy, so Marie gets it in the neck at times, my parents, too. Marie's a brilliant wife, incredibly patient. There's also a friend I go fishing with who is a great help. He's a local umpire, so he doesn't know everything about the game, which means I can say my piece and he won't come back at me. I need to get it out and he understands that. But then you pick yourself up and you want another crack. I'm ready.

Perhaps some of the buzz has gone out of the dressing room, but you expect that when you're losing. Having said that, I still believe we can win here and at The Oval. You have to, don't you? Drawing the series is no good to us. We want to win back the Ashes. We have to tie down their batsmen, not give them so many four-balls, put the attacking option out of their heads, but by the same token we must be prepared to be dried up when we're batting, even during a big stand; we mustn't give them any cheap wickets.

Going to the Eisteddfodd and being presented with that green robe by the Archdruid was the ultimate honour. I've done my bit to help put Wales on the map, and heaven knows we need to sell ourselves. This will be my tenth cap. I'm still pinching myself.

MATTHEW ELLIOTT

From what I can see, Lord MacLaurin wants to give the England players more space between games, reduce their workload. I can see how persuading the counties to make sweeping reforms might be tricky because of all the tradition, which is why board contracts would make more sense. If all goes well I'll sign one in October, so the ACB will be paying my wages and having the final say in what I do. And then it'll be a case of, 'How high do you want me to jump, sir?'

I'm very lucky to be playing alongside some of the best cricketers Australia has ever seen. What drives them is good competition. That's what makes us better. The Sheffield Shield is the best breeding ground for Test cricket. It fuels competitive instincts because there's something riding on every game. Side bets are already being laid on the games between the Vics and New South Wales. There's already some niggles between the players. I've told Tugga I can't wait to bowl at him.

I can always tell when the guys are ready for a Test, because there's invariably a bit of a niggle during the final net session. Someone started mucking around with a yellow ball on the outfield and it went into the net where Alfie was batting. He wasn't happy at all. He must be frustrated to buggery but that wasn't like him. To me it's a good sign. It was the same before the first Test in South Africa. Hayden smacked this net bowler miles out of the net and told him not to bother coming back. It's a sign that we're not blasé.

I'm surprized to see Butcher dropped. He hits the ball well and has improved with every match. I would have picked the Hollioakes from the start, although I do think Ealham is a very good cricketer who gives it everything. I'll miss the challenge but I'm pleased Gough isn't playing, although I don't know why he's been bowling so much between Tests. Pigeon and Dizzy have been rested at every opportunity. I suppose it shows how committed he is to

Yorkshire, but should he really be in that predicament? Still, I'll sleep a bit easier now.

7 August 'Soccer's going bust'

(Daily Mirror)

Before play begins, the band strikes up the theme to *Mission: Impossible.* That's the spirit, lads. The sun? Hat firmly on. The heat? Sultrier than Marlene Dietrich in *Touch of Evil.* The pitch? Creamy and beckoning. The toss? Another Atherton cock-up. So much for ditching his favourite 50p in favour of that Isle of Man coin presented to him by the Lancashire chairman, Bob Bennett. 'They'll probably still be batting on Saturday,' forecasts my good friend Michael Henderson as the news filters through to the press box. Over breakfast at the Holiday Inn, I'd discovered that the *Daily Mail* had asked its admirable correspondent, Peter Johnson, to go for Atherton's jugular after the Headingley Test, informing him that the paper had received 'hundreds' of letters demanding his head. Johnson said he didn't believe a word of it and declined. Whoever said journalists didn't have principles?

Proudly knotting my Devon Malcolm benefit tie, I take a pew at the back of the press box, whose angle to the pitch makes it next to impossible to have any idea whatsoever of what is going off out there without constant reference to the TV monitors. Given that every seat outside is occupied, I might just as well have stayed at the hotel. Still, at least this gives me a chance to renew acquaintances with John Ward, Zimbabwe's leading cricket writer, whom I'd met during the 1989–90 England A tour. His propensity for sly witticisms remains firmly intact. 'I make it only four English-born players in your team,' he said. 'Is this part of the new ECB regulations?' I try to resist the urge to remind him of the racial mix of his own national team, but fail miserably. Qamar Ahmed tells me that that notable Karachi streetfighter, Javed Miandad, just turned 40, now bats for the same team as Viv Richards, taking the Sultan of Brunei's house guests on golfing trips. His response to Lord Tesco's masterplan, according to Qamar, had been characteristically succinct: 'Put me in charge and I'll make them a decent team.'

The crowd are courteous to a fault and wholly restrained, awaiting reasons to be cheerful. Precious few are forthcoming. Matthew, on 5, plays Headley firmly into the turf and looks back askance as the ball bounces fractionally clear of the stumps. Tubs reaches double figures for the first time since Edgbaston then almost plays on to Hollioake Minor's first ball. On the ground where Botham made his Test bow and promptly lured a disdainful Greg Chappell into dragging on a long-hop, it was almost too eerie. Unstirred, Tubs collects 3 with a straight drive. Uh-oh. The other night, while watching a video of his century against South Africa at Melbourne in the last week of 1993, I'd been struck by the frequency with which he struck his drives through the narrowest of Vs. Are we witnessing the Third Coming of the batsman *Wisden* once rather unfairly referred to as 'anonymously effective'?

Surviving a strenuous and concerted shout for leg-before from Headley, Tubs overtakes Matthew, 29 to 28, with a clip through midwicket that sends Malcolm tippy-toeing off on the first of two forlorn chases in breathless succession. 'Watch out Sri Lanka,' warns Ray Phillips. Hollioake Minor retires nursing figures of 0 for 23 from three inconspicuous overs whereupon Croftie comes on and delivers a brace of maidens. Having propelled Caddick past a sprawling mid-off to become the first tourist to tot up 1,000 runs, Matthew swivels to pull Malcolm with the utmost disrespect. The Cobbers are 84 without loss at lunch, the urn as good as gone.

While reading an article in the *Sun* about the Hollioakes on the train, I learn that Minor was expelled from nursery school in Hong Kong for trying to stick his female classmates' feet to the floor so he could peer up their skirts. Six months later, he was diagnosed as hyperactive. At 2.30 I tune in to Radio 1 FM for the news. Sally Gunnell has retired; near Redruth, the country's last tin mine is set to close with the loss of 270 jobs; the recent floods in the west, so the experts say, will have little or no impact on reservoir levels. Not a sausage about the Test. Upon my arrival home I barely issue so much as a 'hello', have a rant about my CDs being de-alphabetized and switch on the TV: 203 for 2 and Junior is flipping Headley off his hips with the air of a man with infinitely better things to do with his time. Headley's cry of dismay is close to a screech: a fine over ruined by a distinctly un-fine final ball. How often has that happened lately? The difference between the sides' concentration levels is beginning to resemble the Persian Gulf.

Replays join the dots: Headley had Matthew caught off a gossamer-thin inside edge for 6; having reaped his 6,000th Test run, Tubs had surrendered his off stump to Caddick for 76. Hollioake Minor obtains a fortunate first scalp when Blewie aims to run a short one to third man only for Stewart to bring off a superlative catch, yards to his right; but the traffic thereafter is strictly one-way. Not that there is anything philanthropic about the bowling. Indeed, when the Hollioakes join forces, their tussle with the Waughs is quite gripping. Making both batsmen fret with deceptive movement and variations in pace, Major almost traps Junior with a booming inswinger; Junior pushes the next ball behind square for four whereupon Tugga scythes Minor square; not a muscle twitches before ball thuds off boards. Junior all but plays on to Major, and Stewart howls; the ball had rebounded off the batsman's back foot and sped away before the keeper could react. With that I head for the computer, still tetchy.

Write a feature on Karen Smithies and her new-look England women's team (Vodafone's backing means they no longer have to supply their own kit) then pick up the rest of play on Sky. The highlights package is sponsored by the Australian Tourist Commission, who are certainly getting their money's worth. When the teams go off – at 301 for 3 – the applause is brief, grudging, almost indifferent. Repeated freeze-frames of Tubs's leg-before escape suggest umpire Mitchley was in a minority of one. Good thing he isn't umpiring in Japan. After calling a strike against the home-town favourite, Mike di Muro, the first American to officiate in the Japanese baseball league, was showered with detritus from a dustbin. Only the intervention of a player saved him from a beating, whereupon he was advised with all due deli-cacy to return from whence he came.

Daily Accumulator: Poms 2 Cobbers 8

8 August '1m drivers are blind'

(Sun)

Well, wang my doodle and bugger my begonias! Three competitive sessions in a row. Nip and tuck, tooth and nail, style and strength, spin and speed: the competitive arts at their zenith. The most riveting day's play since that long-gone Sunday at Edgbaston. Just my luck to be cloistered at Wapping, even if the air-conditioning in our new offices does spare my hayfever from the hottest day of the year.

Headley and Malcolm cock snooks at the faithless, polish-ing off the Cobbers for 427 shortly after lunch, whereupon Stewart goes aroistering in consort with Atherton, the openers raising 100 at 4 an over. Gooch had been in the nets with Atherton earlier in the week, pinging bouncers at him from halfway down the track. Does this explain the captain's apparent ease against Pigeon? For all the fears about him going in first after the best part of nine hours' crouching and leaping – he admits he is only doing so because of the one-off nature of the occasion – Stewart wields his wand dismissively, thrillingly. The shots of a heart unburdened? On Wednesday I'd asked him how his wife was. 'Fine,' he replied. Over the worst, though the epilepsy remains. When Pigeon returns, Mr Adrenalin swishes him noiselessly through the covers. Graham Otway rings up from the ground to check if there are any queries about his feature. I ask him if he's enjoying Stewart's innings. Not really: 'Flawed selection. Should never be playing.'

A few minutes later, Stewart goes to deposit Warney into the Trent, Heals drops the edge, twists, dives back and somehow intercepts the dying quail at full stretch. Not a bad way to get your 300th catch for your country. Hussain labours painfully before Warney squares him up and clips off with a leg-break for the gods; Crawley is caught behind fending Pigeon's armpit ball down the leg-side as Heals perfects his Olga Korbut impression, whereupon the Beeb have the good grace to take us to Athens for the world athletics championships, returning just in time to see Thorpe and Hollioake Major see out the day with a blend of wariness and panache. Leave the office in an advanced state of mild euphoria and watch the highlights to relive the best bits. Richie reckons this is the finest pitch of the series, and so it is. Confounding expectations of a batting pleasure-dome, the new groundsman, Steve Birks, has produced a surface with something for everyone. 'They've got the chance – if they're good enough,' warrants Chappelli, a sceptical twinkle in his eye. Mission: Impossible is now merely Mission: Improbable.

Svetlana has e-mailed from St Petersburg, offering to put me in touch with 'lovely marriage-minded ladies'. After the way I've been behaving lately, Anne probably wouldn't object.

Daily Accumulator: Poms 5 Cobbers 5

9 August 'Investors' cash goes missing in cyberspace'
(Guardian)

It all started so promisingly. Dropped at gully off Pigeon, by Tugga of all people, Thorpe, who is said to be enduring marital problems, plays his most authentic hand since Edgbaston, extending his stand with the impressive

Hollioake Major to 102. Then both exit in successive overs – Thorpe nicking Warney to short-leg, his partner slicing Reiffel's outswinger to Tubs – whereupon normal service is pretty much resumed.

A police siren wails as Hollioake Minor enters, but the scoring rate slows to a shuffle. Taking a step to the off, Croftie sees off Pigeon's initial blast then thumps Warney straight for six, but Pigeon has him in the end as another rib-tickler is plopped almost apologetically to short-leg. By the time I get to the office, Hollioake Minor, having shown his lordly mettle with 13 off a Reiffel over, has just snicked a back-foot biff to slip. Caddick goes without addition and Malcolm clops down the pavilion steps to a roof-raising chorus of approval. 'You'd think it was George Headley or Garfield Sobers,' snorts Tony Lewis, 'but it's only a mortal.' Cue mass rejoicing as the People's Choice wallops Pigeon for three boundaries. The end, almost inevitably, is pure slapstick. Pigeon lobs one out of the back of his hand; the People's Choice, presumably expecting a grenade, jumps out of the way; unopposed, the ball floats under his feet and rattles timber. For the first time since Edgbaston, the Poms have scaled 300; they'll have to make at least that many again to win. BBC Scotland have already made their views clear, opting to replace transmission with coverage of the women's golf.

Yet still the teasing continues. Emboldened by a lead of 114, Tubs and Matthew set off at a rapid lick. Matthew outscores his partner 3–1, the 50 arriving inside 15 overs, then hooks at Caddick for Crawley to take a stunning sprawling catch at deep backward square. Win some, lose some. Tubs follows suit at 105, mishooking Caddick. Croftie performs his customary holding operation, commanding respect but never fear. Fluid and precise in drive and glance, Blewie compensates handsomely for Junior's premature ejection only to glove Caddick just before stumps. Though pushed and harried all the way by the seamers, notably Caddick and Headley, the Cobbers finish 281 to the good with 6 wickets in hand, the urn at the end of their fingertips. Another 50 and the Poms will have to match their record winning fourth-innings total in these matches, 332 in 1928–29. Yet still that little voice whispers. Get Tugga first thing and who knows? I try telling the voice to shut up but fail lamentably.

Daily Accumulator: Poms 3 Cobbers 7

10 August 'US doctors "play" God to breed designer daughters'

(Sunday Times)

I don't want to talk about it. I really don't want to talk about it. Want a definitive account of how the Cobbers retained the urn? Forget it. Tugga did go first thing but what ensued defies dispassionate analysis from a Pom, so let's get this over with as swiftly and painlessly as possible before I say something my lawyer will regret. Perhaps I should examine it from a different perspective? How about this: Punters and Heals speed the lead past 400 in a heroic counter-attack, Atherton and Stewart cling on until the last over before tea, whereupon ten men go down in less than three hours, pounded and mesmerized by pace and spin of the highest calibre. While Pigeon and Warney reaffirm their credentials for the pantheon, the hammer blows come courtesy of Dizzy, ripping out the middle-order with 3 for 65 from 8 overs of unstinting attack. There, that feels much better.

When Malcolm's edge off Pigeon hurtled to Junior at second slip, completing the formalities, Tubs, Warney and Junior embraced. The entire team (plus gatecrashing back-packer) then congregated in a huddle. During the ceremonies Matthew looked pensive. Was he thinking about his knees, about how it could all end tomorrow? Warney hugged Tugga then let rip: boogieing on the balcony, stump in hand, spraying the bubbly, communing with the back-packers, letting it all hang out. A summer's worth of restraint released. The late Leonard Sachs, verbose MC of *The Good Old Days*, might well have described it as a jocular jamboree of jubilant gyrations. I found it rather refreshing.

In the *Sunday Telegraph*, Chappelli contends that these tourists are almost on a par with Bradman's '48ers. High praise, but not undue. 'We've got some class players and it's very hard to keep them down for long,' said Tubs. 'I was never going to say it but tonight I will: I think we are the world's best side.' Cue exuberant cries of 'Aussie, Aussie, Aussie'. 'They're undoubtedly a better side than we are,' conceded Atherton, eyes glazing over. Was it any consolation, asked Gower, to be aware of how good the opposition are? 'Maybe,' came the careful reply. 'It would be disastrous to ignore the players we've played against.' What could be done to improve things? Atherton smiled softly. 'To get ahead in the game would be nice.'

Call Stinger to wish him mazeltov. He'd fallen asleep on the couch. When the ringing awoke him, he was certain I was the hospital. His father has emphysema and may not last the night.

Daily Accumulator: Poms 0 Cobbers 10
Match total: Poms 10 Cobbers 30

MATTHEW ELLIOTT

The way everyone came together at the end in that huddle summed up everything. It wasn't planned. We were all feeling the same things and I suppose we all gravitated together. We achieved what we came here for. Five series in a row. The feeling was indescribable.

Having all the girls there made it complete. Families are really important at times like this. Tubs's two little kids came into the dressing room; he sat one of them, Jack, on a chair and he had the baggy green on – it was one of those special moments. Warney had his release on the balcony, which he was fully entitled to. Then you see Tugga and his wife still at the bar at 3 a.m., really savouring it. That's what it's all

about, that's what we've been working for. Beating South
Africa was special, but it can't compare to this. By the time I
got back to the hotel it was about ten o'clock and I stumbled
into the bar in my spikes and whites and hat. I was gone.
Somebody asked me if I wanted a drink and I replied, 'I'll
have an Ashes, thanks.' Then I went upstairs to get changed
and never made it back down again. I was sick all night.

It can't have hurt sitting on the coach going to the ground
on the Sunday morning, watching a video about Australian
cricket. It started with Bradman playing that famous shot
into the covers, showed some of the most memorable players and moments, then concentrated on the last couple of
years, on what this side has achieved. The music they used
was a big hit back home – by a band called Hunters and
Collectors – called 'Holy Grail'. The words were so perfect.
It was wonderful. We were all cheering.

When we came out after tea that afternoon, Tugga said to
me he reckoned that if we could get another wicket within
the next two overs, the match would be all over tonight. He
was that confident. It was a deceptive wicket. You'd be
jogging along, feeling pretty comfortable, then one would
leap or shoot, so I won't say England should have done
better. I know I never felt settled in either innings. The highest score ever made to win a Test at Nottingham is 208, and
once you're chasing 450 and you lose a couple of wickets
there may be a tendency to lose heart. We encouraged them
to play shots by setting attacking fields, and it's hard to
resist when you see all those open spaces, especially when
you're up against it.

Atherton and some of his colleagues came into the dressing room to congratulate us. Stewart's a good guy. On the
first day he gave me a bit of a ribbing after I'd edged the ball
over the top of the stumps. 'Have you been fucking nuns?'
he asked me. Later in the match I wrote him a note: 'Stewie:
do you want the address of that nun's convent?' When he
came into the room he shook me by the hand and said how
much he enjoyed the note. I felt a bit uncomfortable about

211

sending it, mind. We're there to take them down and I know eyebrows would have been raised among the other guys if they'd known.

I also had a chat with Headley, who strikes me as having real drive. Up to this season, you get the impression he's been saying to himself, 'I bloody deserve to be picked, but I'm not going to go away; I'm going to keep taking wickets until they can't not pick me.' We have something in common.

We were rather taken aback when Adam Hollioake did a TV interview just as we were taking the field at the start of England's second innings. Two of your blokes are walking out to bat and you're talking to the camera! If any of us tried that our life wouldn't be worth living. Not that anyone would ever dare. We'd be thinking, 'let's get up there and support each other'. Hollioake batted beautifully in the first innings but he also broke an unwritten rule, making a lot of gung-ho claims before the game. It wound our guys up. And I don't believe it had anything to do with him being Australian. Nobody could understand how he could sound off like that before his first Test. I suppose you have to earn the right.

It did surprise me to see so few English players on the balcony during the presentations. Atherton was there but not many others. I realize they must have been disappointed but so were we at Edgbaston and we were all there. For one thing, it's the right thing to do; for another, you're all in it together. You win together, you lose together.

ROBERT CROFT

That was the worst day of my career. To hear all those celebrations going on below and you're sitting there with a towel round you, feeling as if you could slide through the floorboards.

We let ourselves down. There was a great deal of anger at the end, frustration mostly. All the high emotions at the start of the series then the gradual slide. When they declared I went into my own little world and I wasn't involved in whatever the coach said to the batsmen. 'Let's bat out tonight,' I thought. See where we can get without losing wickets. But a draw was no good to us. Athers got a good ball, and there were a couple of drag-ons. I played a terrible shot.

I really felt for Athers. He's under immense pressure, and goodness gracious me, the stick he gets. It's not as if he earns as much as the soccer players: they earn more in a week than Test players earn in a year. But at the end of the game he had to go down and face the press, feeling the way he did, and answer every question diplomatically. The strain has not shown at all as far as the players are concerned. I have the utmost respect for him.

Marie was with me and we went back to the hotel for a few drinks with some of the other boys and their wives. It was all rather subdued. In some respects it probably isn't a bad thing having to drive off to Chelmsford today because the NatWest semi-final will stop me dwelling on the disappointment. All the same, the best thing for me now would probably be to have a game of rugby, get rid of those frustrations.

ACT 4

12 August 'Mother killed as driver, 86, dies at wheel'
(Daily Telegraph)

One of Croftie's fastest friends on the county circuit is Mark 'Ramble' Ilott, the chirpy Essex left-arm seamer renowned for his enthusiastic nattering. During the England A tour to the Caribbean in 1992–93 they staged nightly crooning duets for the delectation of hotel guests and colleagues alike. For the latter stages of today's NatWest semi-final at Chelmsford, their wives sat side by side. Most of those watching at home or in the flesh would have been blissfully unaware of all this, but their initial incredulity at the events that unfolded would have been no less marked.

With the game bubbling to a crescendo and Waqar Younis's thunderbolts proving increasingly difficult to pick up amid the gloaming, Ilott appealed against the light, whereupon Croftie intervened. In a trice, the pair were prodding each other in the chest. Given the strain Croftie has been under, some sort of release was inevitable, but this? In the heat of the moment, it was easy to overreact. 'As ugly a scene as I would wish to witness,' intoned an outraged Tony Lewis to BBC viewers. 'Quite unacceptable.'

Tempers had been simmering ever since the light began to fade (another good reason for floodlights). Stuart Law, whose sumptuous thumps had taken Essex to the brink of the Lord's final, had reacted furiously to an accidental beamer from Darren Thomas; Ronnie Irani and Thomas had

214

collided and exchanged unpleasantries. When Ilott and Croftie went chest-to-chest, Essex were 296 for 8, still 6 short. There was no hidden agenda, no festering grudge, just passions momentarily overflowing, fuelled as much by fatigue as the will to win. Ah, but would I feel as forgiving as this if I didn't have a soft spot for the protagonists? Yes, I think I would.

On Radio 4's *Today Programme* this morning, as fate would have it, Hussain had been actively encouraging such vivid demonstrations of commitment. Or seemed to be. 'We have to get a bit of nastiness into our game,' he argued, without quite defining what he meant by 'nasty'. Declaring the county circuit to be 'matey and lovey-dovey', not to mention full of Pimms drinkers, he contended that the sheer quantity of cricket played by English professionals mitigates against maintaining the requisite fire. 'We have several individuals who played brilliantly but the difference between the sides was definitely that Australia are harder than us.' So Junior was right all along! All the same, hard is assuredly not the same as nasty. What will this do for Hussain's captaincy aspirations? It was certainly a poor choice of words, an irresponsible choice. There again, the interviewer did call him before 8 a.m.

Although they must know full well that such considerations are no defence, Croftie and Ilott will no doubt count themselves unlucky to have been caught by the all-seeing zoom lens. After all, when Imran Khan and Mike Brearley had an argy-bargy at Lord's in the early eighties, the witnesses were in the hundreds rather than millions, and neither was punished. There weren't that many more on hand when Steve James thrust a gloved fist under John Stephenson's chin during Glamorgan's second-round NatWest tie at Southampton last month (the incident was only seen by BBC Wales viewers). On that occasion, the Hampshire captain had refused to recall Adrian Shaw even though Shaun Udal had admitted not having executed a run-out strictly by the book, hence the mild-mannered opener's atypical retort. Again, no recriminations. Today's perpetrators will not escape so lightly.

ROBERT CROFT
Mark and I are the best of friends. Twenty minutes earlier, our wives had arranged to go out for a meal. After it all blew up, they were hugging! It was terribly embarrassing for them. When we went off the field Mark and I bumped into each other going to the toilet. We stuck our hands out. 'God,' we said, 'what was that all about?'

The light had been offered to the batsmen before Mark came in, but they'd turned it down. Unfortunately, they omitted to tell Mark this, so when he appealed, I made the point that the light seemed to be perfectly acceptable before Essex started losing wickets, so why not now? It was six of one, half a dozen of the other. We both reacted to the tension of the moment. It had been a long day, twelve hours in sticky heat, and suddenly there was some light for us at the end of the tunnel.

I'm not condoning what we did, but everybody does something they regret at some stage of their lives. For me it was probably the build-up of frustration over the past couple of months, being on the back foot. Things haven't quite gone my way. Ideally, we wouldn't have to play such an important game immediately after a Test, but I'm not seeking excuses. Maybe I would have been better off playing rugby after Trent Bridge? Mind you, I do think it has been blown out of proportion. It was announced after the third bong on *News at Ten*; if I'm not mistaken, it took precedence over a famine.

14 August 'United Ireland "still the top item on Sinn Fein's agenda" '

(Irish Independent)

George Bernard Shaw was holidaying on an island in the Adriatic with Richard Strauss, the noted symphonic poet, and Gene Tunney, the world heavyweight boxing champion, when he discovered the true nature of stardom. 'When all three of us walked together all eyes turned our way,' recalled G B S, 'but when Strauss and I walked alone, nobody took any notice.' Had he wandered into Eglinton Cricket Club today, he would have been similarly humbled.

Warney's Trent Bridge twist did not go down at all well back home. One blast of invective bordered on the histrionic. 'His actions were those of a 5-year-old boasting at marbles,' raged Patrick Smith in the *Melbourne Age*. 'His provocative and immature actions have sullied a fine victory ... It was exhibitionism. It was arrogant. It was unbecoming of an Australian cricketer. With victory comes dignity. With Warne comes a lack of class.' In grade cricket, so Matthew tells me, Smith was notorious for his lack of propriety, so these holier-than-thouisms do seem a trifle rich. Anyway, so far as the citizens of Derry are concerned, Warney's farts probably smell of Chanel. He may be sitting the match out but his presence is all that matters. 'Shane Warne's here, so he is,' exclaims a copperheaded lass in a white T-shirt, fidgeting excitedly. Slumped in a neighbouring deckchair beside the sightscreen at the far end of the ground, a pink-cheeked chap of middlish age and well-fed mien turns to her with a look of untrammelled superiority. 'Saw him last night,' he boasts. 'At the hotel.' A blow-by-blow account ensues. Miss Copperhead turns lime.

Just as Decker Curry, whose audacious blows inspired Ireland's stirring triumph over Middlesex in May, set about trying to do unto Glenn McGrath what he had done unto Angus Fraser, just when the Limavady Lasher needed every available lung in his corner, the PA announcer shows a distinctly unpatriotic sense of timing. 'Shane Warne,' he proclaims, 'has kindly agreed to sign autographs in the car park.' In a trice, the number of bottoms on benches is halved.

Barring the birth of his daughter, and the Friday of the Old Trafford Test when he effectively dashed all hopes of the

Ashes coming home, today was arguably the most enjoyable day of Warney's summer. No boos, no aspersions about his sexual predilections, no cries of 'Fat Boy'. Just a semicircular queue of beaming youths, boyish fathers and blushing mothers. Matthew had a theory: 'I reckon these people were quite pleased we won the Ashes.'

And how. For the Cobbers, the jaunt to Derry, shelved after Edgbaston, was a reward, awarded after Headingley (which implies a certain confidence that the rubber would be dead by The Oval). The replacements for Dizzy (injured back) and Pistol (pregnant wife), Shane Lee and Shaun Young, all-rounders more renowned with bat than seam, are to be recruited from the Lancashire Leagues and Gloucestershire respectively, but official business stops there. A round at Royal Portrush, a tipple or three at the Bushmill's distillery and now a spot of what these chappies do better than anyone else in the known universe. For Punter, greeted by one local paper with the headline 'Ricky's Oul Sod', it was a chance to meet Betty and Mary, the sisters his grandmother left behind when she was dispatched from east Belfast to Tasmania nearly sixty years ago. For the Irish Cricket Union, it marked the latest step on the road to credibility. Yet the occasion was more about selling than winning. 'We're here to promote Irish cricket,' insisted Tubs. Every little helps.

The skies were of a suitable disposition this morning as Matthew and Slats strolled gingerly to the middle amid thick plumes of barbecue smoke. Matthew had declined a helmet, albeit not out of arrogance: his head is thick enough already. 'After the way we celebrated at Trent Bridge and now the past two days, I reckon I'm becoming an alky,' he would later observe. The tuft of hair beneath his bottom lip is beginning to resemble a fledgling forest: 'I reckon I'll grow it right down,' he warns, running a finger down and under that imposing chin. I encourage him, suggesting it would be a unique fashion statement.

Rather than join the gang at Portrush – tramping eighteen

218

holes on those knees has been out of the question all tour – Matthew had elected to go fishing with Alfie. The fish weren't biting, but then he didn't reckon there were any in there. As with so many newcomers to the territory, myself included, he was finding it hard coming to terms with the beastly within the beauty. His companion had been at an even bigger loss. 'Alfie told the bloke we were with that he didn't understand anything about the IRA. Could he tell him? "If I were you," the bloke suggested, "I wouldn't bring that up with anyone.". '

I can understand that, but I'm damned if I'm going to stay schtum. On my way in from the airport we'd passed the Rising Sun, the bar where, a couple of years ago, loyalist gunmen had extracted vengeance for the dreadful killings at Enniskillen. How could you possibly ignore the issue? At Eglinton, Shaun Bradley, a Catholic in an area '70–80 per cent' populated by Protestants, points out a passing luminary. 'See him? That's Judge Nicholson, Judge Michael Nicholson. The owner of the Beech Hill estate where you're staying. That's a sign of the times. Before the ceasefire he wouldn't have been able to wander around with such impunity; he'd have been surrounded by blokes with heads turning 360 degrees.'

I note the number of boys clad in Rangers FC shirts. Catherine, Shaun's daughter, attends a mixed school, which she's glad about, but this reminds her of one of the sources of friction. 'It's provocation. We get boys wearing Celtic and Rangers shirts. It's just about the only problem we ever get.' Mother nods sagely. 'The mindset is more appropriate to 1914. Mind you, I wouldn't let a child of mine wear a Celtic shirt. That's not what we need. Provocative is the right word. Like the marchers in Derry last weekend. The kids carry it on. The only long-term solution is a united Ireland but Shaun's not optimistic.' Shaun is sceptical about the prospects of discussion, let alone lasting peace. 'The Unionists won't come to the table. They're very fearful of being cast adrift by England. There's no industry here, a bit of agriculture, and tourism. The British government has been pumping millions into the country. The Unionists would prefer independence to union with the Republicans.'

Punter's *joie de vivre* brings him a century and the Cobbers top 300. During the interval, teenagers in Manchester United and Rangers shirts chuck rugby balls around the outfield while their younger brethren get stuck in with bat and ball. At the Paddock End, Eurosports of Lisburn have slashed the prices of their Gunn & Moore stocks by a third, but pickings are slim. A few yards away, ADM, 'Ireland's only sports company with its manufacturing base in India', do a roaring trade in £10 willows and 50p poppadoms.

The Irish batsmen go much the same way as the attempts to launch a Mexican Wave: initial vigour followed by swift death. Tubs himself takes the final wicket. To Ireland's batting coach, the former Indian Test all-rounder Narasimha Rao, known to one and all as 'Bobby', disappointment is eased by delight at the bigger picture. 'I told the lads to play straight against McGrath – no hooking, no pulling, no cutting. So what do they do? But they'll learn by experience. Anyway, it's good marketing, good publicity. It's great to see so many kids here. That's the future.'

There are only two blots on this pristine landscape. One is a conversation with Mark MacFarlane, a beefy accountant from Sydney who came to Dublin seven months ago to join his girlfriend. He had been on the Western Terrace on the fourth day at Headingley. 'It was awful. They were chanting "Stand up if you want to kill an Aussie", not to mention the usual crap about Warney. And they were throwing bottles. And glass plates. One almost hit me: I felt the wind as it whistled past. We were really intimidated. They weren't cricket fans, mind. Leeds United supporters. It still left a nasty taste.' So, to a lesser extent, had the series itself. 'I get no pleasure from thrashing England. They're supposed to be the second best team in the world! I don't want them to be weak. I want them to be competitive. Whatever happened to that academy John Major wanted? I'll tell you what: I'd make Gough captain. He's the only bloke with the right attitude.'

The other ruffle is the news that Croftie – already deflated by Glamorgan's eventual defeat when hostilities were rejoined yesterday morning by the River Can – and Ilott have been fined £1,000 apiece by their counties and ordered to appear before the ECB. Much as one would have to be a paid-up member of the Philistine Preservation Society not to reinforce their employers' desire to be seen to be slapping wrists, was it really necessary to take the matter any further? Besides, was the punishment truly commensurate with the crime? West Ham and Tottenham indulged in a free-for-all at Upton Park last night and nobody gave a dicky bird. Two combative chaps in flannels hurl handbags and everyone goes bananas. 'The shameful face of cricket' thundered the *Mirror*. The *Mail* resisted specifics: 'Shameful!'

Croftie and Ilott know they were in the wrong. Still, didn't they kiss and make up for the snappers? Besides, who got hurt? Only the precious sensibilities of those who would like the world a whole lot better if emotions were declared illegal. The selectors should interpret it as a sign of the drive they so crave.

16 August 'Princess flies to Greece for third cruise in a month'

(Daily Telegraph)

According to my rigorously researched poll of the St Lawrence Ground, 78 per cent of the nation believe that Croftie and Ilott were the victims of rough justice, while 22 per cent believe they deserve a lifetime ban and a birching. Sounds just about spot-on.

Catches of astonishing dexterity are *de rigueur* as Kent flay and fluff their way to 201, Kasper proving all but unplayable in his first spell while Lee, marginally less unimpressive than Young, picks up the last four wickets without conceding a run. Watched by Tim May, in town to

221

address the troops on union business, the Cobbers are promptly undermined by three wickets in ten balls from the leggy Alan Igglesden, the affable fast bowler whose affinity for the physio's couch has probably cost him thirty caps, now turning out on a pay-as-you-play basis. Slats scrapes his 100th first-class run of the summer then becomes his first victim. Not every Cobber will return home with joy unconfined.

At tea, the tourists are 65 for 4 – 266 runs and 14 wickets in four-and-a-half hours, skills and spills aplenty for a hearty crowd. Thereafter proceedings snooze as Tugga, captain for this match, chugs along, inexorable and intransigent. By the close he has a throbbing thumb but he's on 96 and his side are in front. Quite obviously, the boy can't help it.

17 August 'Cell test gives hope of slower ageing'
(Sunday Times)

Gough is pretending to be a Spice Girl: mouth agape, right arm outstretched, palm upturned. Hussain looks at him as if he has mislaid at least half his marbles. A flushed Croftie claps the throng below, thanking them for their support. Caddick and Ealham are vying for an endorsement deal with Colgate. Malcolm seems more rueful, sensing, perhaps, that it wouldn't last, couldn't last. At the back of the mêlée, standing behind a smirking David Gower, Matthew fingers his lips, remembering the taste and resolving not to sample it in the future. To his right, Swampy appears to be giving the inside of his left cheek a good mangling. Dizzy glowers from the wings; Kaspar stares into the middle-distance; Pigeon glares daggers at the floor. That was the scene at Edgbaston selected by the *Sunday Telegraph* to adorn Atherton's column today. Talk about rubbing it in.

Tugga recently likened Atherton to a cockroach. This was said, it must be emphasized, with nothing but admiration. It was the way he kept being stamped on but insisted on scuttling back for more. But for how much longer? There are surely more satisfying ways of earning a crust than being a nation's pin-cushion. Especially when the fates have evidently decreed that you will never again divine which way up a coin is going to land. To read his latest observations is to suspect the end may well be nigh, for all that Graveney wants him to lead the winter tour to the Caribbean.

'Cricket really is a simple game,' he writes, 'and the Australians do the basic things very well: play straight to produce partnerships and big totals in good time; bowl with absolute discipline and field with intensity. When you ally that basic philosophy with fine individual cricketers and a couple of crackerjacks, it makes for a potent force.' The inference seemed plain enough: 'Why the hell can't somebody give me men with absolute discipline? Why can't I have some intense fielders?'

In a gentle dart at Hussain's call for 'nastiness', he also stresses that toughness comes 'from within ... a deep unshakeable belief in your ability ... a desire to fight for your country or your team when times are hard and your side are staring down the barrel. It is a knowledge of when the opportunity presents itself, and of ramming home the advantage when the opposition is weakening. It is the ability to stick to your guns when all around you urge otherwise. Those are the characteristics that define the real hard men of a cricket team.' Of whom, one would surmise, Atherton feels his boasts precious few.

19 August 'US building up new nuclear arsenal'

(*Guardian*)

Mrs Croftie was feeling surprisingly chipper. 'To be honest, I think it'll do him a bit of good. If he'd played again at The Oval the media'd be on his back again. Anyway, that poor Phil Tufnell's missed out every game. It's about time he had a chance.'

In advance of this evening's disciplinary hearing at Bristol, David Graveney had informed Croftie he would be surplus to requirements at The Oval, freeing him to play in Glamorgan's vital championship fixture against Northants at Abergavenny. The selectors' decision, the chairman stressed, was not influenced in any way by the Chelmsford affair. 'We feel that a change of angle is needed,' he told the press. 'The Australians haven't necessarily mastered Robert but they've obviously got used to him.' In private, he assured him he was still part of the furniture. When we spoke half an hour ago, Croftie, who since Edgbaston has taken 5 wickets in the series at nearly 63 apiece while conceding 2.5 runs an over, was wryly philosophical. 'My confidence has taken a bit of a blow lately but at least you've got five Tests out of me,' he chuckled. 'Just give me a pitch to bowl on.'

He had arrived home from Bristol at 10.30, relief mingling with mild resentment. At least he'd had a better day than those 190 Laura Ashley factory workers in Caernarvon who'd learned that they were being laid off. 'Mark and I were up before Alan Moss, the Middlesex chairman, some bloke called Gabbitass and Alan Fordham, the treasurer of the Professional Cricketers' Association, which was a bit strange given that he'll probably be trying to score runs off me at Abergavenny tomorrow. I went in with Matthew Maynard, the Glamorgan captain, our chief executive and a committee member who knows a bit about the law. They let us have our say then ratified the fines and gave us a two-match NatWest ban, suspended for two years because of our "exemplary" records. I hope the players around the country don't think of me as a bad lad, but I honestly thought Glamorgan had dealt with it swiftly, that I'd been made an example of and that would be it. Been good for the book, eh?'

As Chumbawumba and lead singer Alice Nutter (I kid thee not) celebrate their first major chart hit with 'Tubthumping', Chris Smith finds a new tub to thump.

Jolted by the reaction to his putative plans for an élite sporting academy devoted to Olympic hopefuls, the Secretary of State for Culture, Media and Sport has consented to consider a separate one for our cricketers. All personal bias aside, the accent on individual sports was baffling. With their emphasis on collectivism and selflessness, successful national teams would surely be far more beneficial to the nation's moral fibre. 'Smith's change of heart clears way for academy' rejoiced one headline in the *Guardian*. When New Labour make a U-turn they certainly don't dilly-dally.

MATTHEW ELLIOTT

I see England have given Ramprakash another chance. He deserves it. But why has Crawley been dropped? One Test at number three, which may well be his best position, and he's out. People have criticized him for only getting runs in the second innings, but that's nonsense, surely. At Old Trafford and Headingley his side were staring down the barrel and he had the guts to stick it out. Isn't that evidence of the mental toughness the same critics insist that England need? Besides, I would have thought runs were runs, regardless of when you make them.

Junior has been suffering with flu for a couple of days but I'm sure he'll make a hundred here. Underneath that cool exterior there's more drive than people would realize. Nobody can put their finger on why he hasn't done himself justice in the series, and I think it's getting to him. At Trent Bridge he was constantly shuttling backwards and forwards between dressing room and balcony, gesticulating, remonstrating, playing air shots, showing whoever had hit the last shot the proper way to play it. I've never seen that side of him before.

If you had given me the option I probably would have gone home after Trent Bridge. Megs is having morning sickness and we've got a tough season in store, six Tests against New Zealand and South Africa then a tour of India. The other guys probably feel much the same; most of them have been on the go for over a year. But that doesn't mean we lack incentive, individually or collectively. We feel a final scoreline of 4–1 would reflect our superiority; we also want to nail our reputation for easing off in Tests when the rubber has already been decided. It'll help having two new guys coming into the side in Kasper and Shaun Young, because they'll give it that extra 'oomph'. Tubs will want to maintain the form he showed at Nottingham, Junior will want his hundred, and I want to pick up the 60 runs I need to complete 600 in the series. Somebody in Macclesfield bet Chuck I wouldn't do it, so I'll be out there trying to win him fifty quid.

21 August 'We've got the worst pensions in Europe'
(Daily Mirror)

It was a cackle more than a laugh. Long, throaty, lusty. Uncontrollable. Unbearable. So this is what it feels like to be humiliated by association.

Apparently, that dismal Sunday at Trent Bridge was merely an hors d'oeuvre to this feast of frippery, this orgy of headless chickenry. During the course of the Poms' ignominious spiral from 128 for 3 to 180 all out, Ihithisham Kamardeen, a charming Sri Lankan reporter working for Associated Press, leaned back in his chair in The Oval's media centre and rendered his unequivocal view of the fare below. The cause of his amusement was Peter Martin. Having just heaved Pigeon for six and poked his tongue out at his team's tormentor, the lofty Lancastrian seamer, a late replacement for the injured Headley, had paid for his temerity, bowled neck-and-crop next ball. It's official. My country's cricketers are now a fully fledged laughingstock. And to think that today marked *Test Match Special*'s debut on the Internet. They've been following all this in Lithuania and the Solomon Islands, for God's sake.

Today I crossed the Rubicon. Goodbye disappointment, hello fury. Granted, my blood boils whenever I see two men

226

get paid squillions to don silky shorts and flirt with brain damage, but then boxing bears as much relation to civilized entertainment as bear-baiting. This is the first sporting event I have ever attended where the on-field antics have driven me to anger. Sheer lunacy, but there you go.

Backed by fourteen of the eighteen county captains as the best man for the job – according to a poll conducted by *The Pavilion End* – Atherton did his bit, calling correctly at last. 'England need Oval win for captain and country' clamoured the *Telegraph*. Unfortunately, a revamped team (Crawley and Hollioake Minor ditched, Butcher, Ramprakash and Tufnell restored, Stewart back at first drop) let down both. Superbly as Pigeon bowled (his 7 for 76 was the most destructive analysis by a Cobber beneath the gasholders for 85 years), relentlessly as the ball swung in the oppressive atmosphere, spitefully as the pitch occasionally played, the complicity defied comprehension. Although Hollioake Major was bowled shouldering arms to a Warney leg-break that pitched middle and straightened the best part of an inch, it wasn't so much the manner of the dismissals as the sheer folly of the mood. The irresponsibility. The what-the-hell. It is not often that Sir Geoffrey of Boycottshire and I are in agreement, but he hit the nail on the proverbial the other day. 'They're not bad cricketers by any means, they're just playing bad cricket.' But why? Is this their way of telling Atherton his time is up? Or have the poundings of the last three Tests left them too nonplussed to think with a modicum of reason. Hussain seemed to be in the grip of a frenzy, lashing at everything. His scorebook entry reads 35, one short of Stewart's top score; he should have been docked the lot for macho posturing. Lloyd, to his credit, refused to duck the bullets. 'The pitch is fine. There is no hiding place. We chased the ball. To me that is a sign of a shortage of confidence. They played nowhere near their potential. It's just not acceptable.'

Before the carnage began, I had an instructive chat with Mike Denness, the steely but genteel Scot who had the decided misfortune to lead the Poms when Lillee first united with Thomson and who now works in public relations. 'To an extent,' he contended, 'the Trent Bridge collapse was down to complacency, a complacent mindset.' He feels for Atherton. He, too, had endured a loss of form while captaining a badly beaten team. He'd even dropped himself during that '74–75 series. 'We don't want to get into a situation like the RFU have been with Jack Rowell, offering the job of England manager behind the incumbent's back then seeing him quit. After forty-six Tests, there are four aspects I'd look at: Mike's own success, his motivational abilities, his man-management and his reading of the game. I can't think of many in my time who have met all those four criteria successfully. Peter May came close, but man-management wasn't part of it in his day. Brears? If you ask Mike he'd say his major disappointment was not scoring the runs he should have. The question now is whether there are any candidates sufficiently different to Mike in any of these areas. I doubt it. Mike will probably be thinking 'hey, I'd enjoy playing solely as a batsman', but I'd question whether he is motivated to play for Lancashire and England from the ranks.'

The question I have to ask is why, five hours after the close, the amount of lava bubbling away inside me could keep Vesuvius going for the next six months. Perhaps I have more in common with that sociopath I met outside Trent Bridge than I realized. I'm not about to hit Anne, but I certainly feel like hitting something. These keys will have to do. (They usually do. That's the wonder of writing for a living. It's an outlet for all that suppressed emotion. Which doubtless explains why so many of the world's best-loved writers have been English.) God knows there are matters eminently more worthy of my seldom-vented spleen. Bosnia, Northern Ireland, the Middle East; the homeless, the jobless, the indolent; anyone without full command of their faculties; the Beeb's refusal to grant *Seinfeld* a regular slot in the schedules; those rubbery rissoles that pass for beefburgers at Stamford Bridge. Maybe I'm angry because I've allowed myself to get angry, because I've permitted something so trivial to play such merry hell with my sense of proportion. Or perhaps it stems from my blatherings at the very start of this odyssey. How much longer will the occasion be sufficient to keep the customers satisfied? How much longer can ineptness and misapplied talent be tolerated? When I'm 64, I want to sit with Laura and Josef at Lord's, sharing an enthusiasm, wallowing in the uniqueness of the five-day play. Days like this only serve to lengthen the odds.

Daily Accumulator: Poms 0 Cobbers 10

22 August 'Spineless, Gutless, Hopeless (and I haven't even started on Athers yet)'

(*Daily Mirror*)

Ahem. What was that I was wittering on about? Only one thing could have atoned for all that angst and, glory be, it bloody well happened. Among all sport's manifold wonders, none, to these eyes, can match the sight of Philip Clive Roderick Tufnell in full flight. Today he soared. Guile, deception and a touch of Nureyev. Hopping, skipping, twirling, spinning: a competitive artist in every possible sense. The schoolboy arsonist with a copy of *Loaded* stashed in the back of his car. The non-conformist who found salvation (and cut down the fags) through fatherhood and a good woman. Pity I can't follow his example.

The lava was still bubbling when I got up. Tugga's Q&A in the Guardian didn't help much:

Are there any umpiring decisions that haunt you?
How many? In my second Test I was lbw for a duck. It was Ravi Shastri's arm ball . . . it was missing leg stump by a foot.

Greatest unfulfilled ambition?
To take 100 Test wickets. I now have 80.

Favourite film?
The Shawshank Redemption.

How would you describe yourself?
As a person who likes to make the most of my abilities.

At the serious end of the paper lurked some heartening statistics. According to an article in the *Journal of Respiratory Medicine and Critical Care,* 15 per cent of those who have been smoking 20 fags a day for less than 25 years showed signs of protein GRP, the substance that spurs lung cells to divide. I gleefully brandished the evidence at Anne. 'You're just looking for an excuse not to give up,' she reasoned with her customary grasp of my feeble-minded ways. 'Well, you've got five years.' At that juncture of the day, cricket had a better chance of being stubbed out of my life.

Almost as soon as I set foot in Wapping I went into a rant: about yesterday's idiocies, about my fears for cricket's future, about my envy for those similarly besotted with football, in which the success of the national team has absolutely no bearing on the game's survival. I was relieved to discover I had been far from alone in my indignation and suffering. 'I'm never going to a Test in this country again,' vowed Dave Rose, a kindly Lancastrian with a fuse as long as a tapeworm. 'If we'd been Italians, we'd have thrown tomatoes at them. People around me were laughing. If they go on much more like this, they'll stop having Tests here.'

I'd promised myself I was going to ignore the rest of the match. Had I been at home I would have accomplished this without the slightest bother. Had I still been a trainee accountant or an estate agent or a standing orders clerk or a record shop assistant or labouring under any of the other guises I have adopted in the past to earn a crust, I would have been home free. A sports desk is another kettle of cod. I had to avoid everything: the voices, the evening paper, the wires, the radio, the TV. I was doing pretty well, too, getting past lunch with an ease bordering on cockiness. Then, just as I passed the infernal cathode tube en route to the smoking room, I heard the sound of laughter. Happy laughter. Gay laughter. Heals had edged, Stewart had pressed his thighs together and Tufnell was racing down the wicket, mane flapping, fist shaking, teeth gritted, eyes dancing. Resistance melted.

By the close the complexion of the contest had resumed its previous pallour. Warney and Punter steered their side into a 28-run lead with a combination of bellicosity and diligence whereupon Kasper and Junior picked off three Poms with the arrears uncleared. But no matter. Seven wickets from the prince who likes to pretend he's a pauper and I'm back in love. Not because they altered the balance of the contest (however briefly), but because the only thing I love more about cricket than watching Philip Clive Roderick Tufnell (don't you just love the Roderick?) is watching him enjoy himself. And to think the last time a Pommy slow bowler bettered his 7 for 64 in an Ashes Test, the Russian tanks had just paid an impromptu visit to Prague, there was no distinction between first- and second-class mail, the Victoria Line was about to open and the Crazy World of Arthur Brown were topping the charts. Funny how I can't seem to overcome my antipathy towards Gooch for hastening Gower off stage yet I can forgive Tuffers for beating up his wife. We all have our blind spots.

'Just give me a pitch to bowl on'? Poor old Croftie. By way of pouring salt on his wounds, the oddest rumours are afoot. Paul Brind's preparations were interrupted a week or so ago, or so the word goes, when his father Harry, the flying pitch doctor, suggested he stop whatever he was doing and prepare a surface offering encouragement to the spinners. So why not pick two of them? Curiouser and curiouser.

Daily Accumulator: Poms 4 Cobbers 6

23 August 'Victorious Aussies want to take the Ashes home'

(Daily Telegraph)

7.20 a.m.: See Anne and kids off to Poole to see Mother and Ralph. Snooze on couch.

9.40: Pick up papers. Yesterday, apparently at Heals's behest, the ACB dispatched a letter to Lord's, requesting that the urn be removed from the museum and sent home with Tubs and co. The buffers really ought to oblige. Having to retrieve the accursed thing literally as well as figuratively might well make all the difference. Another Tugga titbit in Clive Ellis's *Telegraph* cricket diary: seems his wife put in a telephone bid of A$8,000 (£4,000) for Victor Trumper's 1902 cap, confidently expecting to bolster hubbie's extensive collection of cricketana. Sadly, it fell some way short of the eventual buyer's A$30,000.

Concern for nation's sense of humour mounts. Those prissy Booker Prize bods have threatened to take out an injunction against the publishers of the latest verbal meisterwork by that multi-talented self-promoter Jonathan King (author of 'Johnny Reggae', 'Jump Up And Down And Wave Your Knickers In The Air' and *Bible Two*). Unless, that is, he chooses an alternative title to *The Book** Prize Winner.* Conversely, they propose, he could always plaster labels over the cover informing would-be readers that this was NOT the 1997 Booker Prize winner.

11.00: Remain on couch for first session. Having made 2 runs in an hour yesterday afternoon by way of repentance, Hussain goes third ball, top-edging a cut off Warney; Matthew hurls himself forward at backward point to catch after initially losing the ball in the background. Impaired by a torn groin muscle, Warney hobbles over to offer congratulations. Can't have been easy on my boy's knees.

Head over the ball, weight flowing forward, Ramprakash gets off the mark with the silkiest of cover drives as Warney errs in length, but is soon struck on the shoulder by Pigeon.

232

The Ramprakash–Thorpe *v* Warney–Pigeon tussle is utterly hypnotic. Warney clearly cannot bowl with the right side of his body, restricting him to leggies and toppies; assiduous and careful but determined not to tug forelock, the batsmen wait for the short ones, normally about as commonplace as vipers at a mongoose convention but now arriving once an over. Ramprakash's Test stats are posted on the screen: 16 dismissals in single figures; 10 in the 20s; Ashes average in the mid-40s. In Chappelli's estimation, a lead of 150 'would give England a chance'; Richie reckons 125 might be enough.

11.52: Kasper replaces Pigeon: half the battle won. Ramprakash goes walkabout between balls, adjusting his helmet, jumping up and down like a middleweight between rounds. Thorpe pads Warney away with impunity then fastens on to a full toss and on-drives thrillingly. Back comes Warney, making one fizz past the edge as Thorpe shimmies to the off side for that trademark legside flick, flirting with Thursday's mode of destruction. 'Watch it, watch it,' pleads Lewis. Emotion seconded. Ring office: can't possibly leave before lunch. Warney bites his bottom lip and begins another over, a chap in pain. Thorpe edges between Heals's knees to complete the first 50 of the contest at the twenty-fourth attempt. Kasper's expansive swing keeps it tight. That kindly visage and unassuming demeanour are highly deceptive. What was it that Matthew said last week? 'You wouldn't know he was Australian.'

Warney gives way to Young: broad-shouldered, saturnine, lumbers in like an apologetic ox. 'The Aussies are just beginning to get worried now,' asserts Sir Geoffrey as Thorpe carves Kasper behind point. The next ball draws him into a full-blooded drive but pitches a shade wider and moves away, kissing the outside edge; Tubs spins round with the impact but clings on with those ham-sized mitts. Hollioake Major enters to a fearful hush, avoids a pair then bows out, leg-before to Kasper. Ramprakash soldiers on, lunching at 145 for 6. Another 50 more and who knows?

1.15 p.m.: Catch Tube to Wapping and read Warney's disarmingly frank *Telegraph* interview with Mark Nicholas. He checked his mobile phone after they'd been chatting for two hours and found forty-three messages! As a shareholder in the Official All Star Cafe group along with Tiger Woods, André Agassi, Monica Seles and Shaquille O'Neal, he is a fully fledged member of the new sporting aristocracy. He wants to develop his captaincy and play for a county, the clear inference being that the two should go hand-in-hand. 'There's plenty of talent here and I'd like to see if I can make something of the underachievers. It may sound odd but Australians are keen for England to play well, which strengthens the world game in general.' Very odd. Not that the sympathy stops there. 'The newspaper coverage is a huge obstacle, the way that it jumps on the England players' backs and destroys their confidence. This is the hardest country in the world to play as the home team, no question.' Fair point, albeit exaggerated. He obviously hasn't spent much time in Iraq lately.

2.01: Arrive at Wapping – 157 for 6. Before logging on I hear the dread words from Chris 'Campo' Campling, perched in front of a TV three yards away: 'Oh, he's gone!' 'Ramps?' 'Yes.' Dash into his office to see the replay: stumped by yards charging at Warney. Game over? Certainly looks that way as Kasper cleans up with 3 wickets in 5 balls, 7 for 36 all told; 163 all out, 124 to get. Edgbaston '81 Revisited? Who am I kidding?

Press on with the county round-up as Campo supplies updates. Matthew goes at 5, leaving a humdinger from Malcolm that zips back, catching him bang to rights, but runs come briskly and Tufnell is summoned. Deadline approaching so no more sorties in search of visual proof. Fortunately, Campo is a wizz at the precise and concise. Urged by Botham to deepen his concentration and lengthen his run, Caddick traps Tubs: 36 for 2. Then 42 for 3 as Tufnell makes one turn and spit at Junior, whose modest summer ends with a dolly to slip. Interesting. Caddick derives the benefit of some extremely grave doubts as Blewie is adjudged caught behind: 49 for 4. Very interesting. Then 54 for 5 as Tugga nicks Caddick into Thorpe's midriff. Pinch me. Hard. Bodies pile into Campo's office. Then the exodus as Punter and Heals bed down. Almost half an hour passes before Tufnell traps the Tasmanian devil: 88 for 6. Next over, Heals chips a return catch to Caddick and bodies trickle back. 'I got into cricket this summer,' young Pete Watts informs me with a mixture of pride and bemusement; he can't quite believe it himself. A thought occurs. Do the Cobbers fold so frequently in pursuit of small targets because the challenge is insufficiently demanding?

Finish my column and rush to Campo's office. The buzz is incredible. Hampered by that gammy groin, weight falling away, Warney hoists Tufnell towards Neptune; Martin hovers anxiously at deep mid-on, holds his nerve, judges it impeccably and finds himself engulfed by cock-a-hoop colleagues: 95 for 8. Kasper prods at a Caddick lifter after 4 runs in 5 overs; ball balloons off splice to Hollioake Major: 99 for 9 and fists flail the air. Five more balls and Tufnell nets Pigeon, caught via a leading edge at mid-off by a swooping Thorpe. Yesss!

Atherton and Stewart sprint off, arms around shoulders, smiles beatific, just as they did on this selfsame outfield four years ago. Thorpe gallops away, waving a fist, as if he's just won the Cup Final for his beloved Chelsea; Hollioake Major pulls him back by the shirt and hugs most of the breath from his body. Tubs and Warney greet the victors as they drag themselves up to the balcony, drained but jubilant. Below, a lady in a floral hat holds up a placard: 'Stay captain Athers'. Gower interviews Tubs and asks about the request to relocate the urn; double-entendres are exchanged. Gower: 'It's small but it means a lot.' Tubs: 'It's not the sort of size where you want to wave it about very much.' The Ashes, he insists, is merely 'a figure of speech – none of the guys are bothered'. Why did he think they lost? One reason, he felt, was the inability of Heals and Tugga to find the requisite motivation with the series already won; not, he stressed, that this should in any way be perceived as a fault. Lewis nominates Tufnell as Man of the Match (a penny for your thoughts, Croftie); Lloyd nominates Pigeon as his Cobber of the series (36 wickets, half as many again as any man on either side); Swampy's pick of the Poms is Thorpe, the only specialist willow-wielder on either side to average 50 apart from Matthew, whose 556 runs at 55.60 would assuredly have made him the batsman of the series had there been such a thing. The statistics, though, are deceptive. The Poms had the highest partnership of the rubber, more three-figure stands, the best individual score, the best match analysis. The key, though, is the contrast between the collective efforts. While the Cobbers' top six barely outscored their counterparts (2,137 to 2,009), their tail wagged much the more vibrantly (699 to 365). No number, surely, was more crunchworthy than that.

At the press conference, Tubs describes the pitch as 'substandard', the game as 'remarkable'. Atherton declares the opposition to be the most formidable set of Cobbers he has yet encountered, singling out Pigeon and Warney as the fulcrums. He intends to spend the next couple of days as far from the maddening crowd as is humanly possible. Nothing that occurred here, he insists, will alter his decision over the captaincy. Hmm. I wonder.

Daily Accumulator: Poms 7 Cobbers 3
Match total: Poms 11 Cobbers 19
Series total: POMS 83 COBBERS 165

MATTHEW ELLIOTT
A disappointing end to the summer but all credit to England. Ramprakash and Thorpe produced the best batting of the match and that's probably what swung it. The wicket was probably at its best in our second innings and we simply didn't bat well. We should have been more patient, worked harder, rather than trying to finish it with quick fifties.

The dressing room was very quiet while all the wickets were falling. Each time somebody came back after being dismissed you could sense he was low, not just because he'd failed but because that was the end of his tour. Tugga was a bit edgy before he went in. He even had a go at someone, which is not at all like him. 'We've still got a Test match to win', something like that. He was using it to gear himself up for one last big effort but it must be difficult being the one everybody relies on. He probably thought he would be able to sit back and enjoy the other guys making the runs.

A few of their guys came into the dressing room at the end and we had a good laugh, particularly with Atherton. A nice guy, a decent guy, good sense of humour. He copped a bit of stick about the way he objected to Warney having a runner, and how that might ruin Lancashire's chances of signing Warney, but he took it in good heart. England's best chance of winning in the Caribbean is with him leading the side. Tubs agrees. He feels that if a new captain came in the West Indies would rip him apart. I think Tubs will carry on for as long as he can, and I sincerely hope he does. He was definitely hitting the ball better towards the end of the summer, so that ought to help.

If you take Warney out of the equation, the outcome of the series might have been different. We wouldn't have played on wickets like that. I don't want to take anything away from Pigeon because he is a magnificent bowler, but would he have taken all those wickets if the pitches hadn't been prepared to negate Warney?

I'm tired and my left knee feels a bit numb and I'm looking forward to spending two weeks on a beach in Queensland, but I've enjoyed the tour. Considering I've never been 100 per cent fit, I'm delighted to have got through it, although I'm due to go into hospital next week for arthroscopic surgery. I'd be lying if I said I wasn't worried.

I'm obviously satisfied to be going home with a few runs on the board, although I let myself down at The Oval. In the first innings I felt as good as I had all series, really working away, and even though I left a bit of a gap between bat and pad I wasn't expecting the ball to turn that much. Poor execution. That said, Tufnell's control was incredible. When we played Middlesex he bowled all right, no more, but some of the guys were saying that his wife has been really good for him. His batting and fielding were both far better than they remembered.

I really wanted to make 600 runs in the series, because that would have meant averaging a hundred per match. I'd also like to have finished with an overall Test average of 50, and perhaps even made the 100 or so runs I needed to bring my total to 1,000 after 11 games, which is what Tubs managed. Where would we be without goals?

I do feel for Croftie. That altercation at Chelmsford was obviously down to a build up of frustration. Would it have happened if he hadn't had to go straight from a Test to a crucial cup tie? I admire the way he plays the game and I wish we'd had a chance to get together over dinner. We could have compared fishing tales. Thirty years ago we might have managed it, but not now, regrettably.

ROBERT CROFT

At Abergavenny on the Thursday, the first ball I saw from Warney spun a yard and a half. That, I decided, was enough for me, so I went and sat as far from the TV as possible. We'd just beaten Northants when the match was bubbling to its climax and our boys took the mickey out of me whileTufnell was taking those wickets. Stewie had rung me up to say bad luck when I wasn't picked and I'd wanted to ring the guys up during the match, let alone at the end, but I wasn't sure whether they wanted to hear from me, so I didn't.

I thought it would be hard to pick ourselves up after Trent Bridge, which makes the victory even sweeter. I was glad for Tufnell, whom I know reasonably well. Of course it was frustrating not to be at the other end. I wouldn't be human if I didn't wonder what might have happened had we been able to operate in harness all summer. During that squad get-together at the start of the season the players were discussing the type of pitches we ought to play on. A lot of the lads fancied green seamers, but a few of us, myself included, felt that there should be something in it for the spinners. The reasoning was that Warne will turn the ball on any surface, but if you back your own spinners you can reduce the gap, take each other out of the game.

Why did the Aussies win? Look at the breakdown of the runs. If you compare the respective top sixes, there was little or no difference, but there was a huge disparity between the bottom halves of the order. If you look at people like Taylor, Warne and McGrath, they seem to go out knowing exactly what to do and how to win. Warne and McGrath are two of the ultimate bowlers; they attack but they still keep it tight. Another key for me was that Reiffel didn't play at Edgbaston. He made them look a different unit. I couldn't believe it when they didn't pick him in the first place. You could hardly lay a bat on him at Lord's, and he played a key role all the way through. Coming back at the end was a terrific sign of resilience, but I don't think we finished the summer in as good shape as we started it. I honestly felt we had the beating of them but they say the measure of a side is how they bounce back from adversity. They've demonstrated beyond doubt that they are a hell of a side.

Looking back on my first Ashes series, I can safely say that it was every bit as hard-fought as I expected. No quarter asked, none given. Hard but fair. There was no real sense of camaraderie between the teams, but the way the game is structured makes that virtually impossible. If Matthew and I had been staying in the same hotel we might have bumped into each other in the bar and had a drink, but with the teams staying so far apart that was never a possibility. Pity.

24 August 'Rail firms lengthen journey times to avoid payouts'

(Sunday Times)

Watch the highlights on Sky, revelling in the reminders, piecing together the missing links. Ethereal silence as Tubs smacks Malcolm past the diving Ramprakash at cover; the crowd's generous send-off as Captain Sensible bows out, almost certainly departing an English stage for the last time; Blewie's 'fuck' after falling foul of Lloyd Barker's dodgy digit (the ball brushed pad not bat); folk dangling precariously out of nearby apartment windows at the end, a-whoopin' an' a-hollerin'; Captain Sensible bashfully raising a replica of the urn, worth thirty quid and borrowed from a display case at the headquarters of Cornhill Insurance (during the game it had been sequestered in an old champagne box in the Surrey committee room and ultimately had to be retrieved from a bin). During an ad break, a wombat scurries through some parched shrubland. 'Ah, strewth,' it pants. 'These Pommy pitches are rough.'

Catch a cab to Muswell Hill to buy the new Oasis tape. The driver is of Caribbean extraction, Jamaican by the sounds of it. What did he think of it all? 'You'd ha' thought they'd won the World Cup,' he chuckled. 'They do so love coming second, don't they?'

Call Stinger on my return. The papers there are chockful of the Cobbers' own weekend of angst: defeats for the national rugby union and hockey teams as well as the men in white. 'Congrats on a worthy win,' I say, referring to the series. He sounds vaguely disappointed: 'Well, we played well when it mattered.' I tell him about my outburst on the first day. Had he ever been on the brink of renouncing his support? Closer. There was a period when he didn't want his lot to win because Bobby Simpson would take the credit.

Stinger's father had indeed died the day the Ashes were retained. His mother, thankfully, was coping; he himself was over the worst. Besides, at least they'd all said their goodbyes. How many, he consoled himself, could claim that?

240

20 September 'Archers actor dies'

(Daily Telegraph)

In Paris three weeks ago tonight, Princess Diana was killed in a car crash, uniting Poms and Cobbers in mourning. On the day she was laid to rest, Hyde Park was awash with tears as the British people discovered the wonders of emotion; every major TV station from Perth to Brisbane broadcast the funeral live; condolence books and pictorial supplements were common in both lands.

Now the Cobbers have an additional reason to grieve. Last Sunday, Lady Jessie Bradman, The Don's rock and redeemer, finally succumbed to cancer at the age of 88. So integral was she to her husband's triumphs, Charles Williams dedicated his recent biography to her. The Don, who had been taking her for chemotherapy five times a week, is said to have been wasting away with worry. Will his thirst for life be the same without her? We Poms, meanwhile, have lost one of our own institutions. Jack May, Nelson Gabriel in *The Archers* since the nation's favourite radio soap debuted on New Year's Day, 1951, died yesterday. At the time of his passing, Nelson was running a wine bar; when those suave, sonorous tones first crackled through the ether, the damn things hadn't even been invented.

Amid it all, revolution is in the air. Disillusioned by the House of Windsor's tardy public response to Diana's death, the minority parties Down Under have changed tack on republicanism, setting the seal on arrangements for next February's inaugural convention at Parliament House (pundits have cited the same motivation behind the results of the latest public opinion poll, which showed the nation shifting ever more perceptibly towards severing the Gordian knot). Last week, the Scots voted for devolution. On Thursday, albeit by a whisker, the Welsh followed suit. As if by divine decree, the strains of 'Bread of Heaven' rang round Taunton this afternoon as Glamorgan beat Somerset by ten wickets to carry off the county championship. Disappointed to be denied a proxy vote in the referendum ('as a true Welshman, how do you think I would have voted?'), Croftie played his part to the hilt, smacking three sixes in one over en route to 86, his highest score of the season. Hans Christian Andersen himself would have been hard-pushed to match that for a happy ending. Throw in Matthew's clean bill of health from the surgeons and his union's request that the ACB open its books for public consumption, and you have all the makings of a Disney epic.

Nothing, though, can stir Atherton. Revitalized by events at The Oval, and 'not wanting to leave the job half-finished', the nation's staunchest sporting servant has decided to remain its most willing pin-cushion. The counties, somewhat less admirably, are not for turning either. Before they passed judgment on his blueprint earlier this week, Lord Tesco came clean. Having had his original conference plan rebuffed – but still bravely adhering to the 'no change is not an option' line of bullying he'd been pedalling all summer – he confessed that he had always believed a two-divisional championship to be the only way forward, and urged all concerned to support the motion. Denied any guarantees as to their future, the counties declined, opting to retain the competition as a single league. Some prisoners of the past, it would seem, have no desire to leave their cells.

Still, nobody can accuse the counties of being inflexible. They have, after all, voted for an 'enhanced' championship wherein the top eight teams will qualify for a so-called 'Super Cup' the following season. And what manner of matches will these be, pray? Why, one-dayers, silly. I rang Stinger to avail him of the news. 'Most Aussies,' he declared, 'feel like putting their hands around the neck of English cricket.' Now *that's* what I call a special relationship.

First Test at Edgbaston   5–8 June

AUSTRALIA	Runs	Balls	Mins	4/6	FoW		Runs	Balls	Mins	4/6	FoW
*M A Taylor c Butcher b Malcolm	7	16	24	1	1–11	(2) c and b Croft	129	296	398	19/1	1–133
M T G Elliott b Gough	6	13	19	1	2–15	(1) b Croft	66	113	146	12	2–327
G S Blewett c Hussain b Gough	7	15	36	–	4–28	c Butcher b Croft	125	228	303	19/1	3–354
M E Waugh b Gough	5	25	23	1	3–26	(6) c Stewart b Gough	1	7	8	–	5–399
S R Waugh c Stewart b Caddick	12	20	31	3	5–48	(4) lbw b Gough	33	101	137	2	6–431
M G Bevan c Ealham b Malcolm	8	21	31	1	7–48	(5) Hussain b Gough	24	41	44	5	4–393
†I A Healy c Stewart b Caddick	0	1	1	–	6–48	c Atherton b Ealham	30	46	67	5	7–465
J N Gillespie lbw b Caddick	4	8	13	1	8–54	(10) ro Crawley/Gough	0	6	11	–	9–477
S K Warne c Malcolm b Caddick	47	46	63	8	10–118	(8) c and b Ealham	32	34	51	5	10–477
M S Kasprowicz c Butcher b Caddick	17	28	44	3	9–110	(9) c Butcher b Ealham	0	2	2	–	8–465
G D McGrath not out	1	3	9	–	–	not out	0	0	2	–	–
Extras w2 nb2	4					b18 lb12 w2 nb5	37				
TOTAL 31.5 overs	**118**					144.4 overs	**477**				

BOWLING

Gough	10	1	43	3		35	7	123	3
Malcolm	10	2	25	2		21	6	52	0
Caddick	11.5	1	50	5		(4) 30	6	87	0
Croft						(3) 43	10	125	3
Ealham						15.4	3	60	3

ENGLAND	Runs	Balls	Mins	4/6	FoW		Runs	Balls	Mins	4/6	FoW
M A Butcher c Healy b Kaspr'z	8	13	16	2	2–16	lbw b Kaspr'z	14	10	14	2	1–29
*M A Atherton c Healy b McGrath	2	4	10	–	1–8	not out	57	65	87	9	–
†A J Stewart c Elliott b Gillespie	18	33	51	3	3–50	not out	40	54	72	7	–
N Hussain c Healy b Warne	207	337	440	38	6–416						
G P Thorpe c Bevan b McGrath	138	245	294	19	4–338						
J P Crawley c Healy b Kaspr'z	1	14	19	–	5–345						
M A Ealham not out	53	131	172	7	–						
R D B Croft c Healy b Kaspr'z	24	56	70	4	7–460						
D Gough c Healy b Kaspr'z	0	9	9	–	8–463						
A R Caddick lbw b Bevan	0	7	11	–	9–478						
Extras b4 lb7 w1 nb15	27					b4 lb4	8				
TOTAL 138.4 overs	**478–9 dec**					21.3 overs	**119–1**				
Did not bat: D E Malcolm											

BOWLING

McGrath	32	8	107	2		7	1	42	0
Kasprowicz	39	8	113	4		7	0	42	1
Gillespie	10	1	48	1					
Warne	35	8	110	1		(2) 7.3	0	27	0
Bevan	10.4	0	44	1					
S Waugh	12	2	45	0					

Toss	Australia		Close of play	
Test debuts	M A Butcher (E)		1st day	Eng 200–3 Hussain 83, Thorpe 80
Umpires	S A Bucknor (WI), P Willey (E);		2nd day	Eng 449–6 Ealham 32, Croft 18
	J W Holder (E)		3rd day	Aust 256–1 Taylor 108, Blewett 61
Referee	R S Madugalle (SL)			
Man of the Match	N Hussain (Adj: R G D Willis)		**ENGLAND WON BY 9 WICKETS**	
Sponsor	Cornhill Insurance			

Reprinted by kind permission of *Wisden Cricket Monthly*

Second Test at Lord's   19–23 June

ENGLAND	Runs	Balls	Mins	4/6	FoW		Runs	Balls	Mins	4/6	FoW
M A Butcher c Blewett b McGrath	5	26	28	1	1–11	b Warne	87	210	267	14	4–202
*M A Atherton c Taylor b McGrath	1	24	38	–	2–12	hit wicket b Kaspr'z	77	159	222	10	1–162
†A J Stewart b McGrath	1	13	18	–	3–13	c Kaspr'z b McGrath	13	24	29	2	2–189
N Hussain lbw b McGrath	19	73	110	2	6–62	c and b Warne	0	5	4	–	3–197
G P Thorpe c Blewett b Reiffel	21	49	61	4	4–47	not out	30	39	60	4	–
J P Crawley c Healy b McGrath	1	17	21	–	5–56	not out	29	45	52	4	–
M A Ealham c Elliott b Reiffel	7	30	51	1	9–77						
R D B Croft c Healy b McGrath	2	13	18	–	7–66						
D Gough c Healy b McGrath	10	10	11	2	8–76						
A R Caddick lbw b McGrath	1	5	7	–	10–77						
D E Malcolm not out	0	0	2	–	–						
Extras b4 nb5	9					b8 lb14 w1 nb7	30				
TOTAL 42.3 overs	77					79 overs	266–4 dec				

BOWLING

McGrath	20.3	8	38	8		20	5	65	1
Reiffel	15	9	17	2		13	5	29	0
Kasprowicz	5	1	9	0		15	3	54	1
Warne	2	0	9	0		19	4	47	2
Bevan						8	1	29	0
S Waugh						4	0	20	0

AUSTRALIA	Runs	Balls	Mins	4/6	FoW	BOWLING				
M A Taylor* b Gough	1	15	18	–	1–4	Gough	20	4	82	2
M T G Elliott c Crawley b Caddick	112	180	242	20	7–212	Caddick	22	6	71	4
G S Blewett c Hussain b Croft	45	70	83	7	2–73	Malcolm	7	1	26	0
M E Waugh c Malcolm b Caddick	33	60	81	1	3–147	Croft	12	5	30	1
S K Warne c Hussain b Gough	0	4	5	–	4–147					
S R Waugh lbw b Caddick	0	1	3	–	5–147					
M G Bevan c Stewart b Caddick	4	7	9	1	6–159					
I A Healy† not out	13	23	44	2	–					
P R Reiffel not out	1	6	7	–	–					
M S Kasprowicz	–									
G D McGrath	–									
Extras b1 lb3	4									
TOTAL 61 overs	213-7 dec									

Toss	Australia	Close of play	
Test debuts	none	1st day	no play
Umpires	D R Shepherd (E),	2nd day	Eng 38–3 Hussain 10, Thorpe 13
	S Venkataraghavan (I);	3rd day	Aust 131–2 Elliott 55, M Waugh 26
	D J Constant (E)	4th day	Aust 213–7 Healy 13, Reiffel 1
Referee	R S Madugalle (SL)		
Man of the Match	G D McGrath (Adj: I M Chappell)		
MATCH DRAWN			

Reprinted by kind permission of *Wisden Cricket Monthly*

Third Test at Old Trafford   3–7 July

AUSTRALIA

	Runs	Balls	Mins	4/6	FoW		Runs	Balls	Mins	4/6	FoW
*M A Taylor c Thorpe b Headley	2	20	22	–	1-9	(2) c Butcher b Headley	1	2	6	–	1-5
M T G Elliott c Stewart b Headley	40	98	130	4	4-85	(1) c Butcher b Headley	11	40	59	–	3-39
G S Blewett b Gough	8	13	16	1	2-22	c Hussain b Croft	19	35	40	1	2-33
M E Waugh c Blewett b Ealham	12	27	36	2	3-42	b Ealham	55	81	120	7/1	4-131
S R Waugh b Gough	108	175	240	13	9-235	c Stewart b Headley	116	271	380	10	8-333
M G Bevan c Stewart b Headley	7	16	24	1	5-113	c Atherton b Headley	0	16	20	–	5-132
†I A Healy c Stewart b Caddick	9	20	32	1	6-150	c Butcher b Croft	47	78	103	6	6-210
S K Warne c Stewart b Ealham	3	7	13	–	7-160	c Stewart b Caddick	53	77	99	5/1	7-298
P R Reiffel b Gough	31	84	103	1	8-230	not out	45	87	102	6	–
J N Gillespie c Stewart b Headley	0	8	12	–	10-235	not out	28	55	63	3	–
G D McGrath not out	0	2	2	–	–						
Extras b8 lb4 nb3	15					b1 lb13 nb6	20				
TOTAL 77.7 overs	235					122 overs	395-8 dec				

BOWLING

Gough	21	7	52	3		20	3	62	0	
Headley	27.3	4	72	4		29	4	104	4	
Caddick	14	2	52	1	(5)	21	0	69	1	
Ealham	11	2	34	2		13	3	41	1	
Croft	4	0	13	0	(3)	39	12	105	2	

ENGLAND

	Runs	Balls	Mins	4/6	FoW		Runs	Balls	Mins	4/6	FoW
M A Butcher st Healy b Bevan	51	140	178	5	3-94	c McGrath b Gillespie	28	78	102	1	4-55
*M A Atherton c Healy b McGrath	5	29	36	–	1-8	lbw b Gillespie	21	38	70	1/1	1-44
†A J Stewart c Taylor b Warne	30	79	117	2	2-74	b Warne	1	5	5	–	2-45
N Hussain c Healy b Warne	13	29	45	2	5-110	lbw b Gillespie	1	14	16	–	3-50
G P Thorpe c Taylor b Warne	3	7	8	–	4-101	c Healy b Warne	7	29	50	–	5-84
J P Crawley c Healy b Warne	4	26	28	1	6-111	hit wicket b McGrath	83	151	171	10	8-177
M A Ealham not out	24	97	135	3	–	c Healy b McGrath	9	75	97	–	6-158
R D B Croft c S Waugh b McGrath	7	23	18	1	7-122	c Reiffel b McGrath	7	13	15	–	7-170
D Gough lbw b Warne	1	13	11	–	8-123	b McGrath	6	18	22	1	9-188
A R Caddick c M Waugh b Warne	15	57	72	–	9-161	c Gillespie b Warne	17	18	21	3	10-200
D W Headley b McGrath	0	10	12	–	10-162	not out	0	4	9	–	–
Extras b4 lb3 nb2	9					b14 lb4 w1 nb1	20				
TOTAL 84.4 overs	162					73.4 overs	200				

BOWLING

McGrath	23.4	9	40	3		21	4	46	4	
Reiffel	9	3	14	0	(3)	2	0	8	0	
Warne	30	14	48	6	(4)	30.4	8	63	3	
Gillespie	14	3	39	0	(2)	12	4	31	3	
Bevan	8	3	14	1		8	2	34	0	

		Close of play	
Toss	Australia		
Test debuts	D W Headley (E)	1st day	Aust 224–7 S Waugh 102 Reiffel 26
Umpires	G Sharp (E),	2nd day	Eng 161–8 Ealham 23 Caddick 15
	S Venkataraghavan (I);	3rd day	Aust 262–6 S Waugh 81 Warne 33
	J H Hampshire (E)	4th day	Eng 130–5 Crawley 53 Ealham 5
Referee	R S Madugalle (SL)		
Man of the Match	S R Waugh (Adj: P J W Allot)		

AUSTRALIA WON BY 268 RUNS

Reprinted by kind permission of *Wisden Cricket Monthly*

Fourth Test at Headingley   24–28 July

ENGLAND	Runs	Balls	Mins	4/6	FoW		Runs	Balls	Mins	4/6	FoW
M A Butcher c Blewett b Reiffel	24	57	64	2	1–43	c Healy b McGrath	19	18	18	3	1–23
*M A Atherton c Gillespie b McGrath	41	143	226	6	5–154	c Warne b McGrath	2	13	25	–	2–28
†A J Stewart c Blewett b Gillespie	7	24	25	–	2–58	b Reiffel	16	30	41	3	3–57
N Hussain c Taylor b McGrath	26	40	57	4	3–103	c Gillespie b Warne	105	181	251	14*	5–222
D W Headley c S Waugh b Gillespie	22	32	4	2	4–138	(8) lbw b Reiffel	3	17	30	–	8–263
G P Thorpe b Gillespie	15	26	29	3	6–154	(5) c M Waugh b Gillespie	15	30	39	1	4–89
J P Crawley c Blewett b Gillespie	2	13	22	–	7–163	(6) b Reiffel	72	214	262	10	7–256
M A Ealham not out	8	24	41	–	–	(7) c M Waugh b Reiffel	4	47	65	–	6–252
R D B Croft c Ponting b Gillespie	6	8	11	1	8–172	c Healy b Reiffel	3	7	17	1	10–268
D Gough b Gillespie	0	2	4	–	9–172	c M Waugh b Gillespie	0	1	2	–	9–263
A M Smith b Gillespie	0	2	2	–	10–172	not out	4	4	5	1	–
Extras b4 lb4 w1 nb12	21					b6 lb4 nb13	23				
TOTAL 59.4 overs	172					91.1 overs	268			* also 1 x 5	

BOWLING

McGrath	22	5	67	2			22	5	80	2
Reiffel	20	4	41	1			21.1	2	49	5
Gillespie	13.4	1	37	7			23	8	65	2
Blewett	3	0	17	0						
Warne	1	0	2	0		(4)	21	6	53	1
S Waugh						(5)	4	1	11	0

AUSTRALIA	Runs	Balls	Mins	4/6	FoW	BOWLING				
M A Taylor* c Stewart b Gough	0	11	9	–	1–0	Gough	36	5	149	5
M T G Elliott b Gough	199	351	465	23/3	8–444	Headley	25	2	125	2
G S Blewett c Stewart b Gough	1	8	15	–	2–16	Smith	23	2	89	0
M E Waugh c and b Headley	8	18	30	1	3–43	Ealham	19	3	56	2
S R Waugh c Crawley b Headley	4	12	14	–	4–50	Croft	18	1	49	0
R T Ponting c Ealham b Gough	127	202	264	19/1	5–318	Butcher	2	0	14	0
†I A Healy b Ealham	31	46	59	6	6–382					
S K Warne c Thorpe b Ealham	0	5	3	–	7–383					
P R Reiffel not out	54	72	106	5	–					
J N Gillespie b Gough	3	18	17	–	9–461					
G D McGrath not out	20	30	35	1	–					
Extras b9 lb10 nb 35	54									
TOTAL 123 overs	501-9 dec									

Toss	Australia	Close of play	
Test debuts	A M Smith	1st day	Eng 106–3 Atherton 34 Headley 0
Umpires	M J Kitchen (E), C J Mitchley (SA);	2nd day	Aust 258–4 Elliott 134 Ponting 86
	R Julian	3rd day	Aust 373–5 Elliott 164 Healy 27
		4th day	Eng 212–4 Hussain 101 Crawley 48

Referee   C W Smith (WI)
Man of the Match   J N Gillespie (Adj: I T Botham)
AUSTRALIA WON BY AN INNINGS AND 61 RUNS

Reprinted by kind permission of *Wisden Cricket Monthly*

Fifth Test at Trent Bridge　　　　　　　　　7–10 August

AUSTRALIA	Runs	Balls	Mins	4/6	FoW		Runs	Balls	Mins	4/6	FoW
M T G Elliott c Stewart b Headley	69	117	156	10	1–117	(2) c Crawley b Caddick	37	40	62	7	1–51
*M A Taylor b Caddick	76	155	217	12	2–160	(1) c Hussain b B Hollioake	45	100	133	7	2–105
G S Blewett c Stewart b B Hollioake	50	115	143	7	3–225	c Stewart b Caddick	60	94	126	8	4–156
M E Waugh lbw b Caddick	68	124	172	8	4–311	lbw b Headley	7	22	30	1	3–134
S R Waugh b Malcolm	75	102	168	13	8–386	c A Hollioake b Caddick	14	25	59	2	5–171
R T Ponting b Headley	9	15	15	1	5–325	c Stewart b A Hollioake	45	131	167	4	7–292
I A Healy† c A Hollioake b Malcolm	16	18	28	3	6–355	c Stewart b A Hollioake	63	78	104	9	6–276
S K Warne c Thorpe b Malcolm	0	5	11	–	7–363	c Thorpe b Croft	20	36	47	0/1	8–314
P R Reiffel c Thorpe b Headley	26	48	58	4	9–419	c B Hollioake b Croft	22	37	54	3	10–336
J N Gillespie not out	18	34	50	2	–	c Thorpe b Headley	4	19	19	–	9–326
G D McGrath b Headley	1	6	8	–	10–427	not out	1	16	15	–	–
Extras b4 lb10 w1 nb4	19					b1 lb11 nb6	18				
TOTAL 121.5 overs	427					98.5 overs	336				

BOWLING

Malcolm	25	4	100	3		16	4	52	0
Headley	30.5	7	87	4		19	3	56	2
Caddick	30	4	102	2	(4)	20	2	85	3
B Hollioake	10	1	57	0	(5)	5	1	26	1
Croft	19	7	43	0	(3)	26.5	6	74	2
A Hollioake	7	0	24	0		12	2	31	2

ENGLAND	Runs	Balls	Mins	4/6	FoW		Runs	Balls	Mins	4/6	FoW
*M A Atherton c Healy b Warne	27	75	112	3	1–106	c Healy b McGrath	8	32	35	1	1–25
†A J Stewart c Healy b Warne	87	107	137	14	2–129	c S Waugh b Reiffel	16	22	37	3	2–25
J P Crawley c Healy b McGrath	18	14	16	2	4–141	c Healy b Gillespie	33	41	67	4	4–99
N Hussain b Warne	2	22	25	–	3–135	b Gillespie	21	37	49	2	3–78
G P Thorpe c Blewett b Warne	53	118	154	6	6–243	not out	82	93	128	13*	–
A J Hollioake c Taylor b Reiffel	45	94	139	6/1	5–243	lbw b Gillespie	2	6	16	–	5–121
B C Hollioake c M Waugh b Reiffel	28	39	56	5	8–290	lbw b Warne	2	25	30	–	6–144
R D B Croft c Blewett b McGrath	18	34	39	2/1	7–272	c M Waugh b Warne	6	6	7	0/1	7–150
A R Caddick c Healy b McGrath	0	6	17	–	9–290	lbw b Warne	0	10	15	–	8–166
D W Headley not out	10	17	23	2	–	c Healy b McGrath	4	26	34	1	9–186
D E Malcolm b McGrath	12	12	20	3	10–313	c M Waugh b McGrath	0	2	2	–	10–186
Extras b2 lb6 nb5	13					b6 lb2 nb4	12				
TOTAL 93.5 overs	313					48.5 overs	186			* also 1x5	

BOWLING

McGrath	29.5	9	71	4		13.5	4	36	3
Reiffel	21	2	101	2		11	3	34	1
Gillespie	11	3	47	0		8	0	65	3
Warne	32	8	86	4		16	4	43	3

Toss	Australia	
Test debuts	A J Hollioake, B C Hollioake (E)	
Umpires	C J Mitchley (SA), D R Shepherd (E);	
	A A Jones	
Referee	C W Smith (WI)	
Man of the Match	I A Healy (adj: A W Greig)	

Close of play
1st day　Aust 302–3 M Waugh 60 S Waugh 38
2nd day　Eng 188–4 Thorpe 30 A Hollioake 15
3rd day　Aust 167–4 S Waugh 10 Ponting 5

AUSTRALIA WON BY 264 RUNS

Reprinted by kind permission of *Wisden Cricket Monthly*

Sixth Test at The Oval   21–23 August

ENGLAND	Runs	Balls	Mins	4/6	FoW		Runs	Balls	Mins	4/6	FoW
M A Butcher b McGrath	5	24	22	–	1–18	lbw b M Waugh	13	48	69	2	3–26
M A Atherton c Healy b McGrath	8	17	31	–	2–24	c S Waugh b Kasprowicz	8	21	29	1	1–20
†A J Stewart lbw b McGrath	36	73	104	4	3–97	lbw b Kasprowicz	3	9	11	–	2–24
N Hussain c Elliott b McGrath	35	114	139	4	4–128	c Elliott b Warne	2	50	62	–	4–52
G P Thorpe b McGrath	27	35	51	3	5–131	c Taylor b Kasprowicz	62	115	130	9	5–131
M R Ramprakash c Blewett b McGrath	4	8	19	–	7–132	st Healy b Warne	48	110	149	6	7–160
A J Hollioake b Warne	0	6	6	–	6–132	lbw b Kasprowicz	4	10	14	1	6–138
A R Caddick not out	26	36	53	4/1	–	not out	0	37	49	1	–
P J Martin b McGrath	20	19	23	1/1	8–158	c and b Kasprowicz	3	2	5	–	8–163
P C R Tufnell c Blewett b Warne	1	20	20	–	9–175	c Healy b Kasprowicz	0	2	2	–	9–163
D E Malcolm b Kasprowicz	0	1	3	–	10–180	b Kasprowicz	0	2	2	–	10–163
Extras b2 lb6 nb10	18					b6 lb10 nb4	20				
TOTAL 56.4 overs	180					66.5 overs	163				

BOWLING

McGrath	21	4	76	7			17	5	33	0
Kasprowicz	11.4	2	56	1			15.5	5	36	7
Warne	17	8	32	2			26	9	57	2
Young	7	3	8	0		(5)	1	0	5	0
M E Waugh						(4)	7	3	16	1

AUSTRALIA	Runs	Balls	Mins	4/6	FoW		Runs	Balls	Mins	4/6	FoW
M T G Elliott b Tufnell	12	33	51	1	1–49	(2) lbw b Malcolm	4	3	2	1	1–5
*M A Taylor c Hollioake b Tufnell	38	42	60	7	2–54	(1) lbw b Caddick	18	34	47	2	2–36
G S Blewett c Stewart b Tufnell	47	132	158	3/1	5–150	c Stewart b Caddick	19	36	57	3	4–49
M E Waugh c Butcher b Tufnell	19	69	80	2	3–94	c Hussain b Tufnell	1	7	7	–	3–42
S R Waugh lbw b Caddick	22	34	51	2	4–140	c Thorpe b Caddick	6	19	21	–	5–54
R T Ponting c Hussain b Tufnell	40	96	134	3/1	10–220	lbw b Tufnell	20	35	47	3	6–88
†I A Healy c Stewart b Tufnell	2	34	50	–	6–164	c and b Caddick	14	17	36	2	7–92
S Young c Stewart b Tufnell	0	3	7	–	7–164	not out	4	24	42	1	–
S K Warne b Caddick	30	34	39	3/1	8–205	c Martin b Tufnell	3	5	7	–	8–95
M S Kasprowicz lbw b Caddick	0	1	2	–	9–205	c Hollioake b Caddick	4	13	22	–	9–99
G D McGrath not out	1	5	13	–	–	c Thorpe b Tufnell	1	2	5	–	10–104
Extras lb3 w1 nb5	9					b3 lb4 w1 nb2	10				
TOTAL 79.3 overs	220					32.1 overs	104				

BOWLING

Malcolm	11	2	37	0			3	0	15	1
Martin	15	5	38	0			4	0	13	0
Caddick	19	4	76	3		(4)	12	2	42	5
Tufnell	34.3	16	66	7		(3)	13.1	6	27	4

Toss	England	**Close of play**
Test debuts	S Young (A)	1st day Aust 77–2 Blewett 10 M Waugh 12
Umpires	L H Barker(WI), P Willey (E); K E Palmer	2nd day Eng 52–3 Hussain 2 Thorpe 22
Referee	C W Smith (WI)	
Man of the Match	P C R Tufnell (adj: A R Lewis)	
Men of the Series	G P Thorpe (adj: G R Marsh)	
	G D McGrath (adj: D Lloyd)	

ENGLAND WON BY 19 RUNS; AUSTRALIA WON SERIES 3–2

Reprinted by kind permission of *Wisden Cricket Monthly*